Upward Nobility

Upward Nobility

how to succeed

in business

without

losing your soul

by OWEN EDWARDS

Crown Publishers, Inc.
New York

1820

Portions of this work were previously published in different form in *GQ*.

Copyright © 1991 by Owen Edwards

Published by Crown Publishers, Inc., 201 East 50th Street, New York, New York 10022. Member of the Crown Publishing Group.

CROWN is a trademark of Crown Publishers, Inc.

Manufactured in the United States of America

Design by Lauren Dong

Library of Congress Cataloging-in-Publication Data
Edwards, Owen.
   Upward nobility : how to succeed in business without losing your soul / by Owen Edwards. — 1st ed.
      p.   cm.
   1. Success in business.   2. Business ethics.   I. Title.
HF5386.E24   1992
650.1—dc20   91-20443
                                                        CIP

ISBN 0-517-58065-9

10 9 8 7 6 5 4 3 2 1

First Edition

All of the interviews and anecdotes in this book are factual, but in some cases events have been merged, and names, descriptions, companies, and even professions have been changed to protect the innocent from the guilty—and, especially, to protect the author from the righteous wrath of the unrighteous.

for Ezekiel and Oona: may they be happy in their work

for Regine, who keeps me happy in mine

and for Edwin Edwards, an ethical man.

Acknowledgments

Many of the chapters in this book began life as columns in *GQ* magazine. My friend Martin Beiser, the executive editor of the magazine, has polished my words and clarified my ideas with unfailing grace. In the substantial revision and expansion done for the book I hope I haven't added paragraphs (or pages) that will make his blue pencil itch. But then, my editor at Crown, David Groff, has gently reined in my stylistic indulgences without ever losing his enthusiasm for the subject or his instinct for what most needed to be said.

A writer—this writer, at least—is lost without good editors. I'm blessed to have been found by two as fine as these. And to have been prompted to do the book in the first place by another friend and fine editor, the fair Harriet Fier.

Contents

Upward Nobility

1

Upward
Nobility

*I*n the early sixties, I bade an unsentimental farewell to the United States Marine Corps, threw my duffel bag onto the passenger seat of a noisy MG, and headed north toward Mecca, a.k.a. Manhattan Island, to seek my fortune (as my favorite boyhood novels had so alluringly put it).

That fortune, as things worked out, amounted to the $85 a week paid to me as an assistant editor of a small trade magazine. I was the quintessential rookie, incredibly glad to be there and willing to do everything nobody else wanted to do. The people were nice, my boss liked me and I liked him, and my responsibilities (if not my pay) grew at what seemed a magical pace. Things were so congenial and promising that I happily forgot a lesson I'd learned in the military: When things get really good, watch out.

And sure enough, after I'd been there about six months, the family-owned company that published the magazine was bought by a much larger corporation. We were told that no drastic changes would be made, and I chose to believe the official line. After all, why would they lie? But when a meeting was held for the new owners to "get to know" us, I had the undeniable impression that they seemed . . . different. Dour. Implacable. Not like our happy band. Before long, we had a new publisher who didn't know anything about the history of the magazine or about the people who worked there, and didn't seem to care much. He had a set of numbers, our numbers fell short, and that was pretty much all there was to be said. The definition of success had changed, and what had been a marginally profitable, respected magazine was now seen as a serious problem. Belt-tightening was called for, more work was demanded, and all-around profligacy was decried, all in a series of memos distinguished only for their insensitivity.

Soon, anger and anxiety replaced the camaraderie of the office. Sides were drawn up in the classic "Us Against the Corporate Black Hats" mode. I didn't have to think at all to decide where I stood— the proper choice was obvious, and years later, having seen many similar situations, I know I was right to consider the new ownership guilty until proven innocent. The feeling was almost general, but a couple of people on the staff drifted into a kind of no-man's-land between Us and Them, keeping their options open while the shape of things to come slowly became apparent.

Though the editor never stopped giving his all to a magazine he loved, his lack of affection for the new publisher's number-crunching ways showed on his face whenever we were rounded up for pep talks (increasingly spiced with implied threats). But the executive editor, an efficient, pleasant paper-pusher who was one of the few among us who didn't care much about the airplanes that were the magazine's subject, grew steadily more enthusiastic, urging everyone to realize that the changes made sense, were for our own good, and all that. He began having drinks with the publisher and making excuses to miss his customary once-a-week lunches with the editor.

It will come as no surprise to you that within a few months the editor was out, exiled to his home in Hastings-on-Hudson to nurse a bruised ego and a no doubt inadequate severance, and that the executive editor had succeeded him. But it came as a surprise to me, as did the moment not too long afterward when I realized my happy job was history, and that it was time to move on.

Thus came my first lesson in the uninspiring business of office politics. I'd watched someone play it smart and move up at the expense of others, and in doing so I'd seen the future and decided it wasn't a pretty sight. Since then, I've worked at quite a few jobs in at least a couple of professions, and in the process I've grown familiar with the many games played that have little to do with the work at hand, but often an enormous amount to do with the success of the best players.

In the mideighties, the editors of *GQ* magazine asked me to write a regular column called "Office Politics," with the intention of looking at corporate culture on a personal level. At the time, I warned them that the idea was like asking Trotsky to do a column on capitalism. Since that first encounter with office politics in the sixties, one measure of how good any of my jobs has been is how little I've had to be involved with the machinations of relentless, tactically adroit upward strivers. Let me add, lest any self-congratulatory tone be perceived here, that my reasons have had less to do with high-mindedness than mystification and impatience. Wherever I've worked, when I have observed men and women with Kasparovian abilities to plan their moves far in advance and somehow orchestrate the actions of others, I've often been astonished at, occasionally envious of, and usually baffled by the fact that they found the time and energy to do it. Somewhere along the way, I realized that much of the time and energy for office politics simply were stolen from more legitimate work, but it was clear that there was more to it than that; some people are specially endowed for the tactical life, with particularly nasty inclinations, a terrible enthusiasm for nefarious deeds, and few of the compunctions that get in the way when good people want to do bad things.

Looking back over the eighties, a decade of vague ethics (to put it nicely), it's hard not to wonder if there are any effective antidotes to the toxic effects of such everyday pastimes as lying, cheating, and murmuring sweet nothings to the boss. In working on my column for the past six years, the central question I've often asked myself is, Can nobility survive in situations where innocence is a dubious virtue and decent behavior may seem an unaffordable luxury? Much to my surprise, after years of skepticism about the high cost (in soul) of success, I've discovered that ethical behavior doesn't have to be synonymous with naivety or vulnerability, and that there are ways to make it in business without hating yourself in the morning (or having others hate you all the time).

People with uncompromised values and the gifts of humor, irony, loyalty, and innate decency *can* prevail and prosper. Just because you find yourself swimming with the sharks, you don't have to join the feeding frenzy. Every now and then, of course, the only way to do the right thing is *not* to succeed, at least not at any price, but most of the time such dramatic choices aren't necessary if you know what's going on. If not everything I suggest in this book is absolutely noble, the reason is simply that in the real world there are limitations to how good one can be before being perceived as the natural (and irresistible) prey for workplace predators.

This book is about the quality of working life, the limits of ambition, and the possibility of moving up with grace, style, ethics—and your soul—intact. I don't presume to offer a model for business ethics (not being able to imagine what such a thing would look like) but rather a series of suggestions about how you can shape your own ethic of business. I hope I've produced an encouraging book for a chastened time: the days when it was okay, even consummately cool, to be bad, have come to a crashing finale. The sight of rich men going bankrupt (or to jail) has raised the novel possibility that an age of decent behavior may rise from the debris of me-ism. But for all the hope that the millennium has come to business (a few years early), office politics continues only slightly abated; after all, the organizational chart is still a pyramid, with less and less room as the top comes nearer. So the beat—and the beating up—goes on, and despite all the dreams of a utopian workplace it pays to know how to deal with the worst while hoping for the best.

All authors, I suspect, have someone else's book (or books) in mind as guides when they start to write, books either to be emulated or countered. Peter Benchley surely saw his great white shark as a latter-day great white whale, and Tom Wolfe acknowledges the connection of *Bonfire of the Vanities* with *Vanity Fair*. In my case, *Upward Nobility* has been inspired by a desire to create an antidote of sorts to *Power!*, a book of business strategies and tactics written by Michael Korda in the midseventies. With his advice on everything from power dressing and power networking to how to push a senior executive into retirement, Korda—a man not personally preoccupied with power, it would seem—produced a kind of yuppie *Dianetics* that may have helped spawn a generation that believed anything was acceptable as long as you were looking out for Number One. It seems clear to me the time has come for a different approach to success and power, one that, while recognizing the desire to reach the top as an admirable impulse, also acknowledges some limitation to the means of ascendancy.

In the chapters that follow, I offer a battle plan for grappling with a wide range of problems, from bastard bosses to expense accounts, from personal style to office sex. But it is a battle plan that I hope never loses sight of the Geneva Convention (or its business equivalent) and never surrenders the belief that good guys can—and increasingly will—finish first.

2

In Defense of

Elitism

*F*irst, a bit of flinty realism: the venerable firm of Fame & Fortune is not an equal opportunity employer. Like Darwinian evolution, F&F favors not just those who are fit, but those who are fitter than others, and frowns on anyone satisfied to blend demotically into the background with the pallid claim that "Gee, I'm just a regular guy." By definition, it adheres to Gore Vidal's (or was it La Rochefoucauld's?) dour dictum "It's not enough that I succeed, others must fail." This doesn't mean, of course, that very ordinary people don't sometimes have the good luck to rise high—witness any number of important politicians, including the remarkably lucky J. Danforth Quayle—but superiority is a surer bet.

Though the fabricators of corporate policy manuals work hard to make company life sound egalitarian, don't be fooled. If you pick up the phone, as I have, and ask top executives if they foster elitism, they react as if you'd suggested eliminating management

7

bonuses. But elitism lives, despite much new-wave management-speak to the contrary, and the companies that foster it—in an intelligent, unalienating way—are the ones that survive with style. Like it or not, the members of company elites, whether declared or just de facto, are the ones who end up with the hot reputations.

Still, the word "elitism" pings dissonantly on the ears of right-thinking Americans. It has such unappealing, politically incorrect connotations, in fact, that the Republicans used it as a major tactical weapon in the 1988 presidential campaign. Never mind that George Bush attended Andover and Yale and has been deeply embedded in the eastern Wasp establishment for much of his life, he had only to make a passing reference to Michael Dukakis's "Harvard buddies" to cast the dread suspicion that his opponent might be an elitist. There is something almost sinful about the idea that any group should set itself up as better than the rest of us (unless that group wears some distinctive fashion, like the yellow, green, and white uniforms of the Oakland A's). Elitism is the meritocracy that dares not speak its name. And yet it is an inevitable function of what sociologists call "group dynamics," and if you haven't identified the elite in your jolly workplace—and figured out how to join up—you're still depending on Dame Fortune to guarantee you a cover story in *Fortune*.

So let's clear the air, shall we? Despite its bad name in public and political life, elitism is just a phenomenon that raises one group above another, at least in its own perceptions, and in the process generates an ego-driven loyalty that will push its members to rise to any challenge whatever the cost. Simply defined, elitism is Us versus the Civilians, "I'm Chevy Chase and you're not," "Deutschland über Alles," or, as Mel Brooks nicely put it in his spoof of national anthems, "Let 'em all go to hell, except Cave Seven."

If that doesn't seem quite enough to lift elitism over the hump of unacceptability in a democratic society, consider this: at the leading edge of every advance in every field, an elite corps is doing the job (whether or not the "E" word is ever mentioned). And this: when things go drastically wrong, the people who come in to put the lid on are a breed apart, whether or not they happen to be encased in asbestos suits or shining armor. The fat cats may get fatter, the drones will drone on, and diligent bureaucrats can ensure that the trains run on time, but when heroic measures are called for, the hotshots get the call. Sinclair Lewis's Babbitt figured that America ought to be run by "regular guys," and in many cases, for better or worse, it is. But the elites, with their samurai, do-or-die codes of conduct and their Jesuitical presumption of superiority, work the miracles. Once, when a brilliant computer hacker played havoc with networks at the Pentagon and major universities, the press and public fulminated at the idea of secretive young spooks with too much knowledge and power for their own good. But one of the members of this outer-limits in-group at Harvard summed up the case for the defense succinctly: "The fact that the United States dominates the world in software is not a matter of technology. The culture for making great software is slightly crazy people working late at night."

With tough competition ahead, and the old economic givens already ancient history, it's the slightly crazy people willing to work late into the night for weeks and months at a time—people just unbalanced enough to think that their happy few have the exclusive contract for salvation—who are going to make the difference. And the more of these presumptuous supergroups there are—at every level and for every job description—the better our chances for a workable future will be. And you can quote me on that, even if it makes me sound like someone you don't want to sit next to at dinner.

No group is too small or too lowly for the bright mantle of elitism. Case in point: When I finished marine boot camp at Parris Island, my training platoon was sent to Camp Lejeune, North Carolina, for advanced combat training. Several of us were "volunteered" for an irksome thirty-day tour of duty guarding an ammunition depot back in the deep boonies. While our buddies were engaged in the manly pursuit of learning how to misread maps and set ambushes, we were feeding mosquitoes and shouting "Who goes there!" at foraging raccoons. Without rank, without clout, doing a job just one step up from KP, we nevertheless quickly began to develop the symptoms of elitism. We were, after all, the ammo guards, and They—all those faux marines running around on candy-ass maneuvers—were not. We came up with code words and a jargon understandable only among ourselves, invented a strictly nonregulation salute, and spent more time on spit-and-polish than we had even during our rigorous basic training.

Given enough time we might have started to mint our own currency. Despite the fact that there was nothing remarkable about what we were doing, or about us, within thirty days we had become implausibly special, a fraternity so exclusive that even had outsiders known about it they couldn't have joined. Cave Seven revisited, right there in the North Carolina pine barrens.

The Sacred Brotherhood of the Ammo Guards was an elite born of a certain desperation, the bonding of have-nots needing to carve out a piece of psychic turf. Elites in the workplace tend to be meritocracies, but the need is the same: to rise above the crowd, even if that crowd is already a good one. People want to identify with something more tangible than country or corporation, and the best people naturally want to link up with the best. General Motors may be one of the biggest corporations in America, but when elitists get together to build a special car they'll forget the corporate logo and say, with jutting jaw, "I'm Chevy Camaro, and you're not." Though there may actually be such a thing as a "company man," most hard chargers find it difficult to give their all for something as abstract as, say, IBM or AT&T. (In boot camp, one rarely heard about love of country, but loyalty to the Corps was a paramount and indispensable virtue, constantly hammered home.)

Such elitist loyalty can be a powerful motivator, and savvy managements use it gladly. Advertising agencies often create what they call "fast groups" of top talents ready to be mobilized when a presentation for a big account comes along. In fields where research and development are crucial, the function of the elite corps is particularly evident. While the yeomen and squires mind the store, the knights sally forth to conquer new territory, and you can guess who gets the glory. When Apple was working to create the revolutionary Macintosh, the Mac team was clearly separated from the common herd that did the profitable but mundane work of producing the company's well-established products. The Macintosh elite wore special T-shirts, kept to themselves, and generally (it's said) acted as if they were on a mission from God. The cult object produced by this cult of excellence is credited by many analysts with turning a pioneering company into a household name in all the hippest households.

John Hummer, a former Princeton basketball star and professional player who has worked closely with Silicon Valley companies as a venture capitalist, points out that along with the advantages of elitism come significant problems. "The downside of a situation like the Macintosh development is that it creates incredibly bad feeling within companies. After all, it's not the development teams that pay the bills, it's the less glamorous divisions, doing the day-to-day work of putting out products."

Sometimes smart management will try to maintain parity, not by squelching the elite, but by buoying up everyone else. Not too surprisingly, the attempt often fails. At a magazine where I once worked, the editor assembled a small elite corps to produce a special issue that demanded top performance. To those on the staff left with the responsibility for putting out the regular issue he diplomatically pointed out that only the best could be trusted to get the regular job done, but of course there's not much cachet in business-as-usual, and the tacit rift that grew between the regulars and the special forces remained long after the single issue came and went.

Since we're on the subject of elitism's possible disadvantages, let's get the others out of the way:

• **Hubris, snobbery, and fascism.** Thinking that you and your colleagues are the best, even if justified, can lead to a feeling that others are not due the same rights. Some smug corner of the mind starts whispering about *Untermenschen*, and the next thing you know somebody is going to suggest that the bathrooms ought to be labeled US and THEM. Brownshirts, Hell's Angels, and Klansmen are a result of the elitist mentality without the necessary ethics to control certain unfortunate human impulses.

• **Isolation, mania, and arrogance.** Elites tend to stick to themselves, and little by little forget what it's like on the outside. Work becomes reality, excellence the only goal, and everything else a fantasy land where there be dragons and sluggards. The farther up the superiority trail you travel, the less pleased you are at the idea that others are making a mess of the world. I refer you to the curious case of one Oliver North, lieutenant colonel and single-handed savior of civilization as we know it. An ultimate, foolish extreme of elitism is the club or neighborhood mentality, a delusive state of mind that makes someone presume membership in an elite simply because of a name or an address. Inheritors of wealth are inclined to suffer from this delusion, and can pay others to believe it too. Unaccountably, people with "Van" in their last names are susceptible, as are the residents of Tuxedo Park, New York, and Bel Air, California. The corporate equivalent of such elitist venues is the small town of Menlo Park, California, mecca to a greater concentration of high-tech investment firms per square hectare than anywhere else on earth. It happened that a couple of the real masters-of-the-universe outfits had their offices at a four-building complex at 3000 Sand Hill Road. In no time it became very, very important among venture capitalists to have that address on their company stationery, as if there were some divine right of geography. Ditto certain clubs, restaurants, tables in restaurants, and so on.

• **Deprivation, exploitation, and suspicion.** Elitism thrives on anything, or on nothing at all, as illustrated by my story of the paltry but proud ammo guards. Venture financier Hummer, who played basketball at Princeton in the glory years of the late sixties, recalls the austerity of the school's Ivy League athletic program—per diem for road games was $2.50—compared to the luxurious situation of opponents like UCLA, where the locker room was carpeted and each player had an elaborate nameplate designating his dressing area. When someone mentioned this disparity to Princeton coach Pete Carril, he growled that the Viet Cong didn't have carpeting and fancy training meals, and they weren't complaining. This guerrilla mentality makes a virtue of going without—be it sleep or perks or even fair remuneration—and engenders disdain for those who need the soft life of privilege (defined by elite sufferers as almost anything that smacks of human comfort).

One of the troubles with such deprivation pride, in addition to its tendency to give rise to intolerance, is that it can be taken advantage of by people who do have the perks and the cushy offices and the limos, and who are low enough to pretend admiration and even envy for those who go without them. As long as some incredibly selfless elite feels a few cuts above the rest of the world because it can get along with almost nothing, almost nothing is conveniently what it will get.

And what does an elitist get for being extraordinary, working superhumanly long days, sacrificing everything to achieve success for his special band of brothers (and sisters), laughing at hardship? The unhelpful reputation of being an oddball, slightly nuts, out of the mainstream career path, or just a holier-than-thou stiff. Remember, in *Apocalypse Now*, the suspicion Colonel Kurtz (Marlon Brando) aroused because he stepped out of a straight line to the Joint Chiefs in order to volunteer for the Special Forces, determined to be all that he could be? Clearly, Kurtz wasn't a man who might be trusted to do things according to the tenets of prevailing management mediocrity. In going the hardest route (the one an elitist may be required to take just because he *is* an elitist) you can find yourself on a path of no return. Unfair, but not surprising. It's only natural that members of the elite in any organization may deplore the cautious style of top management and chafe at the idea of being managed at all. Even among those who are happy to use an elite corps to get the tough jobs done, little affection is felt for people whose motivation is superiority, and whose loyalty is usually placed elsewhere than at the CEO's wing-tipped feet. Ask yourself why it is that a Jesuit has never become pope, or why King Philip the Fair arrested the Knights Templars in 1307 and had most of them burned at the stake, and you'll have a quick read on the double bind of an elite corps.

But having catalogued the many tiger traps that may await you for trying to rise above the crowd, I'll still give elitism four stars. First, it's simply more rewarding to feel special about your work than to stand off to the side and watch a bunch of other people feeling special about theirs. (If you don't think so, you're either not going to do well, or you're a cold, calculating person who's going to do just fine.) Most of us, even those hard-core materialists who view the Ferrari Testarossa as the highest level of spiritual attainment, want something more than money for our labors. The George Steinbrenners of business will never figure it out, but financial gain is neither everything nor the only thing (though it's a long way from being an insignificant thing). The real payoff is to be able to say, "I'm really good," and to know that others are saying it about you. It stands to reason that those who work as part of an elite team get to say and hear those magic words more often than workaday staffers.

Second, the company that elitists keep is more interesting. The trouble with not being in the fast group is that you may have to spend your days with the slow group, listening to the tedious, methodical thump of an uninspiring drummer. Though it can be nerve-racking hanging out with the crazies, it's rarely boring. A close friend of mine joined the CIA many years ago, not because he hungered for a life of derring-do (though that's what he got) but because during his initial conversation with the recruiter he became aware that the guy had made seventy-five free-fall parachute jumps *and* had actually finished *Finnegans Wake*.

Third, elites go where the action is. When it comes to sheer, fierce fun, it's the SWAT teams, the smoke jumpers, the litigators, the arbitragers, the shock troops, the outriders, the troubleshooters, the wildcatters, and the marines who get to have all the kicks (even if they sometimes end up getting kicked). Whichever side of whatever battle you happen to be on, it would seem better to be in the thick of things than on the sidelines; whether or not you win or lose, you'll at least have experienced a real adrenaline high. On a Hollywood set some years ago, I noticed that the stunt men—an elite group if ever there was one—wore T-shirts that read: "The hell with dialogue—let's wreck something." Not only were these aristocrats of controlled mayhem revered by all the beautiful young script girls, but they seemed to be having a far better time than anybody else in the crew, including the lavishly overpaid star.

Fourth, like it or not, elitism is the hope of the future. And maybe the only hope. I don't mean to inject a note of implausible idealism here, but unless we can turn jobs back into callings, whether or not those jobs entail collecting garbage, running a nuclear power facility, producing television, or transplanting kidneys, the next century is going to be a fine mess. True elitists are constitutionally incapable of saying "What the hell, it's just a job," and the less heard of that pernicious and currently pervasive cop-out the better. When first-quality work is crucial, an elite corps can always be trusted to deliver. Once a woman I was traveling with fell seriously and mysteriously ill in Jordan. In a panic, I rushed her to a local French hospital, where she was whisked away from me by a squad of formidable nuns, dark-clad take-charge types I instantly dubbed the Sisters of Clarity. These women exuded confidence— they obviously understood that no one on earth was as capable as they of curing the sick—and looking back on a frightening event that began to improve the moment they appeared, I'm glad they felt that way.

And last, elitism is nature's way. If you're the kind of person with an uncontrollable urge to be one with the gods, seeking out the elite and joining up is really inevitable for you. And if there isn't an elite in place when you arrive on a scene, you'll find a way to form one. Don't fight it, and don't feel guilty about being un-American. Remember Thomas Jefferson, Ben Franklin, and John Adams, who were such elitists that they felt empowered to declare that all men are created equal. Anyway, you'll just be miserable masquerading as a regular guy. Trust me: I've been red shirt, and I've been varsity; varsity is better.

3

The Ambition Thing

what price glory usually

depends on your currency

I've got better things to do than work seventy-hour weeks!"
I overheard this minor revolutionary manifesto across the locker tops at a health club in downtown San Francisco, during the winter of our economic discontent in 1990. Was this just California dreaming by somebody with a ponytail and a patented software cash cow? Not at all. The young brave thumbing his nose at the grindstone was one of the financial district's finest, someone who not too long ago might have been bragging that he'd slept the night before on his desk (the eighties equivalent of being carried home on your shield). Of all the non-moviemaking professionals in California, stockbrokers as a group have been the hardest working, getting to their offices before six A.M. to jump on the New York Stock Exchange, then staying into the night to track the action around the Pacific Rim. Their social lives were barren, their nervous systems shredded, but they toughed it out because getting ahead in their hardball

business was measured in how many buckets of blood, sweat, and tears you were willing to shed.

But the West Coast investment samurai were hardly untypical in recent times. In places like New York, Chicago, and other notably tough turfs, people in every line of work were unfazed by evenings and weekends at the office, if that's what it took to land the big account or litigate the hot case. The rallying cry of the best and the brightest was the big triple A: Ambition Above All.

What a difference a year or two has made. Though ambition hasn't exactly skulked off the playing field, it seems to be taking on a more philosophical—possibly even a chastened—form. As the bullish rush upward that characterized the Reagan romp is revealed to have been as destructive to companies as it was enriching to some individuals, the land of Milken honey has turned into a rubble-strewn landscape. Even those in the search-and-destroy brigade who never thought much beyond winning and who didn't worry a lot about the finer points of ethics are having second thoughts.

The newly reluctant stockbroker proclaiming his independence from the workweek as endless bummer is not alone. All over the country, former hard chargers seem to be deciding that if today is the first day of the rest of their lives, they're going to sleep late. The change may not be all that dramatic, but the signs that this decade is different have been showing up regularly since the nineties began. During the 1990 World Series, the Oakland A's, who ought to have been fiercely ambitious to take home their second title in a row, began, after Cincinnati took the first two games, to sound like people thinking about their vacation plans. Rickey Henderson, a notorious overachiever (whose financial ambitions are briefly chronicled in Chapter 25), admitted that the team had to play better baseball in order to make a comeback, then added, "But you have to have fun and realize they won't throw you up against a wall and shoot you if you lose." And Jose Canseco, a long-ball egoist who, at $5 million a year, might be expected to be ambition personified, complained that he didn't want to "put the pressure" on himself with the feeling that he ought to carry the team.

Of course (you might reasonably point out), these pampered players already had their rich contracts, so their ambition would be largely satisfied. But there are people saying no to money as well as greater glory, even in big-buck sports. Mike Holmgren, the offensive coordinator for the San Francisco 49ers—a man whose rise in the NFL has been dazzling (in 1980 he was still coaching high school ball)—turned down the number-one job with both the Jets and the Cardinals to stay on as a 49ers assistant. And top tennis player Boris Becker actually turned down an invitation to play in a $6 million tournament in Munich because he felt the huge purse was "perverse."

In the corporate world, the fever of desire to have it all seems to be down at least a few degrees, and the prognosis is for further cooling. Some companies like Monsanto, Pacific Gas & Electric, and GE are actually trying to reduce competition within their management ranks and encourage upward-striving executives to stay in their jobs longer—a once scorned phenomenon known as "plateauing." With moves to make operations more efficient by eliminating high-level positions, many businesses are simply offering fewer top spots to strive for. And, with the last (at last!) of the so-called baby boom generation now verging on thirtysomething, and the population growing older, fewer new strivers are coming in at the bottom. So a corporate policy that encourages a Darwinian free-for-all can end up losing people it will need desperately ten years down the road.

But companies looking for ways to make people feel better about *not* becoming vice presidents may simply be responding to the reality that more and more of their former wildest beasts are opting out of the tooth-and-claw club, suspecting that the reward for victory will just be a more desperate struggle to survive. As the Duke of Wellington once sagely observed, "Next to a battle lost, the greatest misery is a battle gained." The big winners of the past decade have been paying steep prices for their successes, in bankruptcies (both financial and emotional), burnouts, or even sabbaticals at minimum security federal institutions. Some of the paybacks have been very public, and they can only have had a sobering effect on young Turks poised to slash their way to the top. But the most likely cause for the growing malaise may be plain exhaustion, and an increasing feeling that whatever's in the pot at the end of the rainbow may not be worth living the life of a warrior monk to get.

Just as the unremitting grind of the fifties led to the dropout disenchantment of the sixties, the relentless press for success in the eighties is likely to spawn a certain skeptical torpor in the nineties. Even the seemingly indefatigable Japanese have begun to worry about *karoshi,* a word that literally means death from overwork; the government is in the midst of a major research project to determine if ambition is killing white-collar ninja, and state-sponsored ads urge workers to take more time off. In America, parents who have both worked long into every weeknight to give their kids a great life have realized with a shock that what their kids really need is parents.

The result of these and similar revelations is that the old do-or-die spirit seems to be dying in places where it used to flourish. Of course, it would be naive to think that even people with the noblest motives for slowing down aren't also affected by the fact that the lavish rewards of the recent past just aren't to be had anymore, no matter how ambitious and driven someone may be. Greed may not be good, despite Gordon Gekko's pronouncement in *Wall Street,* but it's hard to deny that for a long time the other half of his credo held true: "Greed works." It has certainly played a major part in making ambitious men and women accept preternaturally hard labor as standard fare. Given tunnel vision, fierce determination, and high energy (whether aerobically or chemically derived), almost anybody (it seemed) could be a millionaire by age twenty-five. Now our seven- or eight-year-long Midas moment is over, and at least some of those whose sole motivation was money are going to be looking for other ways to satisfy themselves.

But if during the past several years ambition has been fashioned into the golem of the gold card set, it's not invariably a bad thing. Despite the changes in attitude that have already made this decade distinctly different from the last, to dismiss ambition as nothing more than a servant of greed is to oversimplify something that is varied, complex, and in certain forms absolutely essential to the health of any enterprise. Like elitism, ambition can easily be misunderstood. A certain kind of ambition *is* greedy, not necessarily for money, but for success at any cost, and like certain tricky viruses, this sort of ambition can masquerade as the more benign variety most of us learn from our parents and kindergarten teachers ("Jake, you're trying hard to do better, and that's *good*"). Whether ambition is good or bad, its complete loss is unnatural, to say the least, and possibly psychotic. Given human nature, the disappearance of ambition is not on the agenda, at least in this millennium, so it remains worthwhile to know the basic forms of ambition most likely to be found—making reputations or mischief—around the office (and no doubt inside yourself somewhere). If you can separate the bad from the good, ambition is still indispensable, whether you're climbing the icy cliff or camping out happily on the plateau. What follows, then, is a very general roundup of ambition's most frequently encountered types.

• **Blind ambition.** This is the hard stuff, the ego *über Alles* drive that acknowledges neither boundaries, ironies, nor the sensibilities of others. With blind ambition, the ends—personal success, more money, increased power—*always* justify the meanness. There is something awesome about people on the fast and nasty track of blind ambition—they have the power of monomania uncompromised by the slightest doubt about whether getting what you want is worth being an utter shit. Because they can operate with the friction-free fluidity an amoral vacuum permits (a.k.a. the zipless "fuck you"), they can sometimes seem enviable to colleagues constrained by ethics and ingrained decency. And, sad to say, they frequently get what they're after (even though that seldom satisfies them for long). But don't be fooled; blind ambition is just that, and sooner or later those guided by it go off the edge, too busy being ruthless to notice the danger. Even if they don't, even if they become rich and powerful and adored by an easily duped public, you still wouldn't want to do what they did to get where they are. Believe me, even if you wish it weren't true.

• **Blunt ambition.** Similar to the blind variety, this type carries with it at least a pinch of morality. Strivers with blunt ambition know when they're doing something reprehensible, even if they do it anyway. Their goals are usually specific, however, and when they reach those goals they may actually become bearable, if only until the next goal is decided upon. Blunties are rude, sometimes crude, sometimes dangerous, and usually a pain, but they're not truly evil. Nevertheless, they're to be avoided if possible.

• **Blond ambition.** Though found in its most definitive and literal form in television journalism (Diane Sawyer, Deborah Norville, et al.), blond ambition only rarely has anything to do with hair color. Rather, it's a state of mind that says, "I'm gorgeous, so I can have whatever I want." Looks *do* matter, of course—let's not be coy; if beauty and the beast both have brains, who do you think will get the promotion? (And please, no whining about how unfair life is.) But blond ambition isn't about brains, or ability, or perseverance—it's about a remarkable feeling of divine right, a sense of entitlement, that certain good-looking people begin to harbor in early childhood and have perfected by prom night. This presumption, idiotic from any rational point of view, is always based on a certain amount of empirical evidence—good things frequently *do* come to certain physically attractive people when they've done nothing to earn them. Their belief that the comely shall inherit the earth (or at least a very large office), though base, has a dumb purity that can actually propel them an amazing distance. Our parents always properly told us that looks alone won't get you far, yet we've all seen mediocrities who just happen to be long of limb and fair of face do depressingly well. Health clubs are filled with the blondly ambitious, men and women who know instinctively that only ten pounds or so stand between them and the tedious need to have ability.

• **Bland ambition.** Afflicting even those who don't think of themselves as career-minded at all, this is the most common form of ambition, more institutional than personal but often very powerful. Bland ambition is the Mississippi River of middle-class motivation, flowing inexorably from college graduation to retirement on a good golf course in Palm Springs. It is based on the presumption that one *must* advance simply because one is oneself; there is no other choice for a decent American. Certain schools, particularly the Ivy League, specialize in bland ambition, since a Princeton or Yale (etc.) degree is thought to be a sufficient ticket to ride—the academic version of the good looks that fuel blond ambition. Though strong enough to impel thousands of nice, unspectacular people upward, bland ambition tends to crumble easily in periods of stress and reassessment, when idealism or tougher competition makes the idea of regular, required advancement seem boring and restrictive. Most of the lawyers who became potters in the sixties were blandlings, and the nineties will bring a similar shakeout.

• **Blended ambition.** Take some from column A, some from column B, and so on, and you end up with one of the infinite amalgams of ambition most of us call our own. Whether or not this blend, once mixed, can be adjusted is hard to say, but it is possible to analyze the proportions that make up any given ambition cocktail. Someone like ABC anchor Peter Jennings might be assumed to be motivated in about equal parts by all the types of ambition mentioned above, whereas the ambition of White House chief of staff John Sununu would be heavy on the blind side, light on bland, and entirely lacking, presumably, in blond.

• **Blessed ambition.** This is the rarest sort of ambition, something so enlightened that it might be the sole province of saints, if saints weren't so inclined toward the blind variety. Responding to specific situations, never automatic and overweening, blessed ambition rises and falls according to need. It's the drive to be good at what you do, and to rise as a natural by-product of excellence rather than as an absolute prerogative. People with blessed ambition will work like Sherpas when they're determined to reach a goal (something bigger than their own promotions) but know how to ease off when the job is done. They're more likely to be loyal to their colleagues, self-sacrificing, and generally good to be around than any of the other ambitious types. Sometimes a sheer excess of decency can make them seem a little too good to be true, but surely that's more bearable than the jackboot arrogance of those who believe that destiny has decreed their success. During the past decade, these noble souls were often taken for chumps ("If Yvonne's so damned good, how come she isn't rich?"), but their time has come.

Just as all paths of glory lead but to the grave, all blind, blunt, blond, and bland ambition leads but to that grim reaper of careerists, the Peter Principle. In the end, this great, abiding law of corporate nature waits to ambush those whose self-absorption has kept them from getting wisdom. Men and women who can't imagine any higher calling than their own relentless upward motion are doomed by their loss of perspective to go on taking bigger and bigger jobs, until—incapable of knowing when to be satisfied—they end up one fateful notch higher in the hierarchy than they can handle. And find themselves, ambition, Rolodex, arrogance, and all, out in the cold.

4

Ms. Doolittle, Meet Professor Higgins

gauging the subtle

differences

between mentors

and tormentors

*B*efore I launch into a quick study of the emotionally freighted, often ill-fated mentor/protégé relationship, let's take a look at a spectacular moment early on in the history of management upheavals.

Remember Cronus? (Think back to that Greek mythology gut course you dozed through in college.) He was one of the deities the Greeks called the Elder Gods, primordial power brokers also known as Titans. Cronus had been on top since time immemorial, in effect the chairman of the board of Cosmos Unlimited. Rumor had it that Cronus would be overthrown by one of his children, an unsettling prospect that caused him to implement the drastic personnel management practice of devouring every baby his wife bore. When little Zeus came along, Cronus's wife, desperate to change her role from caterer to mater, spirited the kid away (substituting a rock, which her husband gullibly gulped down). Sure enough, Zeus grew up, went head to head with the Titans in a hostile takeover, and ended up with the company. (This was long before anybody had thought up golden parachutes, and you don't want to know how Cronus and his cronies spent their unhappy retirements.)

What does this have to do with mentors and protégés? Just this: if you're worried that someone you've been helping out may be the one who does you in, you're not necessarily suffering a paranoid delusion. Or if you have a mentor and know in your heart you'd never do anything that might hurt someone who offers you protection and advancement, you may be kidding yourself. Even if Cronus had been a solid supporter of the next generation, he probably would have ended up with a sharp stick in the eye; ambition is no respecter of the old guard, or the old gods.

Some mentors never have a nice day. Well, that's not exactly true, since if they hadn't enjoyed success they wouldn't be in a position to hitch others to their stars. But once they take on the role of mentor, their situation is potentially as disheartening as any in business. Protégés don't necessarily fare better, since they often get shafted by mentors who sniff disloyalty and turn mean, by usurpers who identify them with the ousted boss, or by colleagues jealous of their favored status. Yet despite all the possible disappointments and dangers, mentoring goes on, probably because it represents such deep-seated needs on the parts of both participants that nothing, not even the most harrowing atrocity stories, will ever effectively discourage the practice.

Since the motivations of mentors are the more complex, I'll look at them first. Why would any sane, self-serving, ambitious, successful man or woman want to get close to a younger, equally ambitious, even more self-serving, possibly less ethical, and far hungrier man or woman whose loyalty, however impressive at first, may not be of the till-death-do-us-part variety? One has only to mention the Prodigal Son, Judas, Goneril, Brutus, Lancelot, and Donald Regan to reveal a history of cautionary tales. How can any veteran of the office wars fail to see that giving someone a leg up increases the odds of getting a foot in the face?

The question betrays a certain naivety, a notion that a mentor has entirely charitable intentions. In fact, varying amounts of self-interest always motivate someone to take on a protégé. In this sense, a clear difference exists between mentorship and friendly help, though on a day-to-day basis the two may appear to be the same. A mentor, unlike a friend, rarely gives something for nothing. (Let's leave aside the deservedly discredited tradition of sexual self-interest; it's still around, rearing its horny little head, but the relationship is actually faux mentorship and doesn't belong in a discussion of the real thing.) For a mentor, a protégé represents among other things a comforting presence in what is often a lonely and hostile environment. In a way, the relative youthfulness and energy of the protégé provides a kind of rear guard (if only psychologically) for an executive engaged in the struggle to survive, a protective payback for the reflected luster of a powerful sponsor's favor.

Sometimes a mentor takes on a protégé for less selfish reasons, simply because it lends a noble glow to help shape the future of a worthy young contender (though the desire to say "When I took that kid on he didn't know debentures from dentures, and now look at him" *is* a form of self-aggrandizement); or even for the ultimate good of a profession, though a motive that exalted should arouse at least as much skepticism as admiration.

But whether someone's motive is absolutely pure or secretly selfish, the results of mentoring can be significant and salutary for individuals and professions. The late conductor and composer Leonard Bernstein, having risen almost miraculously from the ranks of assistant conductors at the New York Philharmonic, made the job of assistant a formal protégé-ship when he took over the orchestra. Out of this exercise in multiple mentoring came such star conductors as Seiji Ozawa, Claudio Abbado, Michael Tilson Thomas, and Edo de Waart.

Quality counts when someone with a mentoring impulse is looking for a protégé. Though loyalty may count most of all, it can't be depended on too heavily (more about that in a moment). Ability and dedication are strong attractions for friends in high places, since the worth of a protégé is a measure of a mentor. The original mentor, none other than Mentor himself, chose as his special charge Odysseus, whose remarkable career (or at least terrific publicity) reflected everlasting credit on his adviser. The goddess Athena, recognizing heroic potential, also took a liking to Odysseus, constantly giving him everything from inside information to grooming tips, and ended up with very good press, too. On the other hand,

a low-grade protégé is just as sure a sign of a shoddy mentor. One
only has to think of the late, loathsome Roy Cohn to sum up Joe
McCarthy, the dipso/megalomaniacal senator who took him under
his wing.

Like lucky Odysseus, certain people seem to attract well-placed
boosters. In Ben Bradlee, Jr.'s book *Guts and Glory*, Oliver North is
portrayed as one of these mentor magnets. From his days at An-
napolis, when the boxing coach made a special effort to help him
win a championship over more gifted boxers, to the White House,
where fellow marine Robert McFarlane and chief CIA spook
William Casey each offered powerful sponsorship, North was the
darling of the mighty (and played havoc with several senior careers). Nineteenth-century novels are filled with lucky waifs who
somehow appeal to rich and generous patrons, thus living happily
ever after, and this potentate-of-gold-at-the-end-of-the-rainbow
dream has never lost its charm.

Whatever magic brings about such fortunate appeal, people
destined to be favored usually show signs early; they are touted
by their high school teachers and still remain popular with their
peers. They ought to be easy to hate, being so enviable, but the
encouragement and special dispensations that come to them seem
ordained and therefore beyond everyone's control. And even
more maddening (if, despite looks, talent, and so forth, you don't
happen to be mentor bait), the phenomenon is contagious; the
success of what might be called the "serial protégé"—someone
passed up the line from mentor to mentor—is self-generating. If
young E. Z. Riser III is given special attention by some important personage, other even more important personages become interested automatically—the gilt-by-association effect. Talent may
be almost incidental with born protégés, and the occasional blunder no great crime; the well-known phenomenon of failing upward can usually be traced to a genius not just for doing things
right, but for being lovable in the eyes of the lofty. People who
never do especially well at anything and yet move from good jobs
to better to best are likely to be serial protégés, or in possession
of some very incriminating Polaroids.

Real protégés are not *untalented*, however; they just have an easier time of advancement, like good hitters who tend to get more
walks *because* they're good hitters. (Those who would be protégés

but lack ability usually end up as toadies, a revolting species I will deal with—I hope harshly enough—in Chapter 22.)

What protégés want out of a relationship to a mentor is nothing more than anyone else wants: to better themselves and/or their situation. Fair enough. But though the goal is simple, the ways to achieve it are many, as are the dangers along the way. Ideally, the relationship of mentor and protégé is mutually beneficial, though the balance of benefits may vary widely. It's not unusual, however, for the protégé to serve the interests of a senior figure without much in return except the chance to catch a little reflected light every now and then. In the movie *Wall Street*, the obedient disciple played by Charlie Sheen is nothing more to the greedy Gordon Gekko than an ingratiating cipher who can provide inside information and take a fall if things go wrong. In many ambitious but basically decent young men and women, the desire to have a mentor—to bask in the glow and learn the moves of a master—is so strong that they easily, even willingly, ignore the one-sidedness of the relationship until they find themselves twisting slowly in the wind.

The central problem of a true mutually enhancing relationship is that it's frequently doomed by its very success. If a top executive creates a younger, hungrier—and less expensive—clone of himself, he also creates a viable and very visible replacement. Sometimes, of course, when the mentor leaves the company, the loyal protégé will opt to go, too; but since young upward mobilizers seek out mentors in order to court success, why would they want to spurn it when the offer comes? "Loyal? Well, sure. I mean, I'm going to miss Dave more than anybody. He taught me everything I know. It won't be the same around here without him, but somebody has to stay to make sure everything he put together doesn't go down the tubes. Right?" Simply put, the better you are at picking a protégé, the more expendable you become. And only someone deeply insecure chooses a protégé—or a running mate—so unprepossessing that no one can imagine him or her taking over.

The Attack Dog syndrome is a central problem (with a certain poetic justice) for mentors who are hard cases. When a tough boss teaches his protégé to show no mercy, to look out for Number One, to go for the jugular, and various the other acts of self-interest and aggression, he or she is in essence training a beast with no guarantee it won't turn on its master.

Sometimes a protégé does offer protection, even after the fall. When the once formidable network TV programmer Fred Silverman was unceremoniously dumped by NBC and became an independent producer, scrambling for attention with hundreds of other supplicants, his first break came from his former protégé Brandon Tartikoff. Of course, young Brandon had old Fred's job, but hey, you do what you've gotta do.

The possibility of providing succor to one's eventual replacement, a nightmarish thought daily brought to the fretful managerial mind through thinly euphemized "Et tu, Brute" stories on the business pages, creates a wary and worrisome sort of mentor poised to turn on his protégé the instant he feels even a hint of parity between them. The choreography of this classic situation is delicate beyond measure, with the protégé in the difficult position of needing to do well or lose the mentor's favor yet not so well that he becomes a threat and loses his job. Similarly, the mentor must walk a line between raising a satisfying replica of himself and creating a monster he can't control (bear in mind that Darth Vader was once the protégé of kindly Obe-wan Kenobee).

The venerable idea that mentors were veterans whose task was to train the next generation of warriors simply doesn't make a lot of sense in places where you are as likely to be attacked from within as without. But for various reasons certain kinds of businesses remain mentor-intensive. The most obvious example is professional sports, where the age of playing gives way to the age of teaching relatively early. The picture of a baseball manager and his coaches studying their team from a corner of the dugout is positively Homeric, and legendary mentors like Cus D'Amato and John Wooden have been crucial in shaping the careers of such all-protégés as Muhammad Ali, Mike Tyson, and Kareem Jabar.

Similarly, the military—another profession where one gets old young, or under certain circumstances dead—has a mentor tradition, one that starts with the most tormenting mentor of all, the drill sergeant, a paradigmatic father figure who can never be satisfied fully and thus inspires ultimate efforts. (The implacable, unpleasant mentor appears in civilian life, too. The formidably demanding *Harper's Bazaar* art director Alexey Brodovitch, mentor of such subsequent stars as Richard Avedon and Hiro, was said to be a master whose most encouraging word was a flinty silence.)

Law firms, particularly those with long-established reputations, tend to organize at least an unspoken mentor-protégé system to impress hallowed tradition upon new members. A friend of mine at a prestigious New York corporate law partnership describes a year-long initiation rite for tyros during which they are assigned as protégés to partners, often doing a clerk's chores in a kind of pin-stripe equivalent of a beginning sumo wrestler's domestic servitude. The purpose? To remind young men and women making $65,000 right out of school that however hot they may feel, they are still at the bottom of a slope whose footholds are arduous and slippery.

There may be no more mentor-intensive profession than politics, and no city so overpopulated by protégés as Washington, D.C. Without a veteran's guidance, no one—not even newly elected out-of-town presidents—can safely navigate the fogs of Foggy Bottom. In a parody of the way runaway girls from Minnesota are picked up by raffish "protectors" at Manhattan's Port Authority bus terminal, political mentors (known as "rabbis" in the otherwise Presbyterian parlance of the capital) and first-time members of Congress gravitate toward one another at cocktail parties in the fall of the year. Without the aid of the powerful Georgia senator Richard Russell, Lyndon Johnson might never have become LBJ, and without Senator Johnson, former congressional page Bobbie Baker would never have become a mover and shaker. And so it goes. The freshman class is looked over for future stars, and the rush to mentor is on. (Johnson, an unusually considerate protégé, contended for years that Russell should have become president, but in a way, having his student make the grade, he did.) Separating the mentors and protégés in Washington from the swirling crowds of cronies, toadies, power brokers, hangers-on, and nepotists in search of isms is so difficult that real political mentoring has ended up with an unde-servedly bad name.

Given the problems attached to being either a mentor or a protégé, one might be well advised to keep one's career a solitary affair. But since there are advantages mixed in with all the disappoint-ments and perils, and legitimate needs to be met by the venerable institution, perfectly good people may find themselves in one position or the other, and ought to have a few guiding notions on how best to proceed.

First, advice to the prospective protégé:

- Assuming you can have your pick of mentors, choose one whose position is secure and who is someone you admire (as opposed to someone you envy). Beware of anyone, however important and powerful, who has a track record of sacrificing subordinates; loyalty ought to be mutual, and a perfidious mentor is a daily gamble.

- Try to assess your mentor's motivations. It's okay, and quite flattering, if an established figure likes your style and is willing to trade his or her savvy for your sparkle, and even better if you sense that you have been picked as an heir apparent. But keep your ego in check and retain some objectivity; if there's any chance that you might be drawn into a relationship that is considerably better for your would-be mentor than for you—if, for instance, you might be expected to serve as a scapegoat should things go wrong—it's better to go it alone.

- Assess your own motivations. True, you want to move up, and you want some magical grease for the skids, but power in a mentor shouldn't outweigh wisdom. A good professional relationship can make you more successful *and* a better person. No kidding. If the only reason you want to be someone's protégé is to make life easier for yourself, shame on you.

- Think about the future, which sooner or later may present you with a decision involving that most difficult question, Where does your loyalty lie? Ask yourself how closely you want yourself tied to your mentor's star (which can rise or fall). Someday you may be offered his job, and just in case he doesn't say, "Look, kid, don't worry about me, go for it" it's a good idea to have decided what you're going to do, before the emotions start flying.

And now a few words for those who feel the parental stirrings of the mentor impulse:

- Make sure a prospective protégé is someone you can stand to have as an admirer. Groucho Marx once said that he wouldn't want to belong to any club that would have him as a member, and there are some younger co-workers whose worship would make you feel like a very lesser god indeed. (Irrespective of gender, this sort of thing is called "bimbo love," and can do you a lot more harm than good.)

- Think of mentoring as a calling. Even though both sides of the relationship ought to benefit, the mentor—being the lion—should be prepared to do the lion's share of favors. You may own the present, but the future belongs to your protégé. If the first question you ask yourself when you take on a protégé is, What's in this for me?, you probably don't really want to be a mentor.

• Accept ahead of time that you're likely to end up with one sort of disappointment or another. If you teach brilliantly, your pupil may well end up surpassing you, and no matter how capacious your soul, there's a measure of bitterness in that pill. A well-coached protégé ought to be a natural choice for your job, should things go badly, but despite the logic of that idea it can be difficult to see your misfortune proving only a slightly mixed blessing for your disciple. A protégé of mine now holds a job I loved, and even though he richly deserved it, I've never quite forgiven him. And remember, a good mentor doesn't endlessly claim credit for a protégé's career, and sooner or later the protégé—wretched ingrate!—will stop acknowledging the source of his success.

• Finally, search your soul, or rather your libido. In fact, give it a good ransacking. If a possible protégé just happens to be someone of the opposite sex, and if in the process of considering this person's merits you just happen to have thought (in all innocence) about the wonderful symmetry of her calves or the heft of his shoulders, give up the idea of mentoring until you're older. Much, much older.

5

Laughter in the
Dark

humor is a gift

that ought to be

unwrapped very

carefully

*S*trap yourself into the pilot's seat, and let's run through a little Office Crisis Simulation to check your responses and see how serious you are about making it in the big time. Please note that the operative word here is "serious."

Things are not going particularly well at the company. With the collapse of the junk bond market and an unsure economic outlook, a string of deals have come unglued. The senior vice president in charge of panic and retribution has called a meeting. The atmosphere is thick with dread, as those responsible anxiously prepare their desperate defenses. The VP rises, scowling.

"I'm sick of asking you people how things are going and having you tell me everything is going 'swimmingly, just swimmingly,' when in fact the business is headed down the tubes. Why you feel you need to say how freaking swimmingly things are going, instead of reporting the extent of the disaster while there's still time for me to do something about it, I can't figure out. Deals are collapsing every day, and all I hear is 'swimmingly.' From now on, I want the truth."

At this point, his face flushed, the irate honcho turns to you and demands to know how the Cuddly Software merger is going. You lean forward earnestly and say, (1) "Well, J.D., naturally it's a lot tougher to hammer out an agreement in today's cautious climate, so I'm kind of walking on eggs with this one, but with a little luck I think I can bring it off," or (2) "Swimmingly, Chief, just swimmingly."

If you answered (1), you placed yourself squarely among the sensible majority of your fellow humans that considers life—and especially the business of making a living—absolutely and relentlessly serious. If you answered (2), you spoke for the endangered minority that can't quite believe anything is so serious that a laugh is inappropriate. Or rather, as Robert Redford put it in *The Way We Were*, that everything's too serious to be so serious. These are the people who, finding themselves in the direst of circumstances, war, divorce, an IRS audit, just can't resist the challenge of seeing if they can wring at least one joke out of their malaise.

In a better world, where the laughter-lovers prevailed, an inability to make light of heavy situations would be considered a character flaw so grievous that an entire clan of therapists would grow rich treating it. But unfortunately for those of us to whom utter seriousness is the cause of great discomfort, the world at large and the business world in particular are dominated by those who think of humor as perverse, dangerous and—worst of all—no laughing matter.

And in a way they're right: humor *is* dangerous, at least to those who know that the reverberations of laughter can shake the foundations of an unsmiling establishment. When Vaclav Havel, president of Czechoslovakia and former political prisoner, was jailed in the early eighties, he was allowed to write only one four-page letter a week, only to his wife, and only on personal subjects. There was one further stipulation: he could use no humor. Corporate managers, while not necessarily indistinguishable from Communist thought police, seem to have a similar fear of humor. If, for instance, someone has a problem placing the Cuddly Software merger on a level of gravity with global warming, and feels free to make jokes while discussing the merger's status, how will that muddled thinker accept the idea that he or she should spend every waking minute of six or seven very long days a week worrying about it? Might not such a confused person question whether health, emotional stability, romance, and eventual longevity are worth sacrificing just as long as Mr. Cuddly signs on the dotted line? If you are the troublesome sort who leavens the work of making a deal with even the minimum daily requirement of irony, you might also be the kind of undesirable who tries to tack a private life onto the outermost edges of your career. Those who have risen high in the world without ever risking a frivolous thought will single you out in no time, and are likely to take steps to ensure that your malady doesn't infect your fellow workers.

All right, the above is an exaggeration. You will not be strung up by your thumbs for lightening the mood at a tension-filled meeting. You may even be smiled upon by those who are in no mood to be amused. But don't be misled: the idea that everybody can benefit from a good laugh is tolerated, not celebrated, and in one way or another limits will eventually be imposed on the sound of merriment. So if you are still young and unbloodied enough to imagine that humor will be, invariably, an asset in a working life, let's talk. I'm not going to ask you to take my word for something so dour, but will offer indisputable proof that being funny may be harmful to your future, at least at some times and in some places. Think about some countries where humor is woven into the language and the fabric of life. Italy? Greece? England? All places where the ability to laugh at oneself, and everything else, is considered the mark of a highly evolved personality. Now think about some countries where humor has never played well, if at all. Germany? Switzerland? Japan? All places known for single-minded seriousness of purpose (with occasionally disastrous results). Now think about the relative positions of these countries in the world's economic hierarchy. Need more be said? Looking at that evidence, it's hard not to deduce that gag lines and bottom lines are antithetical. But let's get closer to home. Have you ever heard anybody say, "Man, he's really a funny guy!" when the subject at hand was the boss? Have you ever known a personnel manager hoping to hire people who wouldn't labor at their jobs too grimly? At any given company, who are the least funny people? The financial types and the lawyers. And who are likely to be the most irreverent? The public relations dissemblers. And who are the ones most likely to end up in top management? I rest my gloomy case; it's simply a matter of iron over irony.

But wait, you say, how about the hallowed place of the joke in American business, a facilitator no less essential to deals than the proverbial smile and shoeshine? Doesn't this indicate that humor is an integral part of the workplace? Exactly the opposite. A joke is really humor in its most prepackaged, parenthetical form, segregated from the flow of conversation by the intro ("Have you heard the one about the guy who goes into a bar with his parrot . . . ?") and the punchline. Like a drop of oil, it is meant to lubricate the gears of business, but not be part of the fuel that makes business run. When Donald Regan was White House chief of staff, he is said to have started each morning meeting with President Reagan with a joke. Yet if anything was perfectly clear about Donald Regan, it was that he is a very serious man. The joke was a rite of humor, not humor as such, just as much of television news is a rite of communication rather than an actual exchange of information. Jokes are discrete pellets of humor, in a form most useful for people who wouldn't know a witty remark if it bit them (which it's often meant to do). Jokes are to humor what aphorisms are to wisdom, and they have only as much to do with being witty as a saying like "Sometimes you can't see the forest for the trees" has to do with being wise. Significantly, jokes are not made in response to anything, unless to another joke, while humor is part of a prevailing pattern of thought, liable to pop up at any time. Bob Hope tells jokes; Steve Martin is a humorist. It is possible to imagine Hope as the president of AT&T, but picturing Martin as a corporate honcho is, well, hilarious.

Being able to tell jokes is often the sole criterion among unfunny people for measuring a sense of humor. The heavier-than-lead men who rise so weightlessly up corporate ladders are more likely to have an impressive litany of the latest jokes than the really funny people. It's a mnemonic accomplishment, not a sign of any satirical twist; anyone who can commit to memory the salient points of a company's annual profit and loss statement won't have any trouble tucking away half a dozen little laugh-getters. Ironically, the most humorous men and women I've known in the business world were rarely capable of retaining more than a single joke du jour. Their minds have been too nimble to want that kind of excess baggage.

True humor—the kind that will make someone respond to an overbearing boss using the very word that drives him crazy—is at least mildly subversive and anarchical. Sometimes in working situations it can actually be meant as sabotage, but most often it's just meant to break the lockstep rhythm of the marching orders, throw some monkeyshines into the relentless works, and stick a barb into gasbags of self-satisfaction. The true humorist's uncontrollable, noble urge is to keep people from getting too serious, on the extremely compelling theory that far more harm is done in this world by the serious than by the silly. Someone who seems to take a corporate crisis lightly is probably just trying to get everybody else to back off a little and take a deep breath before deciding how to proceed. Alas, business, like sex, politics, and death, is not generally perceived to be funny, especially by those in positions of power. A gift for witty repartee and an ability to laugh under pressure aren't admired nearly as much as dubious virtues like ambition, rigid self-discipline, aggressiveness, pit bull determination, unquestioning zeal, and, yes, greed. Humor, sad to say, simply doesn't resonate in the managerial mind like a killer instinct when the spoils of victory are being divvied up, though it may be recalled all too vividly when the blame for defeat is parceled out ("It seems to me that O'Wryly just wasn't all that concerned about the Cuddly mess"). The very unfunny lessons of the eighties may strengthen the position of humor in the scheme of things, as rabid behavior falls out of favor, but undoubtedly a tough time will be had by all before the millennium, and it's axiomatic that during times when the bottom line is all that really matters, the most likable human characteristics—like the ability to make people laugh—are woefully undervalued by people high on the chain of command.

Possibly this explains why politicians—in the rare event they are given to witty turns of mind—do their best to disguise this problematic quirk. The public, trained to expect national leaders to speak undemanding platitudes, is presumed to prefer zephyrs to zingers. When Prince Charles, in his role of royal kvetch, suggested that England's city planners had done more damage than World War II German bomber pilots, since the worst thing the Luftwaffe ever put in place of good old buildings was rubble, he was cracking wise in a way that few American public figures ever dare to do (of course, Charles can't lose *his* job). When Patrick Moynihan first ran for the Senate in 1976, a reporter at one of his earliest news conferences asked him if he was aware that his opponent was referring to him as "Professor" Moynihan. The candidate, who was at the time teaching at a university, leaned forward with a theatrical scowl and said, "So it's going to be *that* kind of campaign!" With such a public willingness to tweak both his opponent and the press, Moynihan seemed a sure bet to lose (in fact, it took the reporters at the news conference several seconds to realize he was kidding). Miraculously, New York State's voters forgave him for his ironic style, or perhaps didn't get his drift and figured he was being tough. Since then the senator has been canny enough to keep his sardonic turn of mind mostly under wraps, and seems likely to be one of Capitol Hill's permanent incumbents.

Which is about all he, or others similarly afflicted, can do, since if you happen to have the curse of humor, you're stuck with it. Like perfect pitch, or left-handedness, it's something you can hide but that is always there, ready to burst out at the most inappropriate times (which for humor, of course, are the most appropriate times). I recall, with some pain despite an interval of many years, a pivotal moment in a high school history class. The teacher was one of the best and most demanding I had, and I loved the course, despite a tendency to try to entertain my classmates. More important, I needed a good mark in order to salvage a shaky academic record that year. Yet when, during a discussion of antitrust legislation, the teacher asked, "Why do you think the attorney general singled out chain stores for legal action?" my hand shot into the air and, horrified, I heard my mouth say, "Was it because his family owned a rope store?" Not exactly Oscar Wilde material, I'll admit, but the class laughed on cue as I knew they would. The teacher's finger indicated the door, and I was out. I did not get into Princeton.

Since then, I have never actually been kicked out of anywhere for my tendency to be less than serious, but who knows how often I may have been consigned to the lightweight team from which the first-string stars are never drawn. I remember a particularly tough employer coming into my office after I'd cracked up a meeting with some clever aside. The boss complimented me for being so quick-witted, a quality he sadly admitted he lacked altogether. But a couple of weeks later, when he had to choose between me and a rather stolid colleague for a promotion, guess who got the nod. As I said before, humor is dangerous. To be seen as funny is also to be seen as not entirely grown up (ridiculous, since no one is as serious as a child).

Luckily, there's no urine test for humor. You can be riddled with the stuff, right to your very bones, and—with an extraordinary act of will—you can keep the malady from becoming widely known. In order not to be exposed, it helps to be aware of a few basic problems that face the humorous during their passage along the utterly straight corridors of power.

First, there is the sarcasm problem. People with underdeveloped senses of humor divide funniness into two categories: jokes (being funny at the expense of, say, the Polish) and sarcasm (being funny at *their* expense). This is also known as the "Are you laughing with me or at me?" dilemma, a differentiation of much concern to high school teachers and others in positions of sometimes shaky authority. Since we've already established that upper-level managers are unlikely to have much in the way of native humor left after the erosions of success, anything funny you say in their presence that isn't clearly a joke can and probably will be held against you. Remember, nothing stimulates paranoia quite so fast as laughter.

Then there's the court jester problem. When you spend a considerable part of your time trying to get people to lighten up, it can be difficult to convince them when you really mean business. When was the last time you read about a king's fool ending up on the throne? If you're one of those good souls who sees it as his responsibility to make somber proceedings a bit more bearable (at least for yourself) you'll tend to step in constantly with little japes and asides, until at last, like Joe Biden (another rare politician with irreverence in his heart) during a tense confirmation hearing held by the Senate Judiciary Committee, you'll be forced to add to even your weightiest and most telling statements the lame qualifier "But seriously," or "Really, I'm not being facetious now." And even then, people are likely to suspect you're leading up to a funny line.

The court jester problem leads directly to the hypocrisy shortfall problem. One of the dangers of humor to the nonhumorous is that it interferes with the unspoken agreement to sanctify professional activity. It's one thing to whisper to ourselves "What the hell are we all doing here?" when we're so bored our teeth itch, but quite another to make public fun of the group presumption that we're all on a mission from God. As useful as it would be for those who believe in the divine right of CEOs to have their self-importance lanced, you can be sure no one in their inner circles will take on the job; smart guys know that pomposity is one of the luxuries of life at the top. Funny guys would rather die (laughing) than accept the idea, and thus can often be found working in the small offices near the copying machines.

Underlying all the other problems is the fundamental childishness problem, source of the conclusion that being dour and being adult are synonymous, and that only men and women with the personalities of Junker generals can be trusted with the big jobs. It might seem odd that owning four Porsches or lusting to build the tallest building in the world is considered more mature than poking a bit of innocent fun at the company motto ("In Us We Trust"), but there it is. The childishness problem is frequently expressed as "If Larry would ever grow up, he might get somewhere." Sad but true, the saddest part being that the somewhere Larry will get if he ever manages to squelch his most redeeming characteristic is a place where the heartiest laughter follows jokes about how many Arabs it takes to screw in a lightbulb.

Is there, then, no way that one's puckish wit can be brought into play without damage to the future one holds so dear? As a believer in humor above all else, I want to say there is a way, and so I will. But proceed with care. Use humor so sparingly that when people speak of your "rare wit" they mean it literally. Think of funny remarks and wry observations as if they were insults or social gaffes, which is the way the unfunny often hear them. You'll end up stifling a lot of good stuff, but the reward for this self-restraint is that the occasional mot that does escape—because it's unexpected from such a serious-minded, no-nonsense type as you—will be received as just another example of your willingness to do just about anything, even be funny, to keep those quarterly profits rolling in. And how will things go for you then? Swimmingly, just swimmingly.

6

Meetings, Without Fear

sizing up who's

who around

the conference table,

and who isn't

*B*aseball is nothing if not a constant and dependable source of folk wisdom. In the middle of the eighties, for instance, George Foster—a millionaire outfielder with the New York Mets in the days when middling batters didn't consider million-dollar salaries chump change—was enduring an embarrassing four-year hitting slump. Mets fans, a merciless lot when it comes to demanding their money's worth, greeted each Foster strikeout with high-decibel derision. When Foster was asked by a clubhouse reporter if he was bothered by the booing, he responded philosophically, "Oh, they're not booing me. They're just booing my performance."

Though having a tough time getting a ball out of the infield, Foster *had* hit on a nice distinction: sometimes what matters is not who you are, or even how hard you work; it's what you do when everybody is watching and how you look doing it. For those who test themselves on the corporate playing fields, the success of performance is not a bit less crucial than for those in the big-league ballparks. And the arena in which performance is most meaningful, most memorable, and most likely to be instantly judged is the damnable but unavoidable business meeting.

No one, it would seem, likes meetings. At least, almost everyone complains mightily about them. It's very much the done thing to enter a meeting with a grim smile or a resigned shrug, as if to say, "*You* people may have the time for this, but I've got the bloody company to run." In truth, if the value of meetings were to be assessed by how much true work got done, there really wouldn't be much sense in having most of the ones we endure. But meetings are usually far more than meets the bottom line; they are subtle acts of improvisational theater, and usually matter at least as much for the internal information they provide as for the external changes they may occasionally bring about. What gets accomplished, being psychosocial-political rather than immediately tangible, can be just as important to a career—your career, quite possibly—than how many widgets you sell or how clever an acquisition you engineer.

Some people, whether or not they admit it, relish meetings, for the simple reason that some people are very good at meetings. Understanding the complex grid and the subtle layerings that govern meetings with the implacable force of physical laws, they know how to use variations on a fundamental, effective "meeting style"—a touch of class here, a touch of crass there—to leave the impression of an effective performance, whether or not they happen to be on top of things that day. In this way, masters of meetings have a distinct advantage over baseball players, who either hit the ball or don't. Of course, ethically speaking, getting by on sizzle rather than substance is less worthy than knowing a lot and presenting the facts with wit and brilliance. But sometimes the meeting *is* the message, and accountable results are simply by-products. It is the entirely human inclination of top managers (or even bottom managers) to want a tribal assembly from time to time—the frequency usually varying according to the level of managerial anxiety—not only to communicate ideas and problems, but to see the expressions around the table, to gauge the mood, and, not least, to let others spend a little time watching the boss's jaw muscles twitch. (This is probably why the hopeful new-age notion of the telephonic/electronic nonoffice, with everyone chiming in from their places at the beach, is never going to happen, however much it pains me to unpredict it.)

And anyway, worrying about the ethics of style outweighing substance is decent but pointless, since the two are as inseparable in meetings as in a fine work of art. How well someone performs stylistically can be translated quickly into the power to get real work done later. If someone with good ideas consistently droops during meetings, he or she is likely to be seen as a loser, or at best as someone who may not handle pressure well. Whereas someone who shines when the spotlight hits may end up in a pivotal position with or without good ideas. In the complex culture of the company meeting, a perception of ability often becomes the actual ability to do the job.

Thus there are things to know about performance in meetings that may be somewhat less sublime than "To thine own self be true," but no less vital for progressing upslope. Even such ordinary games as "Who sits where?" can be fraught with peril. If only all conference tables were round, life at meetings might be all harmony; but hardly any are (in part because conference rooms are so often long, narrow, miserly spaces), so the unwritten etiquette of seating comes into play. Naturally, where you sit depends on who you are. If you're Ms. or Mr. Big, go to the head of the table, and heaven help anyone who's there without the clout to back it up. But if you're moving up, and hoping to get something done at the meeting—even if it's only to enhance your power to get something done at the next meeting—make sure to reserve a seat from which you can command the attention of those you need to impress. If possible, figure out where you ought to be according to the hierarchy, then promote yourself by one chair; nobody is likely to complain about such a small breach of the power ladder, and even if they do, the onus of small-mindedness will be upon them, not you. Barring anyone starting a turf fight, you will have placed yourself above the salt, corporately speaking, and with any luck you won't ever have to go back. Don't, however, press your luck by taking a two-seat boost; the gods, in the form of avenging vice presidents, have a way of punishing such noticeable presumption.

Punishment—or at least the possibility of a fairly serious drubbing by a superior—always lurks in the wings at any meeting. In this naughty world, there also exist men and women who use the theatrical setting of business meetings to torture their subordinates in dramatic fashion—an ugly art form, but one that certain types seem to thrive on. The more visible you are, the greater the probability that eventually you'll be pinioned by the Beloved Leader's baleful glare and told, "That, Feldspar, is the single most idiotic idea I've ever heard." How you act at that awful moment will tell everyone present more about you than you might have wanted them to know, so a few disaster drills might be in order. Damage control is usually the best you can hope for, but good damage control can be a very good thing indeed. Behavior to be avoided absolutely:

• Do *not* cry. Not even the sort of suppressed sobbing, where only your shoulders shake. Or that teary-eyed Bambi look that never goes as far as a full ten on the Swaggart scale.

• Do not stick out your chin and say, "And you, Mr. Perforce, wouldn't know a good idea if you stepped into it barefoot."

• Do not slump down in your chair and sulk, hoping someone will say, "Oh, for God's sake, kid, okay. We'll give you the damn funding." They won't.

• Most important of all, do not instantly say (about an idea that's just been stomped on), "Gee, Chief, you're right, I never really liked that approach much myself." That's the toady route, the low road of grovelers, and a sure way to be cast as a lightweight (or merely loathsome) by your meeting mates. (Alas, toadies sometimes do rise—about which more later—but being a suck-up is its own punishment.) If you believed in an idea enough to champion it in the first place, have the guts to make one final defense, and the savvy to drop the subject after that should your last-ditch effort fail. You end up with a reputation as a leader *and* a team player. And if you get fired for not cringing sufficiently, you didn't want to work there anyway (see Chapter 12).

Not the least of meeting sins is the failure to know when to talk and when to shut up. The captive audience of the meeting format, like marijuana, has the effect of making very ordinary ideas seem rare and wonderful. People will listen, because that's part of the drill, but the speaker, self-enthralled, may not notice the middle-distance stares that greet his verbal arabesques. Since almost no one wants to be there, blather as a form of stress management is not only uncool, it's unspeakably cruel. If an idea can't be stated in a couple of minutes or so, it's probably not ready for public consumption. Should you find yourself interjecting words like "I guess what I'm trying to say is . . ." or "Maybe an even better example would be . . . ," you can be sure that more than a few of your colleagues are doodling nooses and knives on their notepads.

Some meetings are held on a regular basis, and after you've attended two or three, you'll know all you need to know in order to hold your own. But coming into a meeting cold, either as a new kid on the block, an occasional participant, or a sufferer at some periodic hell like an annual budget review, can be a miserable, confusing experience, the kind of thing that drives a good mind to dwell on elaborate escape plans. Sitting across from several hard-eyed strangers who also don't much want to be there can induce loss of focus, loss of enthusiasm, or finally, loss of all hope. Given the marathon quality of some company meetings, and the airless, deadening interiors of many conference rooms (never mind the deadening interiors of some attendees), it's lucky if everybody's eyes are even open.

There are ways to get through this slough of despair without cost to soul, sanity, or status. One of the most important is to know what's going on from the minute you sit down at the table. A key to understanding the action, and where everybody fits in the often murky scheme of things (especially at a meeting you're new to) is to come up with a dependable way to decode the proceedings. Along with whatever else they may be, meetings are metaphors: metaphors for management; metaphors for the individual thought process, sometimes able to produce better ideas than any single brain present; and metaphors in miniature for companies and corporations. Since the easiest way to understand metaphors is through other metaphors (according to a dimly remembered philosophy professor of mine who seemed awfully sure of himself), figuring out the nature of a given meeting is best done by finding some equivalent for it. For example, in most cases I use a military metaphor.

Risking a little discount anthropology, I'd guess that meetings probably have their origin in prehistoric hunting and war powwows, with mischievous hairy little men squatting in a circle trying to decide how to steal a meal from competitive hyenas, or swipe a bit of desirable turf from their hairy little neighbors. Perhaps because of this, most corporate meetings still tend to have a military resonance, however faint, whether a man or a woman happens to be in charge. That corporations tend to have what might be called military/industrial complexes—an inclination to overvalue the Stormin' Norman Schwarzkopf approach to problem-solving—is owing to many influences, from John Wayne's film heroics to an often desperate managerial yearning for the clarity of purpose presented by battle (never mind that nothing could be less heroic than most military life and that confusion is the hallmark of war). Whether this is good or bad is not the point; it is simply a persistent characteristic, and useful to take into account.

As a consulting member of a strategic planning group for a venerable manufacturing company in the Midwest, I used to attend quarterly meetings with seven other regular participants at a retreat on Lake Michigan. As an outside consultant, I wanted to seem very knowledgeable very quickly—even if that meant appearing to know rather more than I actually did know (an acceptably pale deceit, I hope). The members of the group were all men (though from time to time women from management sat in), and within the first hour I found myself handing out imaginary military ranks and attributes in order to get a sense of the meeting dynamics. To the CEO, a humane, amiable, and able man in his sixties, I assigned the rank of major general, one of those highly educated military aristocrats who seem somewhat out of place in uniform (since I could just as easily have seen this man as a Dante scholar at the University of Chicago). Yet for all his enlightenment, there was a feeling about him that he might like to draw his sword and charge; he seemed frustrated by the conflict between his role as a statesman general in the style of George Marshall and his occasional hankering for the guts-and-glory abandon of George Patton. As such, the CEO's tolerance for high-mindedness among the others at the meetings was sometimes interrupted by fits of impatience, a wish that we'd all just cut the crap and help him keep the Huns from overrunning his company.

The executive vice president, a former wrestling coach with a powerful physique and an ability to keep things moving right along, was unmistakably a mustang, one of those rough-edged officers who rise from the enlisted ranks by dint of sheer tenacity and field savvy. Whenever he theorized, which was rarely, he treated the moment as one of incalculable luxury. He got the rank of full colonel in my fantasy army, and a full ration of respect. With mustangs, I had learned in the marines, you don't try to blow a lot of smoke.

The chief financial officer had all the parabolic elegance and mathematical certainty of a warrant officer in the artillery. One of the noncompany attendees, a well-known industrial designer, had the slightly rumpled, unmilitary bearing of a bemused major in intelligence. A young architect from Minneapolis would have seemed right wearing a navy lieutenant's uniform (in the earnest Mr. Roberts mode). And so on, down the list of the panel's membership.

With my secret roll call, I had a fast and easy understanding of who was who, and how best to deal with each person. (In the context of my military metaphor, my role was Pentagon specialist, and as such I had to be careful not to act as if I possessed information the others couldn't survive without, yet imply that I knew something they didn't.) Granted, the military-equivalent approach may lead to oversimplification, just like military thinking. And if you don't happen to have spent any time in uniform, another set of analogies (sports, for example, or campus politics) may come more naturally. But in meetings, any shortcut to sizing up relationships and assessing power can be enormously helpful. A lot of time and energy can be wasted trying to make a point with the wrong person, or with the right person in the wrong way.

The obvious fact that more and more women are playing important roles in business doesn't necessarily invalidate the predominantly masculine metaphors that meetings evoke. Despite what ought to be the civilizing effect of the female sensibility, corporations remain adamantly (one might say desperately) male. This doesn't mean that executives at Mary Kay Cosmetics sit around talking about "kicking a little ass," but in order to succeed at most companies, women tend to accept the need to prove they can soldier as hard as those with hair on their chests and mayhem on their minds. A few years ago I sat in on a high-level meeting at a major communications corporation in New York while the company's top executives talked with a businesswoman in her early thirties about funding a multimillion-dollar project she had brought to them. Both the project and the abilities of the woman were said to be of considerable interest to the company (which ultimately provided the funds and later bought the publication that resulted for millions), and if any meeting might have been expected to veer away from strict regimental drill, this would have been the one. Yet before half an hour had passed, classic battle array was evident. The air was thick with smoke from cigars that could have been sold to Iraq as antipersonnel weapons (no, the lady had not been offered one). Flanking the visitor, the men of the general staff launched salvo after salvo of acrid smoke and tough questions in a way that can literally be described as hazing. Clearly, if this young woman intended to join forces with the company, she was going to have to hold her own in a firefight. Not too surprisingly, perhaps, given this initiation, the woman went on to push her own employees as relentlessly as any mean mother of a master sergeant, and is now, as a vice president in the corporation, more or less one of the guys.

Frankly (or maybe I should say, talking man to man), making women conform to the dominant male ethos at meetings can be a distinct loss to all present and ought to be discouraged. One way to be part of the solution instead of part of the problem is to cut back severely on the warspeak and sportstalk that often pass for eloquence at more than a few companies. Even if no one is puffing on a fat Havana, a room thick with phrases like "search and destroy," "take no prisoners," "going one-on-one," "playing hardball," "blitzing," and "blindsiding" is simply filled with cigar smoke of another color, not to mention cliché-mongers who really ought to be dropped from the batting order. Or something.

One hopes that as women reach parity at meetings, the military approach will decline. But it won't happen overnight, and it won't be easy. Contrary to General MacArthur's teary old barracks ballad, old soldiers don't just fade away, they die exceedingly hard. Women, with more than a little help from their friends, will have to change the tone of things rather than going along opportunistically. At the end of the '89–'90 football season, the owner of the Tampa Bay Buccaneers named his daughter to the post of vice president for team administration. She replaced a retired general who had joined the Buccaneers after thirty-three years in the military. If the boss's daughter can raise the consciousness of *her* meetings and someday put Tampa Bay into the playoffs, then the millennium truly is at hand.

Adaptability is central to good meeting style. There are meetings where everyone rolls up his or her sleeves, and meetings where jackets aren't even unbuttoned, with all that both states imply. At a buttoned-up meeting, too much informality can be dangerous. (Bear in mind that even if you don't take a particular meeting very seriously, someone in the room does, and it's likely to be the most important person there.) On the other hand, a chameleonlike adaptability will nullify the impression of individuality that can cause you to be remembered long after the meeting is over. Chameleons, though they may possess a certain reptilian quick-wittedness, can evolve into toadies, than which no life form is lower. The best style, at a meeting as at a dinner party, is one close to the truth of who you are and how you feel about things. Tactful truth, perhaps, truth that stops short of social or career suicide, but truth nevertheless. If, at meeting after meeting, that doesn't seem to be effective, you may have to think about whether you're in the right place.

Perhaps the most important element in effective meeting style is simply focus. As in an athletic contest, the players with the most *there* there are likeliest to end up with the highest point totals. If anything, meetings have become more rigorous as a growing number of humorless careerists move up in companies, and efficiency-dictated consolidations increasingly bring together strangers with sharply conflicting interests. These hard-minded types aren't much fun to have around, but—untroubled by matters of the soul—they often have laser-beam concentration, so keeping yourself precisely aware of just where you are, and where the meeting is going, is more important than ever. Of course, if the future of someone else's pet project is at stake, a few private musings about the pleasures of the coming weekend may not be disastrous. But if the subject on the table is *your* baby, focus is everything. You'll be fielding hard, even unfriendly, questions, and fumbling for answers is bad for you, and very bad for baby. Let your mind drift to the ski slopes or the beach, and you may wake up to discover that funding you were counting on has been diverted to Mr. Keen's plodding research group and their lame scheme to put advertising on Porta Potties.

And since the subject of grim careerists has come up, let's not fail to note a certain prevailing stinginess of spirit. By way of an antidote to this misery, left over in considerable quantity from the eighties, let me put in a word for a couple of elements of high meeting style that have all but vanished, with lamentable consequences for the state of American business of all kinds: passion and risk.

For all the hidden agendas and sly undercutting that may go on across the corporate conference tables of the land, work is supposed to get accomplished. Even meetings that are mostly for show (or show trials) will eventually yield work of some sort. And the quality of that work—or the failure of anything to happen at all—reflects inevitably on the quality of products and services any corporation provides (for despite the prevalent attitudes of recent years, companies are intended to do more than earn money for stockholders or enrich their managers). In that sense, the least important meeting is still an indicator of the well-being of the company and everything it does. As anyone who goes to meetings must observe, self-aggrandizement and the determined covering of one's own ass occupy first place on the priority list of too many key participants. It's a familiar sight to see important executives, men and women charged with charting the courses of their companies, indulging in the modern martial art (the aikido of the cosmic maybe) of dodging decisions, lest—God help them—somebody should ever recall that they'd advocated an idea that didn't pan out. After a gathering at which no one, however powerful, was willing just to say "All right, let's do it!" or even "Sounds like a bad deal to me," there's nothing left but to have another meeting, and another, until an idea finally expires from exhaustion. When something is discussed indecisively ad nauseam, people begin to respond to the illusion that it has been tried and found wanting—and an idea worth at least a tryout is literally talked to death.

The ultimate meeting style is one that incorporates the courage to back an idea you believe in, and back it with eloquence and sincerity, damning the torpedoes of competitive colleagues. Whether you win or lose, you'll have left the impression that you give a damn about more than yourself and aren't afraid to take a risk for something that seems right to you. (The military heart leaps to the notes of the charge, remember, so bravado might just carry the day.) Better yet, you'll have guaranteed that everyone can leave the meeting with the refreshing and distinctly stylish feeling that something actually got done.

7

Send Me a Memo on It—or Better Yet, Don't

the paper trail as

a four-lane highway

to oblivion

*O*f all the memos I've ever read—and I've read too many—the most unforgettably effective came my way when I was serving in the Marine Corps, stationed on Parris Island. The situation was this: On the island at the time, among the omnipotent cadre assigned to train recruits, the swagger stick—an affectation probably adopted from the British Royal Marines—had become de rigueur. Everyone from the lowest noncoms to full colonels seemed to be carrying one. There were all sorts of unwritten sumptuary laws regarding their type and use: Buck sergeants could carry bamboo or ash sticks with brass tops, often the shell casings from .45 cartridges; lieutenants and captains could sport mahogany or rosewood numbers; while majors and colonels could go all the way to the ebony and silver deluxe style; only top officers dared actually return salutes with swagger sticks; and so on.

All this was decidedly nonregulation, but the swagger stick, true

55

to its name, was something that fitted well with every marine's self-image, and those of sufficient rank to carry one tended to love them dearly.

Then the island got a new commandant, a general named David Shoup who would, a couple of years later, leap over a dozen or so more senior generals to become commandant of the Corps and one of the Joint Chiefs. Shoup was already legendary, a Medal of Honor winner for heroism at the battle of Tarawa and a man reputed to write poetry in his spare time. With nothing left to prove, the general's style was adamantly utilitarian. From the minute he came aboard, it was conspicuously obvious that the new top man did not carry a swagger stick.

A few days after he had made his first inspection tour of the island, the following memo was posted on the bulletin boards of all units:

FROM THE COMMANDING GENERAL, REGARDING SWAGGER STICKS:
If you need one, carry one.

The next day, not a swagger stick was to be seen on Parris Island. If you go there now, almost thirty years later, you still won't find one.

I've never forgotten the succinct brilliance of that memo, which achieved its desired effect totally, instantly, yet elegantly. In six words, the general got his way with an ironic twist that made a direct order superfluous.

If all memos displayed even half the quality of that one, how much less cumbersome business life would be. But alas, the art of the memo—that venerable vehicle for clarifying problems, for cutting down the verbal underbrush that grows up so uncontrollably during meetings, for eliminating body English and aggressive eye contact from the consideration of crises, for making a memorable statement all the more memorable—is in a sad state of decline. Used well, the memo can still be a great communicator, and a powerful ally. But its misuse is so rife these days that cautious handling is advised: screw up a memo, or use one for the wrong reason, and it will be held against you.

Consider the difference between "memory" and "memorandum." The first is a mental capacity, the second a written record.

Memory is as malleable as wet clay, and conveniently deniable ("I'm sorry, Your Honor, I just can't recall"). A memorandum, though open to interpretation, is a fact. Unlike the spoken word, memos can't be whispered; they are right there, down on paper, the very souls of indiscretion. (If ever there was a contradiction in terms, "confidential memo" is it. Even when Iran-Contra apparatchik John Poindexter erased secret memos from his computer some clever hacker managed to find them again.) Yet memo writing has become such a compulsion that people involved in all sorts of nefarious goings-on leave paper trails of astonishing complexity. Not all people, of course. Organized crime, please note, is not known for its memos. Can you recall a memo ever introduced as evidence at some dapper don's trial?

> FROM: *Carlo D.*
> TO: *Joey the Mole*
> SUBJECT: *Retirement policy*
> *Pursuant to the forthcoming demise of Tony G, please make sure same does not take place on Mother's Day.*

For obvious reasons, much of what goes on in certain businesses remains firmly rooted in the oral tradition. But where the memo is king—politics, the military, most corporate structures—the validation of words on paper overcomes the logic of stealth. The obviously risky business of Messrs. North and Poindexter, for instance, was lavishly documented in memorandums that described almost every aspect of operations meant to be deeply covert. So much paper existed after a few years of derring do's and don'ts that, according to testimony at a Senate hearing, North and the faithful Fawn Hall almost fried their shredder trying to destroy it all.

Why is the memorandum so appealing, even when its use may be time-consuming, inefficient, and even dangerous to one's health? There are several reasons. One is that the memo substitutes for ad lib eloquence. Few people express themselves as intelligently or as devastatingly as they'd like at just the moment they should. The French have a phrase (don't they always), *l'esprit de l'escalier*— literally "the wit of the stairway"—that describes how we invariably think of the perfect comeback to an insult on our way down the stairs, long after it is needed. When you know you ought to make some unassailably correct point during a face-to-face meeting but your mind goes blank, the automatic response is usually "I have a lot of thoughts on that, J.B., let me put them in a memo for you." Andy Berlin, a partner in a San Francisco advertising agency, sits in an office only a few feet from the offices of his colleagues, yet often communicates with them by memo. The reason, he says, has nothing to do with alienation, simply style. "The truth is I can be funnier when I write." The memo *mot*, being subject to improvement through revision, is generally more trustworthy than even the most admirable ad lib.

Most of us can express ourselves better given time to think and edit. The downside is that while writing a memo, we can't see anyone yawn, so we're liable to go on and on. Then, rather than clarifying, the memo obfuscates, becoming part of the problem it was intended to solve. Somewhere, in business schools or those How to Get Ahead tapes that drone from our airline headsets, the idea is posited that one's ability to compose a great memo will take one far. As a result, almost everyone goes way too far, churning out Proustian tracts (in length, not elegance), unleashing the pent-up novelist within, until the whole get-to-the-point point of a memo is lost in a swirling sea of headings, subheadings, "furthermores," and addenda. When former attorney general Edwin Meese denied knowledge of the details of some dubious plans for a Middle Eastern bribe, he pointed out that a certain consultant's memos were always so long that he never had time to read them all. When nobody has enough time anymore to do all that needs doing, or lacks the inclination to sweat the details, the memo that emulates the Dead Sea scrolls is generally loathed by all but its proud author.

The idea that memos are written with little chance of being read exposes the spastic nature of many practitioners of the form. A perverse notion prevails that every meeting, every half-baked idea, every casual brainstorming minute by the coffee machine, must be—for want of a legitimate term—memo-rized. If it hasn't been the subject of a memo, the thinking goes, it hasn't really happened. And worse, if a memo has been produced, something has been done, and the memo writer is off the hook.

When the memo becomes an action substitute, the game, like a tennis match in which both players exchange baseline shots without risking a play at the net, can end up with memos going back and forth while nothing really gets done. Inevitably in such contests of indecision, someone will sneak into somebody else's office and bury a memo deep in the In-box, so that he can get some real work done and then respond wide-eyed to the question of just where the hell his input is: "Gee, Brad, I sent you a follow-up memo on your memo about my memo early last week."

Another attraction of the memo is that it provides a way to avoid confrontation in our increasingly nonconfrontational age. Adversaries who dream happily of eviscerating one another smile instead and say, "Well, Ellen, I'm not sure your approach is quite the quantum improvement on my plan that you suggest, but let me give it some thought and send you a memo." Then, teeth clenched and hands pounding on the keyboard, visions of Ellen's pelt nailed to the barn door, Mr. Van Spleen drafts a scathing reply. The trouble with the memo as a way of expressing anger is that it's unchecked by the restraints of civilization that usually govern in-person office fracases. Generally, people do not throw punches, or leap across desks and stick fingers in the eyes of those who disagree with them. And, with any luck, after the anger of the set-to has subsided, the intensity of the moment tends to be forgotten. The angry memo, however, can act as a breeder reactor—the satisfaction of venting your ire on paper can be so keen that you don't want to stop, and after waxing wroth for a few pages, you apply another coat, and another.

Once such a memo is sent, it smolders on, and its power to aggravate continues to grow. I once worked in an office where the business manager accumulated real and imagined grievances all week, then put them into a vitriolic memo that invariably got to my desk just around five o'clock on Fridays. Over the weekend, I would brood on this memo, until by Monday I found every way possible to make the sender's life miserable (engendering, of course, the next memo in this diverting and destructive cycle).

Another insidious form of the memo is the instrument of terror that shows up on one's desk periodically, blandly broadcasting someone's ill fortune. Though gentle terminology is the rule, the message is clear: This hapless character sleeps with the fishes, and unless you work much, much harder so will you. At the *Washington Post* a few years back, these falls-from-grace notes were posted in a central location (no doubt saving a fortune in Xerox copies), attracting an anxious crowd every morning. The staff called them "Chinese wall poster memos," and they became a grim newspaper-within-the-newspaper.

One major reason for the proliferation of memos in modern life is their popularity as CYA devices—government parlance for "cover your ass." The underlying idea behind these memos is that something unwise, unethical, or plain illegal may be going on, and a written history ought to be kept that will indicate at some later date that the writer is either innocent or, failing that, no more guilty than others. Sometimes these memos are sent, sometimes they're just filed, occasionally they're leaked to the press, sometimes they're written after the fact and predated. However many pages they may contain, they deliver only one message: "It wasn't me." The irony is that as soon as one CYA memo is circulated, the dive siren starts whooping and everybody rushes to write his own. Within a day or two, not a person in the office remains unimplicated, including the guy who comes by with the coffee cart twice a day.

Not everyone in business is memo-intensive. Like the population at large, those rare birds who aren't tend to fall into two categories: good people and bad people. Or more specifically, straight shooters and back stabbers. Both are a problem, but let's take the latter, more treacherous species first. When you encounter someone who never puts anything down on paper, ask yourself whether you'd trust that person to handle your aging mother's estate. If not, look closer. In the course of considering a job offer, a friend of mine sent a series of carefully thought-out memos to his prospective employer, listing conditions that he considered essential, anticipating things that might be problems, and generally trying to put everything on the record before taking the job. The employer answered each memo with a telephone call, saying that nothing was a problem. The paper flow, however, was all one way, and when my friend took the job and found an entirely different situation than he'd expected, he was left with a handful of copies of his own memos and a boss who denied he'd ever okayed anything in them. No need to narrate the end of that story.

The straight-shooter memophobe is someone who believes in spoken language as a prime business tool, and knows the problems too much paper can cause. Basically, these types can be trusted, but for all their good intentions they can be maddeningly vague about what they've said yes or no to. A well-known adman and corporate rebel absolutely refused to write memos or read them. Though this was good for his legend and no doubt encouraged his co-workers to deal with problems head-on, people who worked at the agency recall that without follow-up memos to clarify what had been decided, a lot of work was done that shouldn't have been done, and work that needed doing never got started.

Contrary to the accepted wisdom of the textbooks, success may reside less in the writing of brilliant memos like General Shoup's bull's-eye than in knowing what kinds of memos to avoid writing, and when not to write any memo at all. A mercifully brief list of rules applies:

• Think twice about the Take No Prisoners memo. If you're furious, try to overcome your genteel upbringing and be furious in person, not on paper. Remember, when your fingers do the talking, it's often the eloquent and indiscreet middle finger that speaks the loudest, and you may have calmed down by the time the target of your memo is putting out a contract on you. Solution? When you care enough to send the very worst, write the memo, rise to Shakespearean heights of invective, then put it in your briefcase, read it immediately upon waking the next day, and put it in a toaster oven set for TOP BROWN.

• Bear in mind that no publisher will ever want your collected memos; no need, therefore, to worry about producing a thick volume. When you find yourself on the third page of your opus on Television Audience Potential for Tractor Puller Contests, cut to the chase. In fact, cut half of what you've written. At a computer magazine on the West Coast, memos are considered excessively long when they fill more than one screen. As your fingers dance across the keys, stop to consider how much you hate the long memos of others. Sure, yours are infinitely better, but try to imagine they aren't. Your recipients will bless you for it.

• Remember, memos are the modern office equivalent of the public proclamation. Don't put anything in one that you don't want everyone—including the Senate Select Committee on Idiocy in Business—to know. Remember the priceless maxim, "Better shred than dead." But if you just can't bear to destroy your perfectly crafted memos, make sure there's nothing in them that can't be shared by the whole class.

• Don't put your memo where your mouth is. On the long-running TV show "thirtysomething," the characters Elliott Weston and Michael Steadman, friends and business partners, knew they had a problem when they began communicating by memo. If you find you'd rather write "Good morning" to one of your colleagues than actually say it, something is obviously wrong. Memos can only paper over fear and loathing for a while, and they usually make things worse. The way out is simple: Write a memo to your bête noire, read it over a few times, then tear it up and go say what has to be said.

• Beware the Queegmire. In the infamous manner of Captain Queeg's "purloined strawberries" broadside, some particularly ill-advised memos seem to take on lives of their own. To the refrigerator at a Los Angeles radio station was taped the following memo from the station manager:

> *Food in this refrigerator is private property. Any unauthorized use of someone else's food will be considered theft and will result in immediate termination!*

The memo was affixed to the door more than a year ago at this writing, and at latest report has begun to turn the sickly beige shade of aging copy paper. Inside the fridge, untouched for that same span of time, is a partially consumed cup of strawberry yogurt well on its way to becoming a new life form. The yogurt's ownership is obscure; many think it belongs to a long-departed staffer in the sports department. Of course, no one will violate the station manager's stern injunction by throwing the stuff out, and everyone gleefully watches this symbol of managerial umbrage grow more and more ghastly, knowing that eventually the memo writer himself will have to reach in and do the janitorial honors.

In the category of mad memos immemorial, nothing is quite so classic as a communiqué produced by *Rolling Stone* editor Jann Wenner in the early seventies. In those days the magazine was located in San Francisco, and one night a moderate earthquake stimulated much apocalyptic talk in the city. "The Big One" is a staple of California speculation, periodically—as in October 1989—brought back to prominence, and the next day a five-page memo issued forth from Wenner's typewriter outlining in manic detail just how the magazine would cover that earthshaking event. Such-and-such a star reporter would head for the beach, a certain columnist would describe the scene in Golden Gate Park, and so on. Last on the elaborate agenda, but far, far from least, were certain internal procedures. The editor's secretaries were instructed to remove his priceless files and place them in indestructible steel cases reserved for that purpose. And the editor himself, in presidential panoply, would be picked up by helicopter and whisked away to the safety of another state (leading his employees to deduce that he was in another state already). Sure, this sounds too weird to be true, and I'll admit I never read the battle plan myself. But remember, it was a memo—somewhere, copies still exist.

8

Look Who's Paying for Dinner

the expense account:

essential tool,

potent symbol . . .

and Faustian bargain

*I*f Mephistopheles has a favorite route into the workplace, it has to be straight down that primrose path known as the expense account. A complex combination of essential tool, basic perk, and Faustian bargain, the expense account can only have been put on earth as an implacable test of its users' moral fiber. Each of us, being of the finest character (I'm sure), faces this test with shimmering honesty, and so ought to have nothing to worry about. Let the devil take those who might slip an Armani tie into the "miscellaneous" column; the upright likes of us are not about to disappoint those eagle scouts who camp out in our souls.

But the expense account doesn't offer a simple question of right or wrong, the lady or the tiger, nice or naughty. Like any self-respecting serpent in Eden, it comes along in various guises, determined to confuse. As an example, brothers and sisters, listen to this story of one man's fall from grace:

The first job I ever held was with a just-breaking-even little enterprise (the aforementioned trade magazine) where the idea of spending company money was considered vaguely subversive. On the road, where we all spent a fair amount of time, austerity was the iron rule; if you took a cab across the frozen tundra of midwinter Minneapolis when you could easily have walked, you'd better have a note from your doctor; order the steak sandwich when a BLT would have filled you up just as well and you might prudently make up the difference yourself. And so on, nickel by hard-won dime. Quickly I developed Spartan ways, and began to think of such luxuries as airplane audio headsets and espresso as shamefully indulgent. My expense accounts were as starkly simple as the grocery lists of an anorexic.

My next job was with a cash-swollen communications empire whose Manhattan real estate alone could have bailed Brazil out of debt, and my first assignment was to visit radio and television stations around the country on a get-acquainted tour. Because I flew the headquarters flag, station managers reserved lavish hotel suites for me—on my expense account, naturally. Trained to be cheap, panicked that my spending would spell disaster, I confined myself to subsistence living in all other ways. If I could have saved money by cleaning my hotel rooms myself, I would happily have volunteered. When I got back to New York, I chipped away at my expense report like a deranged sculptor trying to make a paperweight from a one-ton block of marble. Anywhere I could find a little give I took the hit myself, eventually lowering the final figure by dipping into my own very shallow pockets. With a keen sense of dread, I sent the report through to my boss. Fifteen minutes later I was summoned.

Like a man dispossessed, I slumped into the sleek leather-and-chrome chair (God knew how much *that* cost!) across from the Big Desk and awaited my fate. Pointing an accusing pencil at the first meal entry on my report—which I immediately recalled had been a cheeseburger platter—my boss said, "I see you spent about seven bucks on dinner your first night in Chicago." Oh Lord, how easily I could have done without the cheese. Or the beef. Impatiently crossing out the item, my boss said, "Maybe you can eat for six ninety-five, kid, but I got out of that habit a long time ago."

With that, he penciled in a $24.50 tab (just under the amount requiring a receipt) and then went down the page adding to every entry, inserting phantom cab rides, laundry bills, haircuts, and so forth, until he reached what he considered a barely respectable bottom line. With a stern warning never again to show our corporate bean counters how frugally life on the road could be led, he sent me off to do a new report following his tempter's template.

If this relatively petty bit of larceny were the point of the story, we could just conduct a quick puritanical postmortem, accept my shamed apology, and get on with life. But eighteen months later, the second shoe fell—squarely on my head. My boss and I hadn't been getting along (you'll have to take my word for it that he was at fault) and it was clear he might like to get rid of me if only he could find an excuse. I, of course, worked uncharacteristically hard not to give him one. Finally one morning he called me into his office and, like Claude Rains telling Bogart he was shocked, *shocked* to discover gambling going on at Rick's, he proceeded to announce that he suspected I was doctoring my expense reports and would have to let me go.

And so I learned a hard lesson in the inexact but vital science of the expense account: the thing takes on the coloration of its surroundings, and cannot be trusted to be what you think it is. In the space of only two jobs I had starved in the service of one philosophy and grown fat being served—and ultimately severed—by another, I didn't have a clue what an expense account really was. What I know now, countless cheeseburger platters later, is that it can be many things, often all at once—a straightforward replenishment of out-of-pocket expenditures on the company's behalf; a report card on how hard you're striving; a mutually acknowledged slush fund that is delightful for the employee and deductible for the business (though somewhat less lavishly now, thanks to a tightening of the IRS fist); a measure of personal power; a badge of rank; or just enough rope to hang yourself with.

Let's reestablish here, for the sake of our sense of propriety and upward nobility, that dishonesty is not our policy. Nothing here will suggest breaking the law in letter or spirit. But just because you're determined not to abuse an expense account doesn't mean that the thing won't turn around and abuse you. The more you can understand its shifty character, and the ways of the shifty characters for whom it is the corporate equivalent of crack, the better off

you're going to be. At the risk of oversimplifying what is an ethically complex situation, the expense account is best approached like
one's federal tax account: don't cheat, since sooner or later you'll get
caught, and anyway (to quote Honest Dick Nixon) it would be
wrong; but on the other hand, don't cheat yourself out of either
hard cash rightfully due or the invaluable symbolic currency an
expense account often represents.

If you understand the way expenses are viewed by your company you've found a shortcut into the corporate psyche (besides
knowing something essential from a practical standpoint). In certain places the spending of money is an expression of fitness, the
fiduciary equivalent of pumping iron. The idea is not so much
getting the job done, but showing the competition that nothing so
mere as mere money will stand in the way of victory. A friend of
mine, early on in what turned out to be a very successful career in
real estate development, missed the last plane of the day from New
York to a city where he was due to make a presentation for a
relatively small shopping center project. He called to reschedule the
meeting for later in the week, but when he got back to his office his
boss—a man who had only the day before complained that my
friend was overusing the company's radio cab service—furiously
ordered him to charter a plane and thus be at the meeting as orig-
inally scheduled. "And make damn sure they know we don't have
to depend on the f- - -ing airlines!" he shouted as my friend headed
back to the airport.

Mysteriously, a willingness to spend corporate bucks in high-
rolling public displays often goes hand in hand with an institutional
horror at the idea of personal luxuries like expensive hotels or first
class air travel. Go figure. But it's important—should such para-
doxes be standard procedure at your happy hunting ground—to
know the difference between power spending and just plain over-
spending.

Despite certain obvious risks—and I emphasize that what follows could be *very* risky—it makes strategic sense to test the limits
of an expense account when you first arrive someplace new,
whether a new company or a new position at the old popstand.
Since ambition and presumption are often perceived as springing
from the same self-aggrandizing motive, the person who presumes
like crazy, filling his expense forms with charges for exotic soft-

ware, an impressive desk chair, a rowing machine for the office, bribes to major maître d's, and so on, is as likely to impress those on high (accustomed as they are to their own refined pillage) as anger them. It's a question of tribal behavior: "Hey, this guy spends like a bandit, he must be one of us."

(I'll admit, I've never established this kind of bold expense account beachhead, bedeviled as I am—and no doubt you are too—by reflexive honesty, but I've felt a sense of chagrined envy when I've seen others pull it off. Another friend of mine recounts the highly creative expense reporting of one of his colleagues, a notable rainmaker at a large law firm who managed to find a business purpose for almost everything he ever did. When the head of the accounting department finally brought the big spender's excesses up to the senior partner, she was told to forget about it; when it came to a top producer, acceding to dishonesty was clearly considered the best policy. Such behavior might bring a tear to Abe Lincoln's eye, and mine, but it's hard not to resent the fact that some people have the bravado to get away with it.)

Even if the alarm bells sound too insistently to be ignored, the worst that's likely to happen is a dressing-down and maybe some expenses bounced back. But if you start off spending timidly you may find yourself in the dreaded small-potatoes niche, where you'll be expected to stay forever. Start big and you may get to set your own standard, at the same time establishing a reputation for thinking big. All this may seem academic to those whose companies squeeze a nickel till the buffalo burps (as an uncle of mine used to say), but the point is always to push the envelope (that welcome one with your expense check in it) to whatever size that envelope is.

One key to managing this is to keep preset limits on your spending vague if you can. Conventional wisdom holds that expense accounts should be worked out during negotiations for salary and benefits, but bear in mind that even a generous allowance is an allowance, and you can't always know how much it's going to cost to do your job well until you start doing it. But if you avoid setting up a bottom-line figure on expenses and spend however much you have to, then your employer (as impressed by your big-time attitude as dismayed by the numbers) may be reluctant to rein you in. On the other hand, he won't think twice about saying no to an increase if it turns out some agreed-upon limit doesn't suffice. There are, too, those occasional dream situations where the failure to spend lavishly will cause those on high to wonder if you're doing your job. A boss may then actually encourage you to spend more (as happened to me in one blissful situation where much of my job was done at restaurants, and higher tabs implied a higher profile), but the cost to your waistline and cholesterol count may be considerable. (The solution is to pass up yet another risotto Milanese and treat your client to an afternoon of squash at the club your company is kindly paying for.)

In trying to decipher the ambiguous nature of the expense account, it helps to remember the Orwellian caveat that some animals are more equal than others. The latitude of spending is measured not on a simple scale of one's value to the company, but by an unwritten rule: Money that makes money is favored over money that doesn't. In other words, someone in sales, directly responsible for enhancing profits, will more likely be forgiven spendthrift ways than someone in, say, public relations, where the effect on corporate fortunes is harder to tote up. This is most dramatically evident across the great divide of talent-versus-management typical in businesses like publishing. According to many veteran print journalists, major daily newspapers are notoriously stingy when it comes to the earthly comforts of its reporters, asking them to piggyback stories onto self-paid vacation trips and other Scrooge-like requests. But those on the business side of the same papers can just about order up Nile barges complete with galley slaves without provoking a raised eyebrow. Is this fair? After all, the business types make more money anyway. But fairness, decency, and need have nothing to do with expense account politics; if you produce dollars rather than words (or widgets) you are expected to cost the company more on all levels. So paying close attention to expanding your expense horizons is all the more important if your contribution is not directly measurable in the simple arithmetic of profit and loss.

In the end, the expense account is a thing with a life of its own. Like a breeder reactor, it has the peculiar, illogical ability to be self-generating and to grow as if by magic. The annals of expense account profligacy (a favorite subject of after-work cocktail klatches) are filled with stories of breathtaking spending sprees that miraculously don't end with the satisfying punch line ". . . and so finally they fired her." One talented woman, a marketing guru for a major cosmetics company, legendary for her prodigal ways, mined a rich vein of astronomical expenses for years—traveling from one exotic place to another in high empress style—despite the fact that she worked for a company that furnished its offices in Salvation Army modern. Her secret was simple: she was very good at what she did, an alchemical art no one in corporate management really understood; and she had always left such a cloud of dollar signs in her wake that no one could work up the courage to suggest she might make do on less. And a famous photographer who regularly shoots the covers of a woman's magazine with an infamously tight-fisted editor has for years contrived to blend the entire month's costs for running his studio into his expense accounts for the two-day cover session. Everyone, including the parsimonious editor, knows that this is going on, and has known it for twenty years, but perhaps because it's so obvious (and almost charmingly simpleminded), and the covers sell a hell of a lot of copies, not a discouraging word is ever spoken to bring the costly scam to an end.

At the risk of redundancy I'm inclined, for all of our sakes, to append some warning at the end of this chapter, something like: *These maneuvers are performed by stunt drivers—do not attempt yourself.* So much of success in connection with expense accounts has to do with attitude, arrogance, and presumption that basically honest people can easily come to grief when they try to do only what they see others doing with impunity. For unethical types, the misuse of an expense account is just another episode in that long-running business sitcom "I Love Lucifer," and their ability to get away with murder may lead better people into confusion, pent-up desire, and finally, disastrous imitation. Just remember, if expense accounts were outlawed, only outlaws would use expense accounts. But you have one for a reason; use it ineptly, or fail to exercise it to its fullest effect, or just be so goody-two-shoes saintly in your accounting that you end up giving the company the benefit of legitimate doubts, and you will end up finding that—bitter pill!—virtue is your only reward.

9

Slight
Expectations

how not to be

mistaken for

the Messiah and thus

avoid crucifixion

*W*hen songwriter/comedian Steve Allen rose to give a speech in San Francisco in late 1989, he raised his hands abruptly to silence the applause that followed the chairman's introduction, a fulsome accolade that came close to billing him as the star of the Second Coming.

"I don't mean to be rude, stopping your kind applause," Allen said. "It isn't that I don't like applause, it's just that I don't plan to be that good, so I don't want you to waste your appreciation."

Cute. And canny, too. After all, Allen is not a man without his share of egotism and, with many talents, has no reason to be. But his little "Aw, shucks" ploy was carefully calculated to lower the expectations raised by the moderator's immoderate praise. As it happened, to no one's surprise, the speech about education that followed was smart, funny, and eloquent. But because he had gotten off to such a humble start, his words seemed even better than

73

they actually were. Allen's approach echoed one of history's classic examples of lowered expectations, when Lincoln began his brief, incandescent speech at Gettysburg, "The world will little note nor long remember what we say here . . ."

Expectations can be dangerous, and great expectations can be downright deadly. This is especially significant when the person from whom great things are expected happens to be you. Just think back to your childhood, to the twinge of dread brought on by certain statements: "My boy, your mother and I expect great things from you." Or, "Lorraine, you have the potential to be one of our very best pupils." Or, "Well, Johnny, we know you're too nice a boy to get into that kind of trouble." Expectations are a veiled curse; they are what give you a chance to disappoint people. If nobody believes you're capable of heroic behavior, then no one can be too disillusioned if you just muddle through, and they'll be positively thrilled if you perform brilliantly. But let them stick you with the label of "miracle worker" and anything short of Lawrence of Arabia will seem inadequate. (It's significant that when T. E. Lawrence returned to England from the Middle East, his demigod status snapping at his heels, he changed his name and enlisted as a private in the air corps.)

If George Bush has proved to be a master of anything, it is of keeping us from expecting him to be a master of anything. With calculated clumsiness, he manages to dampen the ardor of overzealous enthusiasts while at the same time stealing from his opponents the opportunity to advertise his deficiencies. What Bush does so cleverly, to almost endearing effect, is point out his shortcomings before anyone else has a chance. During his campaign for the presidency, his predebate emphasis that he was not much good at public speaking lowered expectations so effectively that when he turned in a moderately coherent performance the press acted as if a new William Jennings Bryan had burst upon the scene. During his presidency, Bush has become a far more polished speaker, and he handles press conferences as well as anyone since John Kennedy, but somehow he still gives the impression that he's just a regular guy, putting in an honest day's work, slightly astonished at everyone's attention. Meet George Doe.

Modern politicians have learned, often at great expense, the peril of public expectations. Tell the people you're going to make their lives better, then fail to do so, and the ingrates rise up and throw you out. Remember Jimmy Carter's 1976 campaign: "Why Not the Best?" It's the central irony of television-dominated politics that candidates must offer simpler, even simplistic promises to be elected, yet are less and less able to solve increasingly complex problems. The result is a shorter and shorter effective lifespan in office. (Within the first year of New York mayor David Dinkins's term, he went from a man some saw as a great hope for the future to a man excoriated by everyone for not doing enough to turn around a desperately ailing city—which, of course, he'd promised to do. By his second year in office he was merely, according to the *New York Times Magazine*, a mayor taking things one day at a time.)

But never mind the Olympian concerns of politicians; inflated expectations are a constant and vexing problem for us working stiffs, too. In fact, the whole unwritten script of self-promotion and glad tidings that gets us in the door and up the ladder threatens us constantly with the jeopardy of failing to fulfill high hopes. From the very beginning of our careers, we try to make ourselves look like the answer to some collective corporate prayer. Nervously, our little inner nerd believes in modern artist Jenny Holzer's pop sophism, "Lack of charisma can be fatal." So résumés are carefully constructed to emphasize our accomplishments and camouflage our flaws. We tell prospective employers anything to get jobs, especially early in our careers, including such imprudences as "If you hire me, sir, you'll never regret it." Eager to please, we take on ill-fated tasks and blithely promise to "turn this situation around 180 degrees in three months or, hell, J.W., I'm not worthy of your confidence in me and I might just as well walk out of here."

It's so sad, because we mean well, don't we? And we really believe what we're saying. Self-confidence, after all, is supposed to be a virtue (and it is, as long as we're not caught in its vise). But the treacherous gods who monitor office life are ever vigilant for this sort of new-age hubris. Come on like a hero and they'll make sure you end up with feats of clay. Problems you felt sure were targets of opportunity turn out to be insoluble, hanging you out to expire at the end of your bravado. Minor character defects you can't give up—smoking, for heaven's sake—loom large when you've promised not a moment's dissatisfaction. Do things quite well when you've advertised greatness and you end up looking not so hot after all.

Once you've let the genie of expectations out of the bottle, getting him, and them, back down to manageable size can be almost impossible.

So what's the answer? Shall we just slouch toward mediocrity, trade in self-assurance for the comfortable gray cowl of humility, and let somebody else take the risks and reap the rewards? No, of course not, how could you even suggest such a thing? The solution is just to manage perceptions in such a way that success comes out looking spectacular, and failure seems nothing more than the minor setback it usually is.

The first and most basic way to avoid raising impossible hopes is simply not to oversell your own ability to solve problems. This is not to say that you should emulate the shuffling candidate for ninth-grade class president who stands sheepishly at the podium and says, "My opponent is really a nice guy, and probably deserves to win this election, but I want to be president a lot and I promise to do my best." If you think you're the right one to get a job done, go for it; but let your talents speak for themselves, and just hope they're eloquent. Then, if luck goes against you, nobody will be able to trot out your money-back guarantee of salvation. The trick is to let your real enthusiasm show, without getting carried away with the thrill of it all and saying things you'll be sorry for later. Henry V, you will recall, shouted, "Once more unto the breach, dear friends," and not, "If you guys don't follow me, I'll take this damn town all by myself."

Just as important as not overestimating your chances of handling a job is not underestimating, publicly, the job itself. M. Danny Wall, who resigned under widespread criticism from his position as director of the Office of Thrift Supervision, was as much a victim of this mistake as of any personal limitations. In 1988, when the extent of the savings-and-loan collapse already began to seem huge, Wall testified to Congress that Treasury funds wouldn't be required for a bailout and that the problem really wasn't all that bad. By the end of 1989, with predictions that the ultimate cost of the collapse could exceed $159 billion (the cost has escalated steadily since then), Wall looked appallingly inept, even in our national capital, where tolerance for ineptitude is well established. Yet all he had to do when he took the job was point out that he'd do his damnedest, but that damage control might be the best he could promise. Then, had the situation actually proved as manageable as he seems to have believed it would, Wall might now be posing for an equestrian statue.

A shining example of someone who understood this sort of thing perfectly was David Gunn, who was named New York City Transit Authority president in the mideighties. Stepping into an infamous quagmire of broken-down subways, wall-to-wall graffiti, and serious crime on the thousands of city buses and subway trains, Gunn called his job a "suicide mission," implying that simply ending up alive might be seen as a success. Six years later, when he announced that he was retiring from the position, city officials were lining up to praise him. It happens that Gunn had gone a long way toward pulling the transit system back from the brink of collapse, but though the graffiti have almost vanished from the trains, the danger of violent crime hasn't declined and may even be worse since he took over. But he had let everybody know from the start that he'd be lucky just to survive, so a good effort ended up looking like the Battle of Britain.

Remember, no one ever blames you for taking a problem too seriously, only for thinking it's no big deal and being wrong. Oh, there may be occasional carping about making too much out of a given challenge—the stiff-upper-lip set tends to overvalue suffering in silence. And you have to be careful not to overdramatize the kinds of tasks that are standard fare for the job, since nobody loves a whiner (and nobody should). But if you diminish the importance of a job, you automatically diminish the credit you'll get for doing it well. Fail at a task you made light of, as did the hapless Mr. Wall, and you may never recover. Sometimes perceptions are everything when the A's and F's are handed out.

Inevitably, sooner or later in one's working life, a no-win situation that can be neither evaded nor successfully overcome will present itself, and you will end up a high-profile loser. This is the time for a tactic called postfailure revisionism, which means getting others to look at the debacle as something less culpable. In some cases, it's even possible to snatch the image of victory from the actuality of defeat. Perhaps the most famous example of this ploy was the tactic used by a marine general in Korea who, after breaking out of a Chinese encirclement in what might have been perceived as a retreat, announced proudly, "Retreat, hell! We were just advancing in another direction."

The idea isn't to bluff or dissemble, pretending things went far better than they did; losing is not the worst thing that can happen, but losing and lying about it is pathetic. What you have to do is make the best of a bad situation by highlighting whatever good you can find in it. Saying that it was "a learning experience," for instance. That you'll never let the bastards sucker-punch you again. That you now know enough not to take on such odds without demanding a much bigger budget. All manner of perceptual shadings are available, including the best of all: an excess of guts and glory. Convince people that you simply tried so hard that the effort blinded you to danger, and suddenly you become a tragic hero too big for small challenges rather than a bit player not up to the role. When hotshot yachtsman Dennis Conner ran a twelve-meter boat aground during a race, he admitted he'd made "a silly mistake," but quickly added, "When you're pushing too hard to be a tough competitor, these things happen."

Pre-postfailure revisionism—striving for success but shoring up a defense should things go wrong—is a further refinement of such spin control. One way or another, you let it be known the odds are against you, and that winning will be a miracle. John McEnroe, a bit long in the tooth these days and always a sore loser, once accused the men's tennis system of favoring teenagers. "The circuit's made for seventeen- to twenty-year-olds who have nothing on their minds except tennis. It's not made for thirty-year-olds." If we let old John, with a wife and family and who knows how many mortgages on his mind, talk us into it, we'll give him a standing ovation just for being on his feet at the end of a match.

Another approach, effective if you've been so confident you'd come out ahead that you've forgotten to remind everyone you're only human, is mid-pre-postfailure revisionism. Often, this consists of making the goal unclear, so that when everything's over winning and losing won't be so starkly defined. Pat Riley, former coach of the Los Angeles Lakers, coolly put MPPFR to work during the 1990 National Basketball Association playoffs when his team, dominant for years, found itself a game away from elimination with only one win. Did Riley jut out his manly chin and promise that the Lakers would turn the series around? No, he smiled his brightest smile and said, "We have a great opportunity to do something really significant." The Lakers lost, and in the sense that they hadn't bowed out so meekly in years, the loss really was significant. Riley had coyly made a promise that didn't actually mean a thing.

However wonderful your company may think you are, however much you are depended upon to be brilliant, there's a lot to be said for being perceived as the underdog, that scrappy pup who resides uppermost in everybody's heart. Take a lesson from frail-looking Lou Holtz, coach of Notre Dame's formidable football team. (I've chosen an abundance of examples from sports because coaches and athletes, with no way to evade the issue of winning and losing, become extraordinarily skillful at controlling expectations.) Before each game, whether pitted against powerhouses or pushovers, Holtz sounds the death knell for his winning record, making people think there's no way in the world the Irish are going to triumph this time. And then they do, and even knowing sportswriters wonder how Coach Holtz does it. When fate finally catches up with them, as it did in 1990 when they lost to a true underdog, brainy Stanford, the opponent ends up covered in glory but Notre Dame emerges looking valiant anyway.

Most of all, remember this: you must not for one second believe your own antihype when you whittle away at people's great expectations. Before you take on weighty odds, it makes sense to let the world see you as Clark Kent. But never forget: beneath that understated exterior, you're faster than a speeding bullet and able to leap tall buildings in a single bound. Just remember, bullets are faster than they used to be and buildings are taller than ever, so never let them think you don't sweat.

10

Sex Officio

nine-to-five flirtation can

get you a scarlet letter, a

pink slip, or an offer you'll

wish you'd refused

*S*ince this is a chapter about office sex, let's get right to it with a story that came to me through an innocent indiscretion (and which I'll fictionalize a bit to prevent marital calamity). Some years ago, a friend of mine at a New York advertising agency worked closely with a particularly attractive young woman. The two were friends but had never been romantically inclined. Then a sudden crisis forced the staff on a major account, including my friend and the woman in question, to revamp a month's worth of work on a new campaign presentation in less than a week; the job meant working long hours, feverishly, with no margin for error. The young woman emerged a star, solving problems quickly and well with unflagging stamina and good spirits. Working in tandem, she and my friend got through the crisis, full of admiration for each other's heroic efforts. Finally, alone in the small hours of a Manhattan night, they met their deadline and, with exhausted relief,

81

embraced. From relief to lust was a surprisingly short leap. They sank to the office floor and, amid the debris of five days' frantic work, made love.

My friend admitted that it sure beat going out for a beer with the guys.

I relate that story to make an important point about human dynamics. Offices are sexy places, erotic zones as potent as any Mediterranean beach. That fact makes the bad news I'm about to deliver even more disheartening than it might be, but deliver it I must. Though the workplace remains as aphrodisiacal as ever, anyone who's been around through a few sociopolitical sea changes can see that there's less amorous byplay going on these days than in the patchouli-scented past. There was a time, in offices all over the country, when sex was as fundamental to the basic business inventory as paper clips and phone message pads. For all the turmoil it caused (about which more in a bit), no one thought there was anything remarkable about the fact that everybody seemed to think about sex from punch in to punch out. And at the risk of retrograde thinking, I'll contend that the general preoccupation with carnal musings wasn't altogether a bad thing.

For instance, once, in the pastel-shaded days when a good time was being had by all and nobody much gave a damn, I loved going to the dentist. The ghastly whir of the drill was music to me. No masochist could have looked forward more than I to the needles and nosepieces used to prepare me for the good doctor's ministrations. I didn't even dread the postoperative pronouncement "Your X-rays show a dark area under the crown on upper right six. Better come in next week and let me have a little look."

The reason for my peculiar lack of aversion to having my teeth ground to dust was neither madness, addiction to nitrous oxide, nor nostalgia for the sensations of Marine Corps boot camp. What it was, was desire—suppressed, God knows, by the rigors of the environment, but desire nevertheless. For it happened that my dentist had an extraordinarily beautiful assistant. A recently emigrated Iranian, she exuded an ancient aura of desert hospitality and compassion for those who reclined nervously amid the dread instruments of dentistry. The diverting counterpoint of her starched white uniform and dark good looks was better than novocaine. Sitting by my side while her boss did his noisy business, performing various housekeeping chores with suction tube and squirt gun, she provided a fantasy that made it possible to get my mind off what was really going on.

Once in a while our eyes would meet and she would smile, and into her sympathy I would read some possibility that one day, without warning, she might suggest that it would be nice to see me with my mouth closed, at—let's just say—her place. The thought kept me happily in the grip of my dentist's slender mercies until he retired on my money and she went elsewhere, never to be found again. The fact that nothing ever happened, that her sympathy was just that and no more, has not dimmed her glow in my memory. She made otherwise grim hours bearable with her ability to fill my heart with hope.

I mention this period of my dental history to illustrate how sex—even imaginary sex—could make what went on in an office, even a dental office, a whole lot easier to deal with.

These days, sex in the office (or more accurately, lust in the office, sex after work—only hopeless risktakers and characters in movies would engage in actual desktop ravishing anymore) has become almost mythical, like Sasquatch, except that sex is sighted far less often.

Please don't misunderstand. Sex has not vanished from the office, and never could. Men and women spend more time at work than at anything else, and it is at work that they may appear at their best, doing well whatever it is they do. Excellence is powerfully exciting, and if you can watch an attractive man or woman (take your pick) do a remarkable job for any period of time without feeling at least a twinge of desire, you've probably been forgetting to take your vitamin E capsules. As the opening story proves, a camaraderie exists among co-workers that can easily become genuine affection, and the harder people work together, the closer the bonds of affection grow. If you put appealing men and women together on a task that demands long hours, close teamwork, and intimately shared Chinese takeout meals, it's almost perverse to expect the inevitable result to be nothing more than high-fives and a hearty "Way to go, pal!"

In fact, the increased importance of women at work brought about by the women's movement may actually have enhanced the chances for real mutual attraction to grow, and the longer hours that everyone seems to be working these days (and nights) weight the probabilities in favor of finding comfort among one's colleagues. Add to this the nagging new fears of love with imperfect strangers that have made barhopping a dangerous game of passion roulette, and there's a pretty good case for the idea that a serious comeback of office sex could be imminent. But the new version is so different from what used to go on that it's only just recognizable as the same creature highly evolved.

Veronique Vienne, a French-born graphic designer and writer, has written a wonderful description in *Savvy* magazine of how subtle, nontactile, yet deliciously exciting mental sex games in the office can be:

> I measured lust not in terms of size, but space—and gauged the optimum distance between the sexes in the office to be three feet. I came to this conclusion through a process of elimination, systematically computing the tension down a hall, across a room, inside an elevator and in a doorway, until I figured that my favorite position for sex was standing up, across a desk; it was best done fully dressed, chin up, and preferably in the morning; you did not need to move, moan or sigh. With the door open, the phone ringing and everybody dropping by, any wild expression would have been impractical. My corporate lovemaking became a private piece of conceptual art.

It would be no problem, of course, to reel off epic tales about sexual Iliads and oddities. Anyone who went to work in the sixties, as I did, has a repertoire of steamy dispatches, and I'll probably be forced to mention one or two just for perspective. But these are cautious times, for reasons political, hysterical, and hygienic, and it just isn't done to start reminiscing about how great things were in the old days. It's not even smart to *think* it was so great, so let me go on record as being relieved that we can all get to work early and go home late and get lots accomplished without having to be distracted by all sorts of lewd thoughts. I, for one, would be deeply disappointed to see unchecked passion at the copy machine, or to stumble upon Farrah D., executive VP, casting sexually harassing glances at Scott B., her hard-working secretary. There's just no time for that, boys and girls; it's bottom lines, not bottoms, that make the world grow giddy at the tough end of this censurable

century, and, anyway, with Ann Landers singing the praises of
celibacy and Dr. Ruth sounding more like the Church Lady every
day, who could possibly be in the mood?

For those young careerists who have only lately arrived in the
workplace, it may be hard to imagine a time when sex in the office
was a given, like a regular paycheck. But those who first took jobs
in the nymph-and-satyr days presided over by the none-too-
puritanical President Eisenhower may find it equally hard to imagine how anyone can be induced to work in the unnatural confines
of an office if nothing *but* work goes on there. Simply put, when
you went to work at a new job in the days when Lucy and Desi
topped the ratings, you assumed that one of the perks would be an
intramural affair. The socioamatory climate clearly favored those
inclined toward dalliance. After all, in those jolly troglodytic times
the majority of women coming out of college went to work as
secretaries, no matter what they had studied or how brilliant their
academic record. (How embarrassing to recall that in my first job
I—a college dropout—had a Phi Beta Kappa typing my letters.)
Upper-echelon women in lower-end office jobs had no intention of
staying at them; marriage, kids, and a grassy future as suburban
matrons was the shape of things to come for most.

But if the office was no place for a woman to look for fair advancement, it was at least a fair place to look for a husband. And if
a single man just happened to be there when someone's search
began in earnest, well, so much the better for him. It was all
blissfully uncomplicated.

Big corporations, employing lots of overqualified women bent on
June weddings to junior executives, were especially steamy places.
At some point in my career, I got a job as a press agent for a
previously mentioned communications giant. The relatively minor
position came with a salary, a secretary, and an office that were,
though all distinctly limited, vastly more than I deserved. The best
thing about the job, though, were the parties thrown to celebrate
the more or less constant vice presidential promotions. Oh (to swipe
a fine phrase from Truman Capote) the greedy thrill! The sheer
abundance! Women poured out of the typing pool and the accounting department; brisk dominatrixes strode from the antechambers
of the big corner offices, shy sirens slinked in from research; women
of every face, color, and need, all gathered to pick at canapes, sip

Cutty Sark, and assay the male talent. The air was thick with promise, the chat was slathered with double entendre, and the not-so-secret phrase was "consummation devoutly to be wished." Networking had not yet been officially invented, so the amount of business done was mercifully limited. Affairs were begun, continued, sometimes tearfully ended, all within the workaday context of the corporate structure. Coffee-break conversations on the following days had less to do with who was making big moves up in the hierarchy than who was making it with whom.

All was not fun and games. For every match that actually ended in matrimony, there were many that caused havoc in the ranks. Like love, office sex was blind, at least to consequences. So while some of those involved had marriage on their minds, others already were married. The results could be disastrous. Television producer and editor Carey Winfrey recalls a legendary out-of-town party thrown by "the boys" in the hierarchy at a major New York–based news conglomerate to which the more delectable women from the lowerarchy were invited. "The fallout of that little get-together lasted for a long time," he says. "It started affairs, ended marriages, and changed careers. I sometimes wonder how my life would have gone if I'd skipped it."

At the risk of sounding noble and knowing (and implicitly innocent), I will observe that when office sex involved married men or women—even in the reckless past—the repercussions were rarely much fun. They still aren't. It is an axiom of workplace liaisons that everybody knows about them, no matter how discreet the lovers may try to be. Give them enough grope and they'll hang themselves. Sooner or later, and it's usually sooner, the little blue "We're having an affair" light starts blinking over them, at which point all their colleagues grow uncomfortable, unhappy, unsympathetic, and finally unforgiving.

In an office I worked in sometime during the last dozen years (I'm being vague about time for obvious reasons), a man whose wife and kids often attended corporate social functions began having an affair with an unmarried woman in another division of the company. Unaware of the ties between the man's family and the office family, the "other woman" began dropping by at the end of the day. The face of the red death would have been more welcome. Each time she appeared and the two left together, the temperature in the office dropped a few degrees, until it hovered near zero and turned what had been a happy playground into arctic tundra. As a result of one man's indiscretion, the women in the office began to loathe all the men there, judging them guilty by gender, and life at work became fragile; fights broke out over nothing much, and the friendship that had made a hard job bearable turned surly. Adrift in dreamland, the man causing all this didn't notice, and no one was willing to play the role of morality cop and tell the guy to change his ways. Miraculously, when it seemed that things couldn't get any worse, he was offered a better job elsewhere, and soon left. (The gods rarely undo their mischief so kindly.) Things got better, but they were never quite the same again.

Yet despite such worst-case situations, there *was* something about sex at the office that isn't provided today by all the mutual respect, wary bonhomie, and spirited company softball that has replaced it: people loved going to work, the way I loved going to the dentist. Remember how happy the seven dwarfs became when tall and beautiful Snow White came along? Whether anything was happening or not in the old days, sex was in the air, lubricious and nutritious. Don't get me wrong, people were just as ambitious and desperate for success as any postmodern piranha, but the daily possibility of promising eye contact was more alluring by far than the yearly possibility of promotion.

Now, of course, all that is Stone Age stuff, and the definition of what office sex is has changed along with the dynamics of co-worker relations. No need to go into a litany of all the reasons. Some are welcome—the change of women's professional status, for instance—and some are grim, affecting sex in general. The corporate climate these days isn't friendly to the rascally ways of old. At one time the remedy for office misalliances was simple: when things got out of hand, the female half of the affair was fired. Maybe the male was banished for half a year to the Omaha branch, maybe not. Today, both are fired, lawsuits are filed, and if either is a big enough executive (or a TV evangelist or a congressman), *People* exposes the affair with moist-palmed indignation.

And yet, as indicated by the fact that the nineties seem sure to be vintage years for prurient interest at the checkout stand, it's clear that despite all the new obstacles in its path, lust in the workplace is still a pastime to be reckoned with. Since some of the most attractive men and women known to history (those Nautilus-taut bodies, those six-figure bank accounts!) spend inordinate amounts of time at work these days, it's inevitable that office sex will make something of a comeback (though it never really went away completely). This comeback doesn't herald a return to the slaphappy hedonism of yore, which we can all be glad about. But office sex, in an entirely revamped mode, slimmed down, lightened up, smokeless, and decaffeinated for the just-say-no generation, can bring a welcome relief to the cycle of work, work, and more work that has characterized the past several years.

Unless approached with great care, however, office sex, even in its modernized form, can be very, very dangerous. More than most intramural maneuvers, it requires tactical brilliance and a cool head to survive intact, just when one's head is mostly likely to be addled and overheated. So, loath as I am to present a list of cautions regarding such an illogical, volatile thing as sexual attraction, there's just no way around it.

• **Caution No. 1.** Understand that a new contradiction in terms has been introduced that may be annoying, but must be accepted: Sex in the office isn't sex as defined by, say, D. H. Lawrence or the Mayflower Madam. Titillation, yes, a kind of fully dressed, endless foreplay, maybe even falling in love, but all as chaste as Tristan's night out with Isolde. Don't even think of that after-work martini as the prelude to something wild and sweaty, or you're at risk.

• **Caution No. 1a.** Don't drink that second martini.

• **Caution No. 2.** Acknowledge that flirtation is a worthy end in itself. A good dose of lingering looks over the coffee wagon can go a long way toward making a tough day easier, and isn't going to end up with you circling want ads on some dark Sunday morning. If a horny little devil shows up on your shoulder and starts whispering, "Go ahead, ask her (him), she's (he's) dying for it," go immediately to your health club, punish yourself with half an hour on the Stairmaster, then take a painfully cold shower.

• **Caution No. 3.** Practice safe sex. If, one morning on the way back from the coffee cart, the object of your repressed affection says, "I'm dying for it," feign a headache, or ask, "What's *it*?" I know this is maddening advice, awfully hard to follow, because let's face it, said object looks great today, but what if she (he) has a little horny devil on her or his shoulder? You may not hate yourselves or each other in the morning, but you will find the simple pleasures of the coffee break far more complicated.

• **Caution No. 4.** Consider the benefits of distance, the opposite of what Los Angeles singles call "geographic desirability." In vast L.A. the measure of desirability is nearness (if not the same neighborhood, at least not more than a few freeway exits), but at work just the opposite is true. Given the possibilities that both your devil and your friend's devil may prevail, it's an incalculable help if you are not working too close to each other. On another floor is good. At the Omaha branch is even better. Then, of course, the obvious question is, How does the whole thing get going? Maybe it doesn't. Maybe that's a very good thing. The trouble with proximity attraction is that though it's the most likely, and the most consistently entertaining sort of liaison, it's the most dangerous. As I said before, watching someone at work, doing great stuff with style, can be fiercely seductive, and seriously distracting. And, should things turn cold, daily postdalliance contact can be excruciating.

• **Caution No. 5.** Don't go public. As I pointed out, everybody knows about affairs, but flirtation generates less heat, so the blue light doesn't necessarily go on. Of course, you're not the kind of throwback who's going to grab a friend and blurt, "Good God, Fred, did you see the headlights on the new sales manager?" or "Doris, don't look now but from behind, the hunk who just started in publicity looks just like George Michael." But avoid, too, commenting at length on someone's brains, integrity, vocabulary, or team spirit. I won't go so far as to suggest that these are mere replacements for headlights or buns, but too much gratuitous talk will probably get your name mentioned on the grapevine.

• **Caution No. 6 (men).** Do not flirt upward. If you find yourself working for a woman, no matter how attractive she may be, remain calm and businesslike. Otherwise you'll make her nervous, and it's not good to make the boss nervous. If she flirts with you, be gracious and flattered, but be careful. Play the bimbo role, and she'll never respect you.

• **Caution No. 7 (women).** Do not downflirt. Men working for women are easily confused about how to relate to their bosses (see Chapter 20), and worse, tend to become uncontrollably adoring. Perhaps it's a throwback to goddess worship, or a lingering crush on a third-grade teacher, or a strain of the English malady known as Thatcheritis, but a woman who combines excellence and authority may be a powerful attraction, and the most casual gesture of reflex flirtation can quickly change a reasonable man who ought to be taking orders from you into someone who's trying to imagine what you look like naked. If you can't resist someone who's a few rungs down the ladder from you, wait until he's promoted, or (God forbid) you're demoted.

• **Caution No. 8.** Study your co-workers well. Flirtation can have a wonderful effect on women and men who can understand that when you tell them they make work worth living for, you are not looking for fourteen minutes of bliss in the broom closet. However, some people, women mostly, spend inordinate amounts of time looking for lust in other people's minds, and become very hostile when they think they've found it. Their weapon is the cry of sexual harassment, and they can do all sorts of damage. Luckily, they're easy to spot; they have a Big Nurse kind of aura that ought to warn you off. The trouble is, sometimes these women can be sexy, in a forbidding, Valkyrie sort of way, and to warm them up may seem a droll challenge. My advice to any man so inclined is to join a snake-handling cult instead.

• **Caution No. 9.** If he or she is married, or if you are married, don't do it. Really, just don't. It won't be worth it. Flirt a bit, sure—no need to discriminate or turn yourself into the office nebbish or wallflower. But if you're intent on running your marriage onto the rocks, choose a reef far from the safe harbor of the job. If you just can't get interested in someone not married to someone else, give Dr. Ruth a jingle. Just remember to disguise your voice.

Enough! This is too discouraging. The role of wet blanket is not one I can stand playing any longer. So study this list. Try not to listen to the senior vice presidents when they start talking about how you should've been here fifteen years ago. Practice dry flirting (into a mirror, at first). Put a framed picture of stern-visaged former surgeon general Koop on your desk. Close your eyes and think of paychecks. And keep up those cold showers.

11

The Bastard Factor

sooner or later

you'll work for Caligula;

don't worry,

it won't last forever

*T*hrough thick and thin, bull markets and bears, high times or hard, dizzying growth and daunting recession, one thing remains a constant in the workplace: a plenitude of bastards. Like the poor, it seems, bastards will always be among us, and if things go badly on the personal ethics front, they may even *be* us. Of course, there are all sorts of bastards, at every level of organization, starting with minor mailroom meanies who divert vital memos and personnel department martinets who terrorize with paperwork. But for purposes of the big picture—the macromanaging of survival—the focus here will be on high-level lowlifes, the bastard bosses who not only can make life and work a persistent misery, but play hell with well-deserved advancements either by crushing morale or derailing careers.

There are many kinds of bastard bosses, and many things to learn about their bad breed, but the first and most important is this:

no action is too small-minded, no meanness too petty, no trick too
low, no plot too pointlessly malevolent for a bastard to bother with;
these are not people who stare into the bathroom mirror in the
morning and say, "Frank, you have to rise above this embarrassing
behavior and become a better person." Their bastardism is a source
of joy to them, as sailing or golf is to someone else, and they
practice it every chance they get, polishing their skills as they
heighten their pleasure at the expense of all those who report to
them. Let it be noted that some bastards rise to a level of brilliance
that would be admirable if it weren't so pernicious, just as some
sailors become magically attuned to the sea and their sails. (Sometimes the two accomplishments are even combined; after the brutal
Captain Bligh was forced off the *Bounty*, he performed one of the
greatest feats of small-boat navigation in the history of sailing.) One
of the most distressing aspects of bastardism is that it has a certain
negative magnetism, a dark-star quality, and often the more definitive someone's maliciousness, the more legendary the rat becomes.

Because sheer badness can lend a certain clarity of character to
the perpetrator, mean bosses are a staple of literature, the anec-
dotal equivalent to an author of a martini to a dedicated drinker.
Richard III leaps crookedly to mind, and the Robert Graves version
of Caligula. But some bad bosses are otherwise admirable. Odysseus, despite his heroic stature in Homeric epics, beat up one of his
men, hapless Thersites, for suggesting that Agamemnon's pride
might not be worth prolonged bloodshed. (Similar mistreatment, if
only verbal, was meted out after the Gulf war to those unlucky
Democrats who weren't able to see George Bush as *our* Agamemnon.) Prospero, Shakespeare's main man in *The Tempest*, has only
two employees, slow-witted, blue-collar Caliban and VP for creative deception Ariel, but the play has barely started when each is
complaining bitterly—to an entirely unsympathetic boss—about
miserable working conditions and broken contracts. In Wagner's
Ring cycle there's hardly a worthwhile boss in the bunch, whether
god or man, but Alberich, oppressing the Nibelungs in his neth-
erworld sweatshop, is about as bad as they get. Then there's the
rogues' gallery of hardhearted head men dished up by Dickens, an
author whose collected works could make George Will a socialist.
And so on and on, up through the ages to that very model of a
modern monster Leona Helmsley, who might as well be a fictional

creation, so archetypal is her reputed harshness. Bad people make good copy, which, alas, tends to encourage them.

One of the most popular bastards in pop culture in recent times is one Miles Drentell, the bête froid advertising honcho in "thirty-something." For fans of the show, Drentell (as played by David Clennon) proved irresistible from his first appearance—smooth, impeccably dressed, as all-powerful as Zeus and impenetrable as the Sphinx. The appeal of Drentell for both writers and viewers was so apparent that the original three-episode plan for the character was extended to a regular place for Clennon in the show's cast. In his own ominous way, he gave the bastard boss an alluring image. When, in a pivotal scene, he let the Michael Steadman character go through a humbling scene in order, at last, to find out whether he will get a big raise, Drentell was just an Armani-clothed version of the nasty kid who delights in pulling the legs off a fly— enjoyable to watch, as long as he's safely on the other side of a television screen.

Who can deny that there is something fascinating about bastards, for all their hatefulness? In a world full of smarmy concern for our well-being, where corporate personnel manuals read like something by Leo Buscaglia and company group discussions encourage us to share our feelings, bad people can be almost refreshing—at least they are what they are. The only trouble is, until you *know* what they are, in all their variations, you won't be entirely safe from bastards in high places. In truth, you won't be safe anyway, but it's always better to know about the enemy than to be astonished to find the person you're working for has your worst interests at heart.

Bastards are more than plentiful, they are endemic. If you haven't yet worked for one, you are either long on luck or short on résumé. Ask almost anybody about villainous employers and you'll get atrocity stories to rival the tales of the Inquisition. A phone call to a former staffer of a major metropolitan newspaper elicits testimony about a man who edited one of the weekly sections, a mauler of souls so universally loathed that when he dropped dead in the middle of a weekend tennis game, the celebratory air among his misused minions on Monday could barely be concealed. A poll of a couple of erstwhile executives at a well-known clothing manufacturer unearths harrowing dispatches from life at the front under a CEO with what can only be called a Bligh spirit. "His whole style is intimidation and abuse," one scarred veteran says. "He's a small man who takes great pleasure in hurting people, both emotionally and physically. He's notorious for throwing things at people." The undersize nasty boy's pitching career is alleged to include an incident at a sales meeting when he winged a bagel at one of his top staffers—who happened to be his wife at the time—and called her an extremely rude name. The marriage didn't last, but the man's ironhanded rule continues unimpeded.

It would be easy to fill this chapter with tales of bastards' infamy. Like crime stories and car wrecks, they are gruesome but compelling entertainment. And just as you'll find far more bad news in the morning paper than good, you'll hear far more about mean bosses than benevolent ones. Such testimony is valuable for a few reasons: if we work for a bastard, it's good to know we're not alone in our misery; if we don't, it's good to know how lucky we are; and if we're not sure, it helps to have some comparative research.

Though bastard bosses should be forced by law to wear identifying clothing (hockey masks, Darth Vader cloaks or Freddie Kruger gloves might be appropriate) they tend to look pretty much like everybody else—no fangs, no chain saws, not even a telltale hint of horns. More insidiously, they can behave like ordinary decent folk a lot of the time, too, wrapping their daily bad deeds in a confusing cocoon of typical good-guy activity. Bastards can even be likable, and we may think they're okay right up until the moment they humiliate us, stab us in the back, have us drawn and quartered, or subject us to any other of their grisly specialties. Bastards vary so widely that though most ought to be avoided if at all possible, some are occasionally worth tolerating for what—beyond suffering—they have to offer in terms of expertise. If for no other reason, it may be worth working for a bastard as a way of inoculating yourself against the plague of mean-spiritedness that stalks the land of business; once you've experienced villainy face to face, day after day, it won't come as such a surprise when you encounter it again. And again. But to get the most out of a bastard, or to know when to get out, a knowledge of the species is essential. Though bastard bosses are as different as snowflakes (only much colder), they can all be grouped in certain general types, such as:

• **The Nice Bastard.** Of course there's nothing nice about this example of the creature—geniality is simply the camouflage of choice for a dedication to bad deeds. A nice bastard will do all sorts of thoughtful things, performing a perfect simulation of friendship in the morning while oiling the rack in preparation for an afternoon stretch. The reason for such pleasantness is clear: a lulled victim is an easy victim, someone who will remain to the end unsuspecting of the nice bastard's special brand of "Et tu, Brute" brutality. A friend of mine recently had what is a fairly typical experience with one of these bad good ol' boys (who happened to be a woman, but who's counting anymore?); she was invited out to lunch with her boss, who was leaving that afternoon for a two-week vacation, and told repeatedly what a great job she'd done for the company, what a creative problem solver she was—one wet kiss after another right up through the espresso and cheesecake. After feeling like Wonder Woman all weekend, my friend came in on Monday to find a confidential memo on her desk saying that the company was moving into a "new phase" and she just didn't fit in. You're great, you're special, you're history!

• **Mommy (or Daddy) Dearest.** Imagine a cross between Santa Claus and Jason, or Mother Teresa and Ming the Merciless and you've got the basic blueprint for this paternalistic black hat: periods of familial concern interspersed with nights when you're sent to bed without your supper and given a few whacks for good measure. Superhuman skepticism is required to understand that the solicitous style of this type of bastard is just a means to the mean one's end. Ultimately, the price of that cozy family feeling is periodic parental abuse, ranging from intimidation to towering rages that leave emotional debris all over the place. Like many parents with uncontrollable tempers, these bosses demand absolute loyalty and affection, but are heartless when disappointed in any way. Because they can seem so protective, mommies and daddies dearest are all the more damaging when they're meting out punishment, and tend to warm to the task as they see the devastating effect they're having. Alas, social workers have no jurisdiction in these cases, so it's best to hitch up your Dr. Dentons and run for daylight.

• **The Schizogre.** This is one of the worst bastards to confront, since he (or she) can be just as ingratiating as gruesome. Schizogres differ from nice bastards in that they're actually sincere when they put an arm around your shoulder and ask how your mother's operation went. Then, after putting you through the torments of the damned at a sales meeting (and having a devil of a good time doing it), they'll ask you out for a drink and act as if you've both come from a love-in. Maddeningly, you may find that you genuinely like one of these off (with your head)-and-on-again characters when he's in his sweetheart mode, thus letting down your guard until the next auto-da-fé. Unaffected by their own drastic mood changes, schizogres are devastating for those of us who take it personally when someone calls us "the most pathetic excuse for an executive this company has ever had to endure." They don't remember their invective for more than a few minutes, and they're oblivious to the pain and suffering in their wakes. Despite a degree of dumb innocence, schizogres are not forgivable, because being good some of the time doesn't ever make up completely for being bad most of the time.

• **The Mean Bastard.** All bastards are mean, of course, but some revel in meanness for its own sake. Frank Lorenzo, who took over Eastern Airlines and ran it until being ousted by a federal bankruptcy judge, was often portrayed as nothing less than the antichrist by the unions on strike against the company. Name-calling in labor-management struggles is nothing new, so one might assume a high degree of hyperbole. But a former colleague of Lorenzo's was quoted in *Newsweek* recalling an approach toward employees that, though not directly attributed to Lorenzo, might be assumed to reflect his attitude: "[We use] the carrot and stick routine . . . We take the carrot and shove it up their ass. Then we use the stick to tamp it in."

Mean bastards love this kind of sadistic imagery, and pride themselves on their ability to inflict cruelty on underlings without flinching, deriding those who can't do the same as weak. The infamous Madam Helmsley fired her corporate controller while having a dress fitted, casting him out airily with the observation that though she didn't want to hurt him, she simply didn't see the need for him.

The scariest thing about mean bastards is that they can't see the difference between toughness and beastliness, nor are they even mildly troubled by the enjoyment they derive from causing suffering. Mean bastards are often unacceptable even to other bastards, yet when crises abound they tend to rise, like Robespierre through the chaos of the French Revolution.

• **The Lying Bastard.** Not all bastard bosses lie, though few have any real scruples about it. Lying, after all, is a very useful tool for doing people in. Former RJR Nabisco CEO F. Ross Johnson bitterly described to the *New York Times* what he considered the three cardinal rules that governed the behavior of Wall Street take-over artists like Henry Kravis (who did *him* in): "Never play by the rules, never pay in cash, and never tell the truth." Lying bastards either love to lie or don't bother to differentiate between the truth and mendacity (I've never figured out which). Certainly, they take pleasure in their skill, and sometimes can't resist taking credit for it.

In his book *Confessions of an SOB*, former Gannett newspaper chairman Al Neuharth tells of overhearing (on a phone extension) the head of a company Gannett had just merged with saying to his wife that he'd be running the whole show within six months. Neuharth proceeded to spend those months lulling the man with expressions of friendship while secretly (and successfully) maneuvering to get the board behind his plan to send his pal to the corporate gulag. Whatever the motivation of L.B.'s, they are distinguished by their ability to look you straight in the eye and say things that are completely false. And when you find out the truth, they'll look you in the eye again and say they never said it in the first place. Lying bastards spend an inordinate amount of time looking people in the eye, and their sheer brass when dispensing mis- and disinformation can leave basically honest folk stunned and bewildered. It's this state that the lying bastard strives for, and while others run around wondering how he can lie so shamelessly, he smiles on their confusion and wonders how it can be that so many people were born yesterday.

Just as vampires are said to fear crosses, major liars view paper with undisguised alarm. Needing always to claim they don't remember saying what you heard them say, they will do anything to avoid putting their words in writing. If all else fails, you might try driving a yellow legal pad through their hearts.

• **The Appealing Bastard.** Also known as "one brilliant son of a bitch," "a prick, but damned good," and a variety of other grudgingly admiring terms. These are people with a taste for torment who are, nevertheless, worth enduring because they are so good at what they do, and often quite likable too. I had a marine drill instructor long ago who punched me, shook napalm strikes of Tabasco sauce down my throat, and once made an entire recruit platoon crawl again and again through a twelve-inch high space under a barracks building in ninety-degree South Carolina summer heat, all the while shouting, "You maggots don't even believe in Jesus!" But in all other ways this combat veteran was such an exemplary teacher that after thirteen weeks of his mistreatment I was, I'm convinced, prepared to die for the SOB. Rent the movie *Patty Hearst* if you want a quick refresher course on the allure of this peculiar type. It's the Miles Drentell phenomenon: you'd love to hate him—and he couldn't care less about you—but there's something about the guy . . .

• **The Passive-Aggressive Bastard.** This variation on our lamentable theme is often found in the growing ranks of high-level female executives. (But not all women fall into this category; Dawn Steel, a Hollywood producer and former head of Columbia Pictures, is about as unpassive as anyone this side of an Islamic jihad—so much so that fellow producer Dan Melnick said, "If Dawn was any more aggressive, they would have to lock her up.") But a few thousand years of conditioning don't wear off in a decade or two, so women bosses who may be bad witches to the core will still avoid confrontation (with men or women), smiling demurely while seething inside, until they issue forth a memo with all the destructive power of a pipe bomb.

Passive-aggressive bastards, male or female, are similar to nice bastards except that their vile acts are less constant and therefore less predictable. They can be quite pleasant to get along with, but because they can't get mad openly they constantly want to get even covertly. Passive-aggressive types can deliver fatal surprises to those unfortunates who think everything's okay because no one is frothing at the mouth. Perhaps the worst thing about them is that they *never* lose their tempers, so that even when they're making you crazy enough to blow up, they end up seeming eminently reasonable. Not surprisingly, P.-A. bastards thrive in highly bureaucratic organizations, where they can use the system as a shield for skulduggery.

• **The Megabastard.** Here we have the ultimate prince (or princess) of darkness, the worst of breed, Pol Pot/executive VP, all the miserable traits of bastardism rolled into one predatory package. What distinguishes the megabastard boss from all the other manner of workplace thugs are two factors: sheer expertise and extreme pride of craft. Generally, megabastards have been at their nefarious work long enough to become jackals of all trades, Renaissance meanies, accomplished at all the specific varieties of dirty pool listed above. And while almost all these brigands know who and what they are and feel varying degrees of satisfaction with that, megabastards are so profoundly fulfilled by their evil deeds that the anger and finger-pointing of victims and onlookers only reinforce their self-esteem. One of the reasons megabastards enjoy a certain invulnerability is that the kinds of social sanctions that limit a normal person's behavior tend to drive dedicated bad guys to greater extremes. They are, in short, dead to shame and brought to life by public shock. Al Neuharth actually offered to let one of his ex-wives write a chapter in his autobiography, and she happily accepted, describing him as a snake who "slithers around and sheds his old skin as he grows." One can almost picture Gannett's top serpent preening in front of the mirror, smoothing his scales and murmuring, "Al, you viper you, you're beautiful!"

That bastards feel entitled by power to lie without a blink, blind-side people who trust them, wreak havoc for the fun of it—and succeed in the process—is enough to make those of us who weren't born to raise hell wonder what the point is to being good. High-mindedness may be some comfort, especially for those worried about their place in paradise, but it's not much of a reward on earth when you watch low-down rats move up, amply rewarded along the way. How is it that bastards can do so well that they become bosses, then conduct reigns of terror while everyone busily looks the other way? Why don't people stand up to them the way kids eventually do to bullies in the Hollywood version? A woman who spent one very dreary year under the lash of a famous killer shrew figures it this way: "Most people are not vicious and ugly, so when they see people in power do vicious and ugly things it's like they don't understand what's happening. They just can't realize that these creeps are different than they are. Someone will complain that Mr. So-and-So doesn't have to be such a monster since he's already CEO; they just don't realize that bastards don't *need* a motive—it's their hobby."

Sadly, in a mean-spirited time, bastards are often admired, even revered, by corporate boards, major shareholders, and others whose opinions affect careers. If a company happens to be doing well in the short run despite the misery of its employees, it will be assumed that a bastard's style is the reason why. If a company is doing badly, it will be thought that only bastardism can cure what ails it. Though they usually end up doing far more harm to the heart of an organization than good to the bottom line, bastards have considerable glamour in the war scenarios that influence business. By the time their names appear on the casualty lists, a lot of needless damage has been done.

Inevitably, at some point, you will be asked to aid and abet a bastard's schemes, and by association to take the first steps toward becoming a bastard yourself. (If you're already a bastard, why are you reading this?) The temptation can be great. After all, if it's not always a jungle out there, it's almost never Mr. Rogers' Neighborhood, and one's instinct for survival may whisper that it's better to be on the good side of a bastard than on his (s)hit list. Plus, seeing decent people brought down by dark deeds can make villainy seem nothing more than a smart expedient, a temporary methodology you can dip into without risking any lasting effect. If I don't do it, you figure, somebody else will, and I'll end up on the street.

Sad to say, that last bit may be true. And though it may be easy for me, sitting safely behind my word processor with no lingering ambitions for high corporate office (well, almost none), to urge you to just say no, I'll do it anyway. Bastards are like vampires: once they get their teeth into you, you'll never be the same again. Joining them won't save you in the long run, but you'll have become the kind of person fit only for the company of creeps. So what if the book of nice guys who've finished first is a slim volume? So what if the "wimp factor" unfairly threatens to cloud issues of right and wrong? So what if some Deadly Do-Wrong gets the raise, the raves, the power and the glory? Surely, being a bastard is its own sort of hell, even for the most self-satisfied backstabber. Let's hope so. In the meantime, remember: there *is* a high road, and you *can* get there from here.

12

"You're Fired!"

how to survive

hearing these

dire words, or

saying them

*O*f all the limp clichés to emerge from movies over the years, surely one of the most feeble is the scene—especially frequent in the late forties and fifties—in which an employee who has just been fired leans over the boss's desk and shouts, "You can't fire me, Mr. Thumbscrew. I quit!"

Talk about empty threats. The best the irate employee can manage is a pitiful bit of face-saving, while Thumbscrew, if he's quick enough, can jump at the chance for a resignation and save the severance pay a firing might have cost him.

Of course, it's hard not to feel sympathy for the one who gets fired, and to suspect that in his place we might also try anything, however limp, in order to have the last word. After all, being fired is high on the list of life's most distressing events, a cruel blow to one's self-esteem, and whatever mitigates its dreary effects might seem justified. But for all sorts of reasons both just and unjust, we do get fired, so inevitably that to progress through a career without at least once suffering the indignity is so unusual it might almost be considered a kind of failure, like holding on to one's virginity into middle age.

Almost as unsettling as being fired is having to fire someone. (That's a big "almost," however.) In both situations, considerable élan is required in order for things to go well (or as well as can be expected). If either is botched, word tends to get out, providing highly satisfying entertainment for those uncharitable souls who delight in *Schadenfreude*, the pleasure derived from the calamities of others (which is, at last count, everybody). Stories about firings are the Grand Guignol of the workplace. We listen to them with that mixture of awe, terror, and relief that springs from any disaster that could have happened to us but didn't. And such is the maddening eventuality of life that no matter how high you scramble up the ladder of power and attainment there is always some heel capable of tromping on your knuckles from above. In other words, everyone can get fired, and except for a few blindly arrogant dictators and blithely addled CEOs, everyone knows it. Thus, the subject is always hot, and the business pages of newspapers are usually perused by all of us (come on, admit it), searching to discover what big shot "has decided to leave the company to pursue private interests" or has "resigned, citing personal reasons." The euphemisms are well known, but everybody is acutely aware that they all spell F- - - - .

Despite the fact that people lose their jobs all the time, and that a business section without a body count is as unlikely as the social pages without weddings, the act of firing has a bad name. This may simply be because it is a word that evokes the image of the stake (as in "Hey, Pierre, I hear Joan of Arc got fired yesterday") or the bullet-pocked wall ("Ready, aim, fired!"). Small wonder that the term never appears in official memos announcing some executive's untimely retirement. Corporate personnel types react to the word like vampires confronted by a cross, and will often agree to pay lucrative severance packages if the firee will promise to go along with the company euphemism. Probably the last boss to actually say the words "You're fired" (shout them, in fact) was Dagwood Bumstead's tormentor Mr. Dithers. And Dithers probably only said them because his creator, Chic Young, couldn't fit "leaving by

mutual agreement" or "will continue with the company as a consultant" or "as a result of fundamental policy differences" into car-
toon balloons, and there's nothing funny about the awful
contemporary jargon "let go" or worst of all, "terminated."

In the delicate negotiations that usually attend executive job loss,
face-saving is priority number one for both firee and firer. In my
own first encounter with the process—though by no means my last,
as you'll see—a boss who wanted me to vanish (for no good reason
as far as I was concerned) promised to get me a lavish cash going-
away gift if I would agree to including some phrase like "Mr.
Edwards' departure was a mutual decision" in the memo announcing my downfall. There was nothing mutual about it; security
guards were almost required to drag me from my precious cubby-
hole on executive row. But in return for helping the company avoid
admitting they'd dumped yet another employee (it had been a year
of living dangerously for everybody there) I got the bankroll for a
year on a Greek island to salve my hurt feelings. Ultimately, the
trade-off seemed worth its weight in lotuses.

The raw facts of being bounced can't have changed much in the
past couple of millennia: one minute you have a job, and the next
you don't. But the need for neatness and perfection that applies a
gloss to almost everything in our smoothly synthesized times has
led companies to make firing seem almost pleasant. What was once
a brutal shock is now more like a lethal injection. Corporate personnel specialists have become expert in the sly art of easing the
doomed employee out with enough anesthetic to make the process
seem painless, at least until the next morning, when the victim can
no longer make a scene. Witness the following well-orchestrated
denouement in the career of a woman in a high-level job in New
York (as written for *West* magazine):

> Without taking her eyes off me, she reaches toward her desk. The
> upper right-hand drawer glides silently. Her expression is so com-
> passionate one would think it's a mercy killing. But instead of an
> elegant revolver, the personnel director extracts a box of tissue from
> her secret compartment and pushes it across the polished teak sur-
> face.
>   "Sorry," she whispers. "It's not working out."
>   I am fired.

Called for what I have assumed to be an emergency production meeting, I haven't taken the time to go to the bathroom. Now I realize I am disheveled and *I don't have my lipstick on.*

"What are you going to do next?" she asks. *What am I going to do next?* Does she expect me to have a tantrum, call the newspapers, threaten to sue?

"Well," she goes on, "I took the liberty of making an appointment for you *right now* with our outplacement service. They are very good at helping people in your situation reassess their options and market their talent. You'll enjoy talking with them . . . They'll help you prepare your exit statement. You'll rehearse how you are going to break the news to your staff and your friends. You may not want to say that you've been fired. Think of it as a press release."

But as much as this cool, well-oiled lifeboat drill is meant to divert anger and delay pain, there's a limit to how far an employee can go to save face, especially if the company involved feels the delicate balance in the firing game has been upset. When, on an early summer day in 1990, the Metropolitan Opera announced the resignation of its general manager, who had been in the job for only eight months, the man released a statement saying that he "had not found fulfillment in the position." The attitude may have been a bit lofty for someone on the Met board of directors to take, because a few days later, over a story filled with insider detail that could only have been leaked from high places, a banner headline read: GEN-ERAL MANAGER OF MET OPERA WAS DISMISSED.

Despite the low status of the word "fired," it's probably time to put in a good word *for* it. Because it's a rare firing that does no one any good, sometimes even the person on the dirty end of the stick. After all, few situations that end up in a firing can have been particularly cozy, so once the sting of the experience has eased, being fired can be a blessed relief to the bounced one. (Nothing heightens that relief quite as well as a good contract and a testy lawyer; when CBS chairman Tom Wyman was ousted by the company's board of directors, he managed to leave with the shirt on his back, plus $4.2 million, stock options, and a secretary on the CBS payroll. Many observers felt that Wyman, who joined CBS from Polaroid, had failed to figure out the broadcasting business, but he'd obviously mastered the art of parachuting.) From a management point of view, if the firing is justified, it has the distinctly tonic effect of reminding everyone who didn't get fired that working hard is worth it after all, and that there is a comeuppance for slackers. Of course, getting the ax for a good reason can be a worthwhile learning experience for people who haven't yet understood that all play and no work make Jack an unemployed boy.

It might be argued (though a more earnest writer than I will have to do the job) that one of the things demoralizing Americans these days is the suspicion that a lot of people can be absolutely rotten at their jobs and never be called to account (see Chapter 23). Even when a firing seems whimsical and unjust, the victim's co-workers may experience at least a momentary feeling of elation. They, after all, have survived, if only temporarily. The point is often made that public executions did nothing to deter criminals, but no one ever mentions that those law-abiding folk in the public square who have not been hanged may tend to feel keenly the justification for their goodness. Capital punishment, I suspect, isn't meant to frighten criminals, who will likely do what they do no matter what, but to encourage the righteous to continue along paths that may be fairly boring and relatively unprofitable. In the same way, a firing can make everyone else cherish their good fortune: "Tough about Chuck, and all that, but let's look on the bright side—it wasn't me."

When a firing ought to happen but doesn't, or even ought not to happen but seems inevitable—hanging in the air like a guillotine blade photographed in midfall—the effect on others can be disastrous. Those who don't want to be the ones to hint at the bad news can hardly bring themselves to ask the person about to be fired how things are going. Nothing is more agonizing than having a lunch, or even a conversation at the coffee cart, with someone who seems unaware that the Fates are busily sawing away at his thread. And even those who don't care particularly about the intended victim begin to get depressed by the countdown-to-disaster syndrome that takes hold. Nobody wants to start each day with "Morning, everybody. How 'bout those Lakers? Linda get the ax yet?"

One of the eeriest sights in nature is the way wildebeest in a herd graze apparently unconcerned as hyenas assemble for a kill, but quietly move away from the intended victim. How do they all know which one of them is doomed? And how can they be so sure that said victim won't escape, leaving each of them possible targets?

Whatever the answer, they do know, with a mysterious assurance. And probably through the same anxious herd instinct, so do most of us in working situations. No matter how subtle are the tremors of discontent, an impending firing gets into the air, and often the only one not aware that something's up is the person soon to be the subject of one of those terrible, euphemistic announcements. (One sure sign that you're the ill-fated wildebeest, by the way, is that fewer and fewer memos find their way into your in-box as the day of reckoning approaches. Another sign of danger is a boss who is feeling vulnerable and may plan a firing or two to give *his* boss the impression that others were to blame for his mistakes.)

The burden on everyone of this awful open secret is one of the most onerous aspects of a decision too slowly made. Because of this, even an unjust firing may be better than placing someone in the purgatory of not-yet-fired and asking others to go about business as usual. I once got a phone call from an executive headhunter who asked me if I'd be interested in a very attractive position that, unknown to the recruiter, happened to be the job of one of my closest friends. Calling to break this news to her was not the high point of my week.

Shopping a job around before it's been vacated, before the current jobholder even knows there's trouble ahead, is just one of the many ways the act of firing people is mishandled. Most types of business, however widespread they may be, are communities in which people above a certain level know one another, or at least about one another. No matter how discreet an executive search may be, word inevitably gets out, putting colleagues in the demoralizing position either of delivering bad tidings (as I did) or pretending not to know what's up. Other common firing crimes are such bloodless methods as the fatal phone call, or (worse yet) the letter, especially when either of these is delivered on a weekend, or when the person being fired is on vacation. In 1991, the entire staff of a publication in the Midwest was fired by fax. At least one well-known executive was fired while she was at the hairdresser, which may be more civilized than the treatment Albert Anastasia got at the barbershop, but still bears a certain similarity. And then there's the professional hit-man approach described earlier by the woman wafted out of her job before she had time to get her lipstick on. These experts will write your statement, pack your belongings, leak the agreed-upon cover story, and discreetly collect your keys and parking garage pass before you've had a chance to wonder what it is you did wrong. I once heard an interview with one of England's two last official hangmen, a cheerful chap who proclaimed that what made him proudest of the work he and his colleague did was their ability to get condemned men from the holding cell to the noose and through the deadly trapdoor in the space of a few seconds, before the "poor bloke" knew what was happening. A similar pride, no doubt, fills the innocent hearts of personnel persons when they have cleanly carried out someone else's dirty work.

Management style is much talked about these days, and there can be no effective management style without an effective firing style. The evasions noted above are unstylish, to say the least. Not that the act of firing is something that any nonsadist wants to feel good about being good at (in the manner of Her Majesty's hangman), but doing the job badly just because you have no heart for it is no favor to anyone. Ronald Reagan is said to have disliked intensely even reprimanding those who worked for him, much less firing them. But politics, like baseball, is a game in which heads sometimes have to be served up to the public for reasons of ceremonial exorcism. Questions of fairness are irrelevant. When it became clear that someone had to go for the mishandling of the administration's growing Iran-Contra problems, and that White House chief of staff Donald Regan was the likeliest candidate, the president wasn't up to the role of terminator, and the weeks of speculation, press roasts, and jockeying for position that followed were not pleasant, inside or outside the Beltway. In the end, the body politic was squirming uncomfortably under the impression that Regan's successor had been put in place (through a flood of press leaks) before Regan had been allowed a dignified departure (which was true) and worse, that the chief executive and commander in chief of the armed forces had let his wife, one hundred pounds of pith and vinegar, do the firing for him (which may have been false, but who besides Kitty Kelley could know for sure?). Though it's hard to come up with a fan club of three or more for the abrasive Regan, the clumsy mishandling of his departure made the president look inept and—ironically—heartless.

Thus, the first rule of firing: *If you've got to fire someone, do it fast, not through the death of a thousand cuts.* And if you suspect you're going to be fired but feel you're being left to twist slowly in the wind, figure out a way to bring things to a head even though the head is yours.

Symbolic firings, of which Donald Regan's was an example, often seem remarkably unjust, because they are usually nothing personal and rarely have much to do with job performance. They just *are*. People in certain jobs, notably team managers, ministers of state, generals, and television programming vice presidents, understand that they may be sacrificed for the sake of appearances, and tend to be fatalistic about it. In the movie *Prizzi's Honor*, when the Jack Nicholson character is ordered to kill his wife, the Mafia don comforts him by saying that the hit is "just business," and certain firings are like that. In the late eighties, the Argentine armed forces chief of staff was unceremoniously dumped by the country's president for carrying out a just policy put in place by the president himself—the arrest and prosecution of army members involved in the murders of civilians during the seventies. But when a group of rebellious officers had demanded the chief's ouster, the pragmatic president decided it would be less trouble to fire a faithful ally than open fire on his enemies. Even those with no heart for kicking people out can accept symbolic bloodlettings, perhaps because everything seems decreed by fate ("Sure, it was rough, but we all knew Mike had to go"). If you find yourself on the business end of such a firing, try to be comforted by the fact that being bounced for symbolic reasons means at least that you've risen high enough to be a symbol.

Ronald Reagan's reluctance to fire people is a common problem, but by no means a universal trait. Some people have plenty of heart and stomach for firing, even an unhealthy enthusiasm for the rites of human sacrifice. The lore of termination (an epic bloodier than the Norse sagas) is filled with tales of men and women who seem to find their truest sense of self-fulfillment when they are saying, "Callahan, I thought it was time we talked about your future at the company," or any of the other classic opening gambits of executioner's chess.

At CBS in the sixties, network president James Aubrey earned the epithet "the Smiling Cobra" for his habit of lulling subordinates into thinking that a crucial meeting was going well, then suddenly striking a deadly blow. One story, which quickly became part of

Aubrey's legend, told of a meeting between him and the network's program director. The programmer was presenting his suggestions for the network's fall lineup of shows. "All right, M——," Aubrey is said to have interrupted, "you're through."

"Well, not quite, Jim," the unsuspecting man reportedly replied, "I've got a couple more shows to go over."

To which Aubrey genially responded, gesturing toward the door, "No, M——, you don't understand. You're *through*."

More recently, the mayor of a midsize American city made short work of the firing of his police chief with the following sentence (a model of economy rare in public life): "Read my lips: Good-bye." A lawyer I know heard one of his regular seatmates on their commuter train brag that he had asked his secretary for a cup of coffee, thanked her for it, and in the same breath told her to have her desk cleared for her replacement by noon.

Despite the fact that such brutal behavior earns the perpetrators a certain dubious fame and gets them mentioned in books by authors who would rather not, it sets a bad example for our young and, like terrorism, should probably be ignored by the press. Which leads me to the second rule of firing: *Do the job without malice, as civilly as possible, even if the targeted employee deserves nothing better than keelhauling.* The point of this rule is simple self-interest; the way things go in most businesses, you may eventually end up asking someone you once fired for a job (a gloomy but entirely plausible thought). Gentleness may not always be remembered, but savagery will never be forgotten, nor forgiven.

The subject of civility brings up rule three: *Do the job in person, face to face, not by phone, fax, or memo as mentioned earlier.* Firing someone indirectly is the moral equivalent of sending a letter bomb. Perhaps the best test of how much you really want to fire someone is whether you're up to the confrontation. On the other hand, not being able to do that may simply be a telltale sign that one lacks not only decency but guts. A well-known publisher of men's magazines had a particularly ignoble way of avoiding personal involvement in what is certainly one of the most personal of all transactions; he simply had the lock changed on a person's office during the noon hour, then posted a security guard to break the news when the castaway returned from lunch. Late in his brilliant career, the legendary editor Harold Hayes was fired by telegram while on vacation in London (by a publisher also rumored to have "terminated" an ad saleswoman the same way, a few days before she was scheduled to return from maternity leave—and who, happily, was summarily dumped a few years later by his financial backers). I was once fired by—trust me on this—a swinish fellow who called me at six A.M. while I was on an out-of-town business trip. These indirect sneak attacks happen all the time, but they are bad form at its worst.

The ability to handle a face-to-face firing, even when you're up to the task, is not a given; it's a skill that needs careful development. The problem isn't always one of behaving decently, but rather of going overboard while trying not to be the bad guy. A decent person, wanting to do the right thing, can end up handing out a promotion instead of handing someone his head. It happens. How else could all those idiots who have fired *us* have risen to their levels of incompetence? The best way to administer a decent coup de grâce without botching things with faint resolve is not to spend too much time at the task. Firing, even done with style and charity, shouldn't require the same amount of time as hiring; after all, the person in question is no longer a mystery, but is known well enough to have been found wanting. The trick is to find the right balance between abruptness and therapy. Presumably, every firing scene has its moment of perfection, like the fullest rising of a soufflé; if you stop just there, the person you're firing will accept the inevitable, and even think well of you (given a certain interval of time). But if things go on just a few minutes more you'll end up feeling guilty, sometimes so guilty that you may hear yourself offering to resign yourself in sympathy.

One of the unwanted side effects of the overly therapeutic approach—besides the fact that at some point the concern of the firer, who will still have a job after the meeting, can begin to seem cruelly counterfeit—is that the boss becomes the star of the scene. Even if things work out for the person being fired, the actual moment is invariably a hard one, and belongs to him or her. Part of doing the job right is making sure not to take over center stage. During the darkest days of mass layoffs at Wall Street brokerages in 1989, a young broker at Drexel Burnham Lambert was told that he wouldn't be needed after the close of that day's business. Stunned, he started to leave his boss's office, only to be asked by the anxious headsman, "Uh, Dave, did you think I handled that okay? 'Cause I have several more to do today, but you were my first." Tacky.

You'll have noticed that while talking about firing style I haven't said much about how to behave while *being* fired. This isn't because style isn't required to make a good exit—just ask Charles I, who worried less about losing his head than failing to maintain good form—but simply that there are far fewer options for someone on the receiving end of a pink slip. And knowing how to handle losing a job isn't a skill you want to polish with constant practice. But there are certain rules of conduct useful for those dark days when the sky does fall.

Basically, for white-collar, nonunion types, despite all the muttering about "That bastard can't do this to me!" and "By the time my lawyer and I get through with this company . . ." and so forth, the grating truth is that the bastards usually *can* do this to you, and battling them too loudly can make other possible employers wary. This is not to say that you shouldn't fight the good fight if you've been the victim of contract violations, or of sexism, racism, ageism, or any other wicked ism, but just that you have to make sure it's a good fight that you can win. Going after an employer because you think you were fired whimsically or unjustly may seem like a good idea at the time, but in the end you probably won't get much satisfaction. (Some states are better than others for disgruntled employees—California is a paradise compared to hard-hearted New York, for instance—but except in cases where illegality can be proved, the odds are with the company.) Once in a while, justice triumphs, as when Philadelphia securities analyst Marvin Roffman, who predicted the Trump casino woes in the high Donald Days of early 1990 and was fired when he refused to retract his statements, won a $750,000 settlement from his former employer a year later. But don't get your hopes up.

The best thing to do is wax philosophical and look at the good aspects of being fired. Happily enough, there are usually quite a few. First of all, most severances carry some sort of payoff, and even if your parachute is aluminum instead of gold the chance for a bit of paid time off should be welcome. Second, being fired lets you drop all the hypocrisy about liking your boss and company, which is a relief since you probably didn't think any better of them than they did of you. (The most recent time I was fired—yes, it's true, I do get tossed out frequently enough to make you wonder—I had the distinct pleasure of pointing out to my friends that though I would sooner or later be reemployed, my firer—an exceedingly drab character on her best days—would have to go on being herself indefinitely.)

In the end, the best thing about being fired is that it can do wonders for your self-esteem. When you've done a good job and your employers have been villainous, you can enjoy that rare experience you dreamed of as a kid: dying without actually becoming dead. The ecstasies of an out-of-body experience can come with a firing: friends gather to raise their glasses and praise your virtues, everyone denounces the sins of your enemies, your good deeds are remembered while your faults are forgotten, and—with just a touch of luck—you end up with a better job, riches, fame, and the adoration of the multitudes. And someday the person who did you in will be sitting on the other side of *your* desk, and then . . . But now we're back to Hollywood clichés.

13

Just Deserts

perks can be beautiful

and important,

but don't expect them

to appear by magic

 he job offer was just what I'd been hoping for, a terrific opportunity, a great leap forward along what I once earnestly called my "career track." And the pay was good, a third more than I'd been making. As soon as I delivered my breathless "yes" I called a friend, someone slightly older with whom I felt competitive and, whenever possible, whom I tried to impress. The latter wasn't easy, and this time was no exception.

"Yeah, yeah, that's all terrific," my friend said laconically after hearing me gush about the money and the title and the corner office. "But did you get the car?"

Instant deflation. The car! I didn't get the car, as my friend had when he'd become *Obersturmführer* of a computer software group. Worse, not only had I missed out on the ultimate Manhattan wampum of a free and unhassled ride to and from work, I hadn't even thought about asking for it. Like many upward-yearning working stiffs, I had let the excitement of getting a better job and more money blind me to the essential business of making sure I got the perks.

The Perks. Almighty perquisites. The bennies. Those mostly untaxable extras that separate the kids from the grown-ups, the wheat from the chaff, the players from the nudniks. Thinking about the lost chance to bracket my working days with rides in some roomy American sedan, I might have slapped myself on the forehead and moaned, "I could have had a V-8!"

The problem was, I just didn't understand perks, even though I'd spent plenty of time envying those who did. Early in my career, filled with astonishment that anyone would trust me with even the slimmest responsibility, I thought of a paycheck as a perk, and considered anything beyond that as a party favor, or—if occasionally something special came along, like a trip to Dallas, perhaps, where I could spend three days drifting through seminars in windowless Marriott conference rooms—as a beneficence from above, manna dispensed by gracious employers. Like Rick, lured to Casablanca for the waters, I was misinformed.

I know now, and you should too, that however magical perks may seem, they are really currency of another color, an indispensable part of the package that also happens to include the Friday check and the Fourth of July wienie roast at the chairman's country lair. In fact, with salaries in a lot of professions high enough to make your withholding look like a salary itself, tax-dodging perks may have become the part of the package that matters most to some people, the deal maker when two companies are competing for the same executive. As a stockbroker from an upstate New York firm said on the verge of the nineties, "I don't need any more bucks. If someone can compensate me in another way, that's a good deal." (Never mind that he probably *does* need more bucks these days.)

His thinking is not unusual. An executive recruiter who often helps me understand the ways of the world says that the level of sophistication about perks rose fast in the past decade, and goes on rising. In other words, while I was neglecting to get the car, others were making damn sure they got the airplane. The reason is simple, according to him. "During the eighties, people changed jobs far more often than they used to. Once, five jobs on the résumé of a man or woman under forty was seen as an indication of instability. These days, if you don't have at least that many, prospective employers may figure you're not ambitious. Things seem to be stabilizing now, but there's been a lot of movement during the past ten years, and each time someone changed jobs they discovered a couple more goodies they should have had at the last place."

Not surprisingly, after a long rise through the managerial ranks, some men (and more and more women) bring to bear on the venerable concept of perquisites an inflationary greed that verges on larceny, of a moral if not necessarily legal variety. Before Ross Johnson lost his job as chairman of RJR Nabisco in a takeover battle with Kohlberg, Kravis, Roberts, he had a habit of commandeering two of the corporation's jets for trips, one for himself and one for someone listed in flight manifests as "G. Shepard." This mystery VIP turned out to be Johnson's misanthropic German shepherd, flying in regal isolation—at shareholders' expense, needless to say, and presumably with an in-flight serving of Nabisco Milk Bones and maybe a private showing of old Rin Tin Tin movies. From such excesses do perks get a bad name.

Which is a shame, because, sought out fairly and used with discretion, perks are useful and pleasurable and, surely in your case and mine, richly deserved. Aside from frequent abuses, both major and minor, one of the problems inherent in the perk biz is that knowing all about employment benefits, even studying them from job to job, is no guarantee you'll get them, any more than ignorance of them will necessarily keep good things from dropping into your lucky lap. Some companies are mean-spirited by nature, and, yes, Virginia, some are real Santa Clauses. From the former you'll get nothing unless you have considerable leverage, and from the latter largess will flow as if by bountiful magic. Figuring out why this is so is the job of earnest corporate anthropologists fit for the deprivations of jungle research (I'll pass, thanks), but companies, like individuals, have characteristics that are difficult to judge and often impossible to change. Thus, wanting perks, even demanding them as one's due, may not cause them to happen. A company that views executive privileges as shameful luxuries may be a good place to be for many other reasons, but if you consider coach class a form of purgatory and feel that a ski lodge in the Rockies (a nice extra for upper-echelon Time Warner executives) is a crucial incentive for creative thinking, you may want to move on sooner rather than later.

Whatever your chances of getting the goodies you crave, it's important to understand the nature of perks, because if you *might* have gotten the car, or the dacha, or the personal trainer, or even the personal train car (as did the chairman of Bechtel Construction in San Francisco), and you didn't, then you're probably not as hot a hotshot as you could be. Or you'll be perceived by others as not hot, which can be just as bad. Remember, though perks are currency, they are also potent symbols, like the field marshal's baton or the knight's charger. The obvious purpose of luxe extras is to massage the morale and intensify the incentive of important employees, but underlying that purpose is the equally urgent motive of declaring the importance of those perquisite bearers, thus keeping what companies may consider the more pernicious effects of democracy from confusing the hierarchy. When Charles Keating, the deposed and imprisoned tsar of Lincoln Savings (a multibillion-dollar junk bank taken over by the federal government in 1989), flew to meetings in an airplane said to have had gold-plated bathroom faucets, he tacitly reminded those who flew with him, and those they talked to later, of his royal standing, instilling through his glittering panoply a sense of awe that permeated the company, got some senators in trouble, and surely muted criticism of Lincoln's allegedly wanton ways until the damage was irreparable. Keating also hired and transported the better part of a tribe of Tongan Islanders to look after the gardening at Lincoln headquarters when he became dissatisfied with the Mexican groundskeepers. Such imperious shows of power may be unnecessary, or ethically unsound, but they impress people.

Even on a less grandiose (and egregious) level, perks are power; those who possess them are treated differently, which is the ultimate perquisite. So despite the fact that many advisers say the smart money always opts for the big money first, there are times when the little extra that sets you apart is worth more to your reputation than being able to afford a better grade of truffle.

Symbolic perks should never be used modestly, since their value is in the declaration of *your* value. Don't be abashed, keep your social conscience in check; those who master the ability to behave presumptuously, as if that Franz Kline on the wall were theirs by the right of sovereignty, tend to be rewarded. Modern gods don't punish hubris anymore, they punish uncalled-for humility. You don't have to lord your perks over those without them—very bad form, by the way—but you can enjoy them fully, knowing you'll inspire others to strive. (Try not to worry that one of the things they may be striving for is to knock you off the perk perch.) After all, if there's a seat up for grabs in the company's stadium suite, why shouldn't it go to you rather than to some hateful suck-up?

The perk/power/presumption connection is wonderfully illustrated by a fine moment in the John Ford western *She Wore a Yellow Ribbon*. John Wayne, as a cavalry captain during the Indian wars, is leading a column on a forced march. At some point, while walking his horse, Wayne stretches his arm to one side without looking back, not imperiously, exactly, but with a certain unmistakable assurance. Instantly, a trooper double-times forward and places a plug of tobacco in the captain's hand; Wayne takes a chew, puts his hand out again, and the tobacco is quickly retrieved. The captain was a soldier's soldier, ready to suffer along with the troops, but the demonstration of special status served as a minor yet explicit reminder that he was top dog. Trust me, no one in the ranks would hold this little tobacco ritual against him—as long as he was good at his job (which, being John Wayne after all, he was).

Refusing the benefits that go with a position of power can actually have a negative effect. When Jimmy Carter became president, he made a show of carrying his own suitcase. Maybe the idea was to emphasize his plain-guy-from-Plains image, or to provide a populist antidote to the remote ways of Richard Nixon's White House, but whatever the motive, the gesture seemed ridiculous. Though Americans draw the line at crowns and sedan chairs, they don't necessarily want their leaders to be just folks. Did anyone feel more confident in Carter because he didn't delegate his bag-toting duties? Or did the voters instead get the impression that he was too nice a guy to—in George Bush's parlance—kick a little ass? As my friend who got the car says, "Only jerks refuse perks."

But because everyone wants everyone else's bennies, the nature of extras changes over time. What might have been a perquisite twenty years ago—a dental plan, say, or a generous moving allowance or an office filled with Knoll furniture—may be a prerequisite now. And when everyone gets a perk, by definition it ceases to *be* a perk, an evolutionary leveling that constantly results in imaginative new concepts about the nature of extras. I won't attempt to catalogue all perks to all people, since just when you figure the very last possible goody has been discovered, someone invents another. Was Eddie Murphy's 15 percent of the profit on *Harlem Nights*, on top of his multimillion-dollar salary, plus his $50,000 entourage slush fund, as much blood as anyone can reasonably expect from a given stone? Not as far as Murphy's agent is concerned, so he had a $5,000 weekly "living allowance" tacked onto the contract. There's no end to creativity in the perk zone. But generally, the bennies fall into the following groups:

• **Paper perks.** This category is low on glamour and symbolic clout but high on real value, the kind that concerns people who already have the car, the first-class airfares, and a platoon of helpers. A paper perk, at its simplest level, is just a contract that lays out what the job is and what the remuneration will be. Though that sounds more like a given than a perk, many companies dislike the idea of contracts ("What's to like?" a corporate lawyer asked me) and thus a written agreement is a significant goody, especially early in one's career, the first step along a paper trail that leads eventually to the promised land of rich stock options, termination agreements that can make getting fired almost a joyful occasion, and finally the shimmering golden parachutes that make high-level risk a win-win-win proposition. One of the most important paper perks is to get your perks on paper, but as the increasingly global nature of competition reduces the number of management jobs available and strengthens the bargaining position of employers, the elusive (but maybe not impossible) dream of the nineties will be a little delight borrowed from professional sports known as the signing bonus, significant money paid up front in order to induce you to sign a contract paying significant money all the time. I should live so long, but you just might.

• **Food perks.** This category might seem frivolous, since a benefit you can eat doesn't have the durable appeal of a stretch limo or the cash cachet of a hefty bonus. But if we are what we eat, then perks measured in calories really do count. Whether in the form of fancy sandwiches that arrive miraculously on rainy days, a Dom Perignon fund to be dipped into on the flimsiest pretext, membership dues to exclusive eating clubs, or an expense account that doesn't set off alarms at a C-note lunch, food perks are a visible and palatable signal that you're quite literally in fat city. When the presidential speech writers in the Bush administration lost the privilege of dining in the White House mess (not *that* White House mess, the other one), an insider said, "It's a symbolic rebuke to the power of rhetoric."

Long ago at CBS, I happened to have an office near several top executives, and thus was included in a morning ritual breakfast service that consisted of having a distinguished-looking man in a white jacket bring me a Limoges pot of good coffee and a croissant on a silver tray. It was a small thing for the big fry down the hall, perhaps, but for me it made the savage life of press relations a bit more civilized, and represented a daily Christmas bonus for the soul. (For me, this perk was strictly accidental, and when someone figured it out and my tray stopped coming, I was devastated.)

One of the most famous food perks of all can be seen at work any weekday at lunchtime in the Grill Room of the Four Seasons restaurant on the East Side of Manhattan, where a loyal clientele of heavy hitters in New York's media and business worlds gather to eat very expensive food and be witnessed in this highly significant tribal act by others doing the same. In a city where fine restaurants are plentiful there is no particular reason to go regularly to the Four Seasons, except to remind everyone that you *can* go there, day after day, and nobody at your company is going to squawk.

• **Shelter perks.** The most obvious of these is the office, and one of the better office perks to ask for on getting a new job or being promoted is the right to redecorate so that the place has a personal look, not the generic "current resident" style that says you don't care enough to demand the very best, or aren't cared enough for to get it. Office perks can indicate how much someone really wants to hire you, since they represent a certain amount of trouble. After years spent working in sealed office towers where the air seemed as weary as the ancient atmosphere inside an Egyptian pyramid, I demanded from a new employer a fresh-air duct leading directly to my office. Possibly because the job was in health-conscious California, I got what I wanted, but the concession told me and those who worked for me that I had measurable clout. A woman executive I know always insists on having her new offices painted in an elaborate and decidedly uncorporate color scheme, partly to make herself feel at home, but mostly to establish what she calls her "squatter's rights" not only over her space, but over her professional fate.

Shelter perks are crucial when you're relocating from one city to another. Not just the moving costs—everybody gets those—but all real estate costs where you've been and where you're going, an extended stay in a good hotel, lots of help finding another place, maybe even low-interest loans for a new house or condo. Remember, if a company wants you enough to import you, they ought to be willing to pay some duty. Large corporations like IBM, in which mobility is often a requirement of the executive climb, have long experience in making transitions as painless as possible. But smaller entrepreneurial ventures may be more naive about costs or simply less willing to spend the necessary money. The smaller the company, the more important it is to spell out all the moving costs you need in a contract. Don't leave home without it!

• **Transportation perks.** Once, when I was on assignment for a story on the Marine Corps, I toured a base with its commanding general in his personal helicopter. Arriving at one of our destinations, the chopper landed on the playing field of the base soccer team, causing a game to be suspended until the general and I made our way to a waiting staff car. Like John Wayne with his tobacco carrier, the general was dramatically reminding everyone that his needs came first, and doing it with an impressive transportation perk.

We civilians, though, start at a humbler level. First, naturally, comes the business of the car. In Manhattan, this is such a lust-provoking perk that when a new president was hired at the *New York Post* in the late eighties, *USA Today* reported breathlessly that part of the deal was a "private car and driver—considered the perkiest of perks for New York media sales executives." But a car and driver doesn't mean all that much in places where high-level execs commute to work in their own Jaguars, so a prime benefit outside such chauffeur-intensive venues as Manhattan, Washington, D.C., and the Chicago loop is the car allowance. Whittle Communications, a publishing company in Knoxville, Tennessee, offers money toward its executives' wheels, starting at the Saab 9000 level for junior partners and working up to the BMW Seven series for top dogs. The parking lot reads like a who's who at the company, and by some unspoken agreement or abiding folkway it seems as if nobody augments the allowance to buy wheels beyond his or her station.

To be impressive as well as practical, transportation perks have to offer a distinct advantage in the context where they're offered. The Catholic bishop of Los Angeles, as bedeviled by freeway congestion as any other Angeleno, managed to negotiate his own helicopter (bishops and generals occupying roughly the same niche in their respective hierarchies) plus the promise that he could learn to fly it himself. File that under blessings from above.

• **Person perks.** Until quite recently, a good job in the business end of a certain major New York–based media company meant the privilege of hiring a gorgeous Wasp princess fresh out of Smith or Wellesley, one of the last of that vanishing breed of well-off young women working for a while because it's less boring than the Junior League. The ability to type was optional, but bloodlines and perfection of profile were matters of great moment. For many years, at one of the big three television networks, assistants of powerful executives were often young men who functioned as combination acolytes, disciples, aides-de-camp, and flunkies, walking in step to the left and a pace or two behind the great man, appointment book (in lieu of tobacco plug) at the ready. There are many such variations on the person perk, and they can be both tricky to talk about and treacherous to handle ethically. The most important person perk of all is simply to have the budget to hire the best, from secretaries right up to executive vice presidents (though by the time you get to the level of hiring the latter you'll probably be deciding on the budget yourself). Resisting the lamentable luxury of having your very own lackey is easier when you're surrounded by excellence.

• **Quirk perks.** Rumor has it that Hugh Hefner can't stand to eat broken potato chips, so it's someone's job at the Playboy mansion to cull the imperfects from the imperial snack bowls. Sportscaster John Madden has a morbid fear of flying, so CBS Sports has outfitted a special bus for him to get from one pro football game to the next. A top saleswoman at a commercial real estate firm in Chicago insists on an office full of fresh roses of a particularly rare color. And so it goes, in the annals of the powerful and demanding. Quirk perks are famous, sometimes infamous, because—being eccentric—they make great copy. As contributors to one's legend, they're worth working up the chutzpah to demand. More important, even more than most perks they are an accurate measure of your value to a prospective employer. If somebody is willing to make sure you have a dozen oysters flown in daily from Puget Sound, they want you bad, and they'll treat you right.

Alas, the tendency among the best of us is to be meek about going after perks. There *is* something greedy about asking for favors that others don't have, and ignoble about petulantly demanding absurd bennies like a corporate jet for your dog. And it's only natural to figure that if you work hard and do well, a company won't need to be asked to come up with things to make you feel special, but will do so on its own. Well, it's been known to happen, especially during the seduction phase of recruiting. But a wise old proverb points out that the squeaky wheel gets the oil, so taking the initiative to ask for things is the best way to make an employer behave generously. Timing is important, too; generally, not too many corporate minds are preoccupied with dreaming up new goodies for people who are already aboard, just as *Time* magazine doesn't offer free phones to those who are already subscribers. So perks are best negotiated before you sign on. And never mind feeling squeamish; perks are just bucks, and nobody's embarrassed to ask for as big a salary as the traffic will bear. Ask for everything you can think up (making sure to call any friends currently being chauffeured to work), since even those perks you don't get may result in an imbalance in your favor, with your employer feeling a little inadequate for having fallen short of fulfilling your needs and looking for ways to make it up. Not many companies are so sensitive, but, as the bishop of Los Angeles might put it, ask and ye may receive.

Frankly, I've been perk poor in most of my jobs. Now I work for myself, which pretty much eliminates my chances for a golden parachute or a valet serving my morning coffee. But at last, with myself as boss and principal employee, I did get the car. The trouble is, I'm paying for it.

14

What
I Learned
from
Peter Falk

a few buttoned-down

reasons why

you can't let a style

be your umbrella

*I*n an early book by Heinrich Böll called *Billiards at Half Past Nine*, a young architect arrives in a provincial town to hang out his shingle. After unpacking his bags, he goes to the town's best restaurant and orders an unlikely concoction of his own invention—cottage cheese mixed with paprika—going into considerable detail with the bemused waiter about the proportions. Each day from then on he goes to the same restaurant and orders the same odd dish. Within two weeks, with the waiter's unwitting help, the architect is known to everyone in town, and his new business begins to flourish.

I must have read the Böll book at just about the time I took my first job in New York as an editorial assistant (dim lights, big city) and been profoundly influenced by that story, because with far more energy than tact or taste I frantically set about establishing stylistic trademarks. Somehow, it didn't occur to me that New

York has little in common with Böll's provincial German city, and that if eccentricities were enough to achieve recognition there'd be even more famous freaks in the big town than there actually are. My nearest equivalent to the architect's regular notable meal was a daily shave at a subterranean barber shop in the Daily News Building on East Forty-second Street. I thought it was stylishly retrograde and eccentric to endure the old-time shave ritual, but Vito the barber wasn't really that pleased to confront my stubble at 8:30 A.M. and failed to spread word of me through the streets of midtown. The rest of my hopeful legend-making ploys were all fashion statements. Or rather, misstatements. It's hard to think about them now without wincing. The one shred of photographic evidence that remains from those days is a closely guarded secret.

In a relatively informal office, I wore three-piece suits, bought at Brooks Brothers on a badly abused (and eventually revoked) charge account. From my lapel each day sprouted a boutonniere, the type of flower depending on which of yesterday's blooms was sale-priced. I sported a fedora or a boater, according to the season. And—cottage cheese with paprika!—I grew a luxuriant mustache on which I affected upturned, carefully waxed points. Yes, I was a sight.

Given my lowly status, last on the masthead of a very minor magazine, these aggressively attention-getting tactics must have struck my less self-conscious colleagues as hilarious, but no one had the heart to tell me. Two years and one job later, however, I had my first brush with reality. By then, I had signed on at CBS, and the first flush of flamboyance had faded a bit. In a highly corporate environment—and within the austere monolith of the then brand-new CBS building—the three-piece suits that had been out of place at the trade magazine were a perfect fit. The boater had launched itself from the windy deck of a Staten Island ferry one afternoon, never to be replaced, and the boutonnieres had withered in a money drought brought on by romance (women had not yet demanded their inalienable right to go dutch). But the mustache remained, waxed like a stretch limo, and this at a company where facial hair was as welcome as an FCC investigation. In my own mind at the time, I was the second coming of Gable in *The Hucksters*; in my secret photograph I look like Groucho Marx in Hart Schaffner & Marx.

Feeling very, very good about myself one morning, I stepped

into an elevator at Black Rock and found myself alone with the actor Peter Falk. The star was much in demand in those days and no doubt was on his way to a meeting with CBS chairman William Paley, whose office suite was on the floor above my somewhat smaller digs. As the elevator ascended, I felt Falk studying me closely. In full regalia as always, my mustache polished to a high gloss, no doubt I suspected that Falk was as impressed to be on the same elevator with me as *I* was.

When we arrived at my floor, I gave Falk a collegial "just us big shots" smile and stepped out. I looked back to have a last reassuring peek. From his best slouch, Falk was giving me that weird look Lieutenant Colombo always saves for the guy you know he knows is the murderer. Actually, he was giving my mustache that look. And just as the doors were sliding shut, he said, "You'll never get away with it."

Stricken, I looked quickly left and right. Had anybody heard? More to the point, had Falk somehow heard something about me? Was my upper lip the subject of hot debate among the board of directors? Had Frank Stanton decided that facial hair was inconsistent with his Knoll interiors? Confidence, so often based on self-delusion, is a fragile thing, and from that moment on mine was never the same. Falk was right, too; I didn't get away with it; within the year I was in another line of work. Though I've never been sure just how much a part of my decline and fall could be blamed on my mustache, I prudently shaved it off. And though, even today, I'm given to certain affectations of dress, my style is far more subdued than in those headlong times, reflecting a change that began with the actor's prescient warning.

I relate this incident to illustrate the fine line between establishing a personal stylistic trademark—a reasonable tactic—and setting oneself up as some kind of sartorial oddball, a Duke of Windsor wannabe. Of course, you might not be the type who would ever intentionally turn yourself into a Rose Parade float in order to make a lasting impression. But excess isn't necessarily adopted all at once, as in my case; like an ample girth, it can creep up little by little, so a cautionary note is always in order. Considering how dire is the fear of invisibility at a time when only cars and pickpockets glory in a low profile, to put on airs is human, and to guard against going too far is only common sense.

Of course, if you've arranged to be exceptionally good looking, you might reasonably be expected to forgo the search for a stylistic signature, or bribing venal maître d's to give you the same table every day. Then again, we all know men who look better than Kevin Costner yet never get particularly far, or women more splendid than Diane Sawyer whose looks may not help them at all. (The best-looking man I've ever met labors in the hardscrabble vineyard of Las Vegas dinner theater.) So the urge to redesign oneself—to slap on a new, more marketable label—can strike at any time. The point is not to fight it, but to make sure you don't walk into your job as an up-and-coming bank officer looking like Wayne Newton in heat or an early Madonna video.

Before hoisting warning flags, let me point out two things: the workaday world is a lot more tolerant of individuality than it was in the pre-Beatle sixties; and if you are as good at what you do as, say, Magic Johnson is at what he does, you can probably show up for work in a chenille robe and get away with it—assuming you've been given a chance to prove your abilities.

Women are less at risk than men in the dangerous game of stylistic overkill, in part because women's fashions, replete with jewelry and other pleasing accessories, don't require extremes to be individualistic, and in part because women concerned about their image tend to be conservative, preferring to blend in rather than stand out. If anything, it's this conservatism that leads to the most common female excess—an excess of caution and a loss of femininity. A man doesn't have to be a cross-dresser to envy the wonderful array of styles available to a woman. What's sad is that given an unspoken license to dress in interesting fashions, so many women have chosen to hide themselves under stern, shapeless imitations of men's suits (a felony of sorts, since women ought to feminize the workplace in ways that make it more bearable for everyone, instead of allowing the workplace to masculinize them). When a woman does decide she needs a trademark, however, her hair is usually called upon to do the job. The result isn't often as extreme as, say, singer Sinead O'Connor's buzz cut, or Whoopi Goldberg's dreadlocks—show business and regular business being only vaguely related. But women like Gloria Steinem, with her center-parted eternal seventies style, or massively maned movie producer Dawn Steel (whom *Spy* magazine describes as "hair-obsessed") are as stylistically distinct as any man with a pointed mustache, and far less absurd.

Coming up with a personal trademark is a kind of stylistic roulette: sometimes it will work real mnemonic magic, and sometimes it will make people remember all the wrong things. For instance, Tom Wolfe's neo–Beau Brummellian exaggerations (spats!) have made him visible to a large public that has never read a word of his dandy prose. A Wolfe in sheepish clothing would still write as well, presumably, but might not be as likely to end up on the covers of major magazines. Conversely, when former presidential adviser Lyn Nofziger was standing trial for influence peddling a few years ago, news reports regularly mentioned his "trademark Mickey Mouse tie." On televised news conferences after court sessions, we saw an extraordinarily unkempt, overweight man with a funny little beard, and might have been forgiven for wondering if somebody who wears Mickey Mouse ties ought to be allowed to wander around the White House.

Senator Paul Simon's bow ties and glasses gave him instant recognizability during the 1988 campaign for the Democratic presidential nomination (and a look that caricaturists had wicked fun with), but the ultimate effect of his trademarks was to trap him in the deadly amber of times past (remember Dave Garroway?). Modern presidential politics, in general, illustrates the perceived risks of trademarks. Since FDR's photogenic pince-nez and cigarette holder, chief executives have been wary of adding much juice to their natural look. With star types like Kennedy and Reagan, this unadorned approach worked well; their natural charisma took the place of fashion statements. But one wonders how the election of 1980 might have gone had Jimmy Carter been inclined to face the Washington summer in pale linen suits, or, Patton-like, walk a bull terrier in the Rose Garden. Clearly, there are times when some sort of singular advertisement for oneself makes sense, and times when it makes trouble.

One of the saddest sights in the trademark game is the manqué-see-manqué-do phenomenon, in which unsuccessful types desperate for a way out of their ruts copy the distinctive look of a gutsy major player. A few years back, you could spot this approach in a proliferation of suspenders, particularly red suspenders, particularly at Wall Street brokerages. Whoever was the first to brace himself in such a distinctive fashion—possibly some estimable senior figure who had been wearing suspenders for forty years—his effect was so powerful that in no time he had spawned a required look for the legions of brokers, traders, and lawyers who ply their mysterious trades on the stock exchange. Off the record, of course, we all know that suspenders aren't wonderfully comfortable, no matter how tough Michael Douglas looked in *Wall Street*, but because one man's hallmark became a mimeographed fashion manifesto, a lot of people were stuck with them, and still are. More recently, flamboyant ties have aroused the herd instinct in businessmen. When the ties are right—tastefully radical Armanis, for instance—the effect is a welcome break from the itsy-bitsy polka-dotted and paisleyed things we've worn for too many years. Bryant Gumbel, who may have given momentum to the trend in bold ties when he anchored the Seoul Olympics in 1990, happened to make great choices. But bright ties as a mandatory item in the dress-for-excess look simply single a man out as mindlessly obedient to trends, thus drawing all the wrong kind of attention to him.

The pressures on women to follow a given look are harder to track, since female fashion is more varied and changes more quickly. But the power suit with exaggerated shoulder pads has for years been something close to a required look for women who figure the Victor-Victoria style is required for entrance into the upper sanctum. Women's suits can be chic, without doubt, but somehow, when women think of them as uniforms, they end up looking like uniforms.

One of the big pitfalls of co-opting someone else's trademark is that the originator's purpose may be misunderstood. Take the case of an earlier neckwear phenomenon, the dreaded red tie. Sometime early on in the eighties, one of the network White House reporters —I think it was Sam Donaldson (it *would* have been)—decided that if he wore a red tie he might better be able to attract the president's attention during press conferences. The ploy seemed to work, which led to the semimystical notion of the "power tie" and resulted in a red sea of ties (or rather, a sea of red ties) calling for more attention than anyone (especially President Reagan) had to give. The rumored magnetism of the red tie spread quickly, until all of Washington, D.C., had fallen under its spell. You couldn't find a congressman bellying up to the microphones on C-Span who wasn't wearing a red tie. Soon business got the message, Donald Trump placed an order for what appears to be a lifetime supply, and— though nearly unsellable in the past—red ties flew off store racks like silk possessed.

The trouble was (and is) that red (according to psychologists and bulls) attracts attention because it signals danger. Though it doesn't make us afraid of Santa Claus or Ferraris, it's as likely as not to set off psychic alarms (fire engines, STOP signs, the Red Phone, the devil). Red ties may make some sense in the harsh context of a press conference, but not on a sales call. When some unaggressive fellow like sportscaster Jim McKay wears one on camera—as he did during his broadcasts from the last winter Olympics—the effect is all wrong, and you know that genial Jim and his producers have missed the point entirely. Sitting at the center of a television screen, he already has our attention; what he needs to get is our affection, and a red tie is a very funny valentine.

Such confusion over trademark styles probably indicates the need for a national policy on the whole concept. But clear policies have been increasingly hard to coax out of the federal government, so let's settle for an unofficial short list of good and bad approaches:

• First, consider the coloration of your particular jungle. The best trademark is one that sets you apart without at the same time making you a marked man. All work environments have their unwritten sumptuary laws; just as untitled folk in the Middle Ages were forbidden to wear ermine-trimmed cloaks, entrance-level types fresh out of school may be expected not to show up in Savile Row bespoke suits. Among other dangers, such splendor can make one's superiors unsympathetic when the subject of a raise comes up. Even at top law firms, where tyros right out of law school are paid indecently high salaries, it's not a terrific idea to make the senior partners look shabby, or stylistically passé. If the top guys all look like John Houseman, learn to tie a bow tie, and try not to do your Sting thing during business hours.

On the other hand, don't adopt the local camouflage so completely that you vanish altogether. After all, top management can wear the wallpaper and still get noticed, since they hold the fates of many in their hands. Those with less obvious power need more individualistic trappings, but of course those "me, myself, and I" accessories ought fall short of knickers and a pet falcon.

If drabness is dominant, the effects of conformity can reach far, and you may walk a tightrope between looking good and doing well. A case in point is the low profile garb of power players in Washington, D.C., where the prevailing fashion credo seems to be that men who don't wear anything unusual are not likely to do anything unpredictable. This sartorial "no comment" begins at the White House, a stylish piece of architecture whose recent residents have apparently felt that all they have to fear is flair itself. George Bush, current exemplar of presidential style, clings resolutely to the all-purpose prepster look that dominated male fashion in the fifties (as the trilobites once dominated the earth). With his middle-of-the-road natural-shouldered suits, innocuous Yalie ties, one-size-fits-all golf hats, baggy L. L. Bean khakis, and poly-blend windbreakers, the man is a square pol in an Oval Office. For obvious reasons, those around him don't cut particularly dashing figures, but choose to look (or were chosen *because* they look), as Poppy Bush himself might put it, "steady as she goes, not gonna try anything fancy, wouldn't be *prudent*."

Dressed-down style is so crucial when serving in the capital that when the administration hired a new image maker from Las Vegas, the man is said to have called a reporter to ask that he not be portrayed "as some flashy Vegas gambler who's plopping into the White House in Italian suits and expensive watches." Heaven forbid! One can picture this new guy in town—a man known to favor Hermès ties, Bally slip-ons, Bertolucci watches, and, yes, those illicit Italian suits—frantically pleading with Brooks Brothers to fly him in an emergency supply of shapeless gray suits and button-down shirts.

• Second, avoid plagiarizing the ideas of others. While you may have to be careful about going too far in creating your own style, it's visual toadyism to pick up someone's elegant trademark and mimic it as a way of saying, "You, boss, are the one we all dream of being." A few years ago, a fashion magazine reported on the sudden popularity at the *Washington Post* of dark-rimmed reading glasses shortly after top editor Ben Bradlee appeared wearing a pair. A similar co-optic approach was taken by the people working for a demanding woman in the clothing business who wore impenetrably dark sunglasses in her office during the day. Before long, executive meetings looked like get-togethers at the Lighthouse for the Blind. Frankly, this sort of thing looks really bad, and however flattering it may be for the boss to feel he or she is a trendsetter, counterfeit trademarks tend to highlight a lack of substance among the copiers. Imagine what the world of boxing would look like if every ambitious deal maker tried to get the Don King look. Picture, if you can, dilettante promoter Donald Trump with his hair swooping sky-ward in order to take on the style of a proven winner. (Things being what they are in Trump's empire, we may yet see it.)

• Third, don't try too much, too soon, in the righteous quest to break away from the herd. Most personal styles are a mix of things gleaned from magazines, movies, friends, street sightings, and even the occasional fresh idea. A real look takes time and self-knowledge, as anyone who has tried to be just like James Dean can testify, and it's usually a mistake to force yourself into someone else's look—or into a lot of other people's looks. If you find yourself tempted to create a signature look overnight by taking a little something from Michael Douglas, a nice touch from George Plimpton, an insouci-ant detail from Joe Montana, and just a hint of a bit from Lee Iacocca (or a similar female pantheon of Cher, Joan Lunden, Eliz-abeth Dole, and so on), try to recall how such eclecticism ended up looking when Dr. Frankenstein tried it.

As for the "too soon" part, remember that one of the compen-sations of age is that stylistic license seems less licentious. As one gets to know oneself better, a process that can take a surprising amount of time, one of two improvements takes place: either fewer mistakes are made, or else they don't seem like mistakes. What may be weird, pretentious, and off-putting in someone twenty-two years old may be perceived as eccentric, unique, and intriguing in some-one only a decade or so older. I seriously doubt whether a showy mustache will ever darken my lip again, but I suspect I might actually get away with it now.

• Fourth and finally, the cardinal rule of the personal trademark: Never depend on style to make up for content. Though it's unde-niable that style is one element of content, gaining attention with a particular fillip makes sense only if you can deliver the goods when you finally get noticed. The paprika-and-cottage-cheese-eating ar-chitect in that Böll book was good at what he did, not just good at putting himself on the map. George Washington Hill, a famous advertising man, was renowned for wearing a wide-brimmed hat indoors and out, in meetings with new clients and at lunches with old ones. But Hill was a brilliant sloganizer—his "L.S.M.F.T." copy line made Lucky Strikes one of America's most popular cigarettes—and the hat was just one of his advertising coups. In the late eighties, publishing hotshot Peter Diamandis publicly thanked

New York's Paul Stuart men's store for his success. But when the elegant Diamandis parlayed a leveraged buyout into $90 million in profits for himself and some lucky associates, it wasn't his impeccable tailoring that did the thinking. You can wear power ties without a letup or a dazzling repertory of Chanel suits with Hermès scarves, but there's no style trademark quite so memorable as success.

15

Mighty Spouse

anyone married to the

boss can be a problem,

but certain very significant

others are helpmates

from hell

*B*ack around the time when Jimmy Carter was gently rubbing our noses in the drab fact that life isn't fair, someone I knew (let's call him Eugene, which, meaning "wellborn," nicely describes him) worked for a small, very profitable company with plush headquarters in Manhattan. The place was owned by a man whose wife, a thin, pale woman, was always drifting in and out of the office to check, it seemed, on what her husband's employees were up to. As far as Eugene could tell, she had no position with the company, though she did have an office. The vagueness of her status was unsettling, because though she clearly wasn't part of the solution, it was hard for Eugene to tell how much a part of the problem she was.

He remembers deciding that she seemed harmless enough. Other than a rather spooky tendency to appear, wraithlike, in his office to nose around on the pretext of assessing the decor, she did nothing particularly annoying. Most of her energy was devoted to the task of raising her social standing, using the leverage of her husband's recently coined millions. She had changed the spelling of her first name in such a way that it took on a tonier tone, followed the dietary laws of the Ladies Who Don't Touch Their Lunch, and volunteered for work on charitable committees for causes one suspects she cared little about.

At some point in her image-rebuilding process the boss's wife had wandered into a major Manhattan art gallery with an open and indiscriminate checkbook and begun buying art by the square meter, filling home and office with third-rate paintings of which she was naturally very proud. Recognizing a good thing, the gallery sent over someone every Thursday afternoon to "curate" the collection, making notes and discussing with the eager patroness in what areas the collection might be expanded.

After a while, Eugene decided the lady was not a tiger, and paid little attention to her. Having her demanding and impatient husband for a boss was hard enough, he realized, without adding complications. The abundance of bad art was harder to ignore, however, and eventually he did something that revealed how seriously he had misjudged the house spouse. On the wall of his office hung a particularly tasteless silkscreen, the kind of thing galleries love to fob off on instant collectors. Rather than endure looking at it every day, Eugene—an art history major who had taken the job in part because he loved the idea of working in a great Deco skyscraper—took the thing down and put it on the floor in a far corner, facing the wall like a naughty child. On the next Thursday, the house-call curator stepped tentatively into his office and asked why he'd removed a piece Mrs. X especially liked. Undiplomatically, Eugene replied that he thought the thing was a piece of crap and couldn't stand looking at it. With a disapproving cluck, the curator vanished.

When Eugene passed the lady in the hallway that afternoon, she withheld her usual queenly smile and swept past. Looking back on that moment, Eugene now figures he was already being conjugated in the past imperfect. By the next morning he had a new picture in his office. By the end of the month he was looking for a new job. So much for one man's initiation into the perils of crossing the boss's spouse.

If there is anything in the Serengeti of office life more unpre-
dictably dangerous than the wife or husband of the boss, a more
gothic imagination than mine is needed to envision what it might
be. I don't want to go so far as to say the only good boss's spouse
is a dead boss's spouse, but if you're interviewing for a job and
happen to hear that your prospective employer's mate has just
passed away, let me suggest that your chances of being happy in
your work are at least marginally increased.

A qualification here: not all boss's spouses are bad, or dangerous,
or even a pain. Some are the Disney version, real den mothers or
jolly uncles. And, these days, more and more are working too hard
at their own careers to worry about messing up yours. But the
problem types are such a common menace that it makes sense to
consider all members of the species as you would a snake—deadly
until proven otherwise.

The real danger of a boss's spouse is, in fact, the difficulty in
assessing how important he or she actually is. The usual hiero-
glyphs of rank and function are not reliable indicators. A spouse
who is a full partner, or a senior executive, may actually wield less
power than someone who scuffs around making sure all the aspi-
distras are watered. I once worked for a woman whose husband, a
busy movie producer, put in an appearance at the office once a year,
at the Christmas party. Yet his behind-the-scenes effect was enormous (and, it happens, entirely positive). He reviewed all the major
hires, and was often asked by his wife to look at staff memos and
reports. More recently, I worked for another woman whose husband (now her ex-husband) walked around rubbing his hands together in anticipation of catching someone putting company postage
on a letter to mom. He was so inept that his specious title of
company "co-founder" was changed by a derisive staff to "co-
flounder." But for all his blustering self-importance, his buffoonish
clumsiness and his hilariously pompous pronouncements of "company policy," he was no less dangerous than if he'd been as eloquent and obviously evil as Richard III. His destructive significance
wasn't understood by those at the office, including myself, because
no one thought his wife could possibly take anything he said seriously. But any veteran observer of the in-house spouse could have
pointed out that no matter how foolish he might have seemed, this
Laddy Macbeth had one major advantage over everyone else: he

was married to the power, and thus was always around to whisper in Number One's ear. If, at this very moment, you are underestimating some dithering twit who happens to have said "I do" at your boss's wedding, you are probably overestimating your chances of success at the company.

The power of the boss's spouse is a venerable tradition, almost as central to literature as the bastard boss. Think of Zeus's querulous mate, Hera, endlessly meddling in her husband's management plans, or Freya, always sabotaging Wotan's favorites, or Livia, a.k.a. Mrs. Augustus Caesar, arranging to have all sorts of faithful workers fired (well, killed, actually) while the boss concerned himself with lobbying for promotion to the rank of god. Some of this century's notorious examples of the type are Eva Perón, Madame Mao Tse-tung, and Imelda Marcos. (Though these infamous sweethearts all happen to be female, the rise of women into positions of power is currently producing a bumper crop of the male variety—as evidenced by my two examples above.)

In business, the spouse factor tends to diminish as the size of the company grows. At large, publicly owned corporations, management spouses are essentially ceremonial figures (if they don't have companies of their own). A well-founded distrust of nepotism holds down the number of boss's spouses active in corporate management. In privately held companies, such discretion need not be observed, and as a result some extremely large organizations are simply vastly overgrown mom-and-pop shops. In fact, when an organization grows so large that the boss has more power than any one person can wield effectively, spouses can take on formidable shares of power. U.S. presidents' wives, depending on their ambition and the energy and disposition of their husbands, can end up as true vice presidents or even de facto chief executives, as was the case with Mrs. Woodrow Wilson and, if Kitty Kelley and more than a few others are to be believed, Mrs. Ronald Reagan.

There are myriad types and styles of boss's spouses, and each of the bad ones probably deserves a chapter or two of tender loathing care. But it would make gloomy reading, so let me offer instead a quick look at the more notable general examples. Some varieties share characteristics, and often a given spouse could fit, forbiddingly, into two or more categories. The following examples are arranged in ascending (or perhaps it's descending) order of toxicity.

- **The Significant Bother.** As office spouses go, this is the least worrisome variety, and usually the least noticeable. Significant bothers rarely have big ambitions, but are brought into play by bosses in unofficial capacities to help figure people out, the way diviners use willow wands to find water. On the surface, this may seem like a ceremonial social function, but don't overlook a bother's capacity to mess up your life; if the conversation goes badly or your bow tie offends or you've been a bit lavish with the kiwi-and-musk after-shave, your future could be history.

- **The Hex Officio.** This category, almost invariably a wife, makes up for having little real clout by claiming supernatural powers, thus throwing the monkey wrench of irrationality into the already gremlin-inhabited machinery of office politics. As silly as these Broomhildas are, they can strike fear into the boss's pragmatic heart (however small and hard that heart may be) and for that reason they get listened to. A woman I know once took a job at a major media company where the boss's wife also worked. The first time the two coincided in the same elevator, the wife pointed at the newcomer and proclaimed to a captive audience of colleagues, "I am a witch, and I know absolutely that this woman will hurt someone I love." From that moment on, the job was almost no fun at all, and not surprisingly turned out to be temporary. (My friend is very good-looking, which was not a smart thing to be; hex officios play "Mirror, mirror on the wall" no fewer than five times a week.)

- **The Bitter Half.** This is someone, usually a wife but not always, who has given up a career (invariably described as "a promising career") and won't be satisfied until someone pays. Whatever her career might have been, she figures she knows all about your job, or at least more than you. The double bind presented by the bitter half is that the better you stand with the boss, the more of a target you'll be, since she will feel you're reaping the esteem that's rightfully hers. The most effective way to cope with a bitter half is to pretend the two of you are in a partnership, an alliance without which you'd never get any good ideas. "Gee, Mrs. Grimly, could you take a look at this marketing plan? With your background in French literature, you could really help me get it right." Not a pleasant lie to live, but not inherently evil, and maybe your only chance.

- **The Mom-and-Pop-Shop Cop.** When a couple runs a business together, one of them is probably along for the ride, and he or she will often gravitate toward the role of inspector general, ferreting out the tiniest expense account inconsistencies, drafting memos that decry the increased use of yellow legal pads, making sure no one has any unauthorized office furniture, and generally making life miserable in miserably petty ways. The worst mistake you can make with this troublesome character is to imagine that, since everyone else thinks he's a small time pain-in-the-tail, the boss must surely agree. Bear in mind, they are married, and there must be reasons for this. The chances are that the mom-and-pop-shop cop is just doing what the boss is too busy to do, not too big to do, and, in being loathsome, lets the boss seem more admirable. Since much of what the cop/spouse does will be mean-spirited and picayune, you can often win in a specific showdown. But your resistance to the loved one will be noted by the boss and taken personally, and the victory is likely to be Pyrrhic and short-lived.

- **The Queen Maker.** Picture James Mason in *A Star Is Born*, but less futile and far more fatal. As women earn more opportunities to move into business leadership, more and more men are finding themselves riding their wives' skirttails. They often justify this unseemly means of transportation by imagining that they are the reason their wives have done so well. Since the queen maker knows his wife is his meal ticket, he may become extremely paranoid about anyone he perceives as a threat to her success. He will feel no less threatened by someone becoming important to the business. In these ways, they resemble bitter halves, but, in their need to re-masculate themselves, they can be even more destructive. A wife may be willing to stay behind the scenes, but the queen maker will co-opt as much of the limelight as he can. A photographer I know in New York whose wife is notably more talented with the camera acts as his spouse's manager, and invariably refers to her work as his. When picture editors point out that they are interested particularly in *her* photographs, he intones loftily, "My work and hers are inseparable." With a queen maker you're damned if you do well, and damned if you don't. Hang in there and pray for a divorce.

- **The Bride of Frankenstein.** Sometimes, wives of bosses become bosses themselves, and they are inclined to be fiercely determined to show their husbands—and everybody else—that they're as tough as the old man. And once they've been helped, they may want any evidence that they ever needed help destroyed. Heads will roll in the process, you can be sure. If you have the bad luck to be given the job of showing a B. of F. how to do something, you'll likely find yourself with a dangerously ungrateful pupil. A friend of mine with a safe and happy job at a privately owned publishing company was asked by the owner to be the resident pro at a magazine he had given his inexperienced wife to edit. "I want her to look good doing this," said the boss, "and you're the only one I can trust to make that happen." The start-up was a success, but as the nominal editor gained confidence and made more editorial decisions, quality suffered. Before long, as is the ironic nature of these transactions, the lady decided the fault was my friend's and fired him. Did her husband leap in and save the day in the name of truth and all that's right? Not a chance. Only a husband can bridle a bride of Frankenstein, but he'll usually prefer peace at home to justice on earth. If you work for a B. of F., anything you do well will be leapt upon as her work and any screwups that might be construed as hers will be dealt with mercilessly. In the desperate battle to get out from under, the bride of Frankenstein takes no prisoners.

• **Brand Ex.** This chilling creature—a variation on both the queen maker and the bride of Frankenstein—is someone who has divorced a powerful spouse and sets out to find vengeance in separate success. The brand ex's major motivation is anger, and all problems and achievements are seen through its distorting lens. When Frances Lear, the ex-wife of television producer Norman Lear, was asked by a consultant to describe the reader of her eponymous new magazine, she's alleged to have answered, "A woman in middle age, smart, with plenty of discretionary income, lots of time and ambition . . . and a husband who's messing around with some twenty-three-year-old bimbo at the office!" An office headed by a brand-ex boss is not likely to be a sunny place.

• **The Ignoble Savage.** This is the worst of a bad bunch, a spouse straight from the depths. Springing from the classic case of a boss marrying an underling and turning him or her into an overlord, the ignoble savage syndrome can be very dicey indeed. If you happen to be at an office where such a transhierarchical marriage takes place, buckle on your golden parachute and head immediately for the emergency exit. The ride is bound to get bumpy. Typically, after someone rises magically from obscurity, purges follow, since the new VIP is rarely comfortable with those who were around during his or her days as a nobody. The harshness and immediacy of the purges is directly proportionate to the anointed one's level of incompetence.

If the great leap upward happens to someone talented enough to have made it eventually anyway, which it sometimes does, things may not be so bad. But if marriage to the boss is the only conceivable way a person could ever have ended up on top (in a manner of speaking), then no one is safe. Ironically, the closer you've been to Cinderella (or Cinderfella), the sooner you'll get the ax, since you know far too much. So if you've been especially nice to that lushly padded receptionist the boss is always flirting with because you sense hers may be the shape of your future, don't bother; if she ascends the throne, that friendliness will get you nothing but a very early retirement.

Ignoble savages who have caused the end of a boss's previous marriage often exhibit a deplorable born-again puritanism. With the self-righteousness of reformed smokers, they'll sniff out any hint of sexual indiscretion in the office and demand that such conduct be punished, if not by death, then at least by banishment. Working life anywhere an I. S. has assumed power is a no-win-and-no-sin situation, in which those wedding bells will definitely break up that old gang of yours.

Is there anything to be done about the varying perniciousness of boss's spouses? Frankly, not much. Just as love is blind, it is also very hazy on ethics. A mate has many ways to get from one point to another, and a straight line is rarely one of them. Even a consistently decent boss will give in to a spouse's demands, cajolings, or wheedlings just to get a little peace and quiet. You may have justice on your side, but compared with the promise of domestic tranquillity, it's a very small-caliber weapon. Like droughts, earthquakes, and other calamitous acts of nature, boss's spouses can often be avoided by the good luck of being elsewhere. Some fortunate folk never encounter them. But if and when one befalls you, be prepared to endure difficult days, or to move on to a place where the problem doesn't exist. A position in market research at the Vatican, perhaps?

16

Don't Let This Get Around, But . . .

how to block innuendo,

ride out rumors, and

master the art of spin

control

*L*ook, don't let this get around, but I heard (from somebody in a position to know, believe me) that leaks, rumors, and gossip—the secret incantations of the information age—are the only word to be trusted anymore. Just read the papers—all the best clues to what's happening come from unattributed sources quoted in the smug, knowing columns of former insiders like William Safire or Pat Buchanan. Or hang around the photocopier for ten minutes or so; you'll end up a lot better informed than if you put your trust in the company newsletter. It has become an article of faith, in this time of shameless dissembling by those in high places, that a rumor is more likely to contain at least a grain of truth than a carefully crafted public statement.

These days, inquiring minds tend to distrust official sources and seek out instead articles based on leaked memos and deep-cover indiscretions. Press releases? Real journalists play Nerf ball with them, then place calls to their pet informants. The reason for the ascendancy of leaks and rumors is obvious: we all suspect—given ample precedent—that anyone willing to be quoted publicly is either lying or saying nothing of importance. No self-respecting snoop in Washington, D.C., would be caught dead going to lunch with Marlin Fitzwater at the White House or Margaret Tutweiler at the State Department to pump them for information. Every section of the federal government has an official mouthpiece who is officially disbelieved or genially ignored. And what is true of national affairs applies equally to the office. By the time we find out anything in a memo or at a meeting, it'll be too late to mitigate the damage, doctor the spin, or make the most of any edge the information may offer. We'll be out of it, like all the chumps who shuffle back from the coffee cart, shaking their heads in amazement and mumbling, "Gee, if only I'd known."

Almost nothing happens in any kind of work, from the Oval Office to Hole-in-the-Wall Realty, that isn't the subject of leaks and rumors, info tidbits as packed with omens and ripe for interpretation as the entrails of a luckless sheep in ancient Greece. Nobody gets hired, fired, praised, raised, or braised without the news spreading with uncanny speed, sometimes before the reported event has actually happened. The ability to read accurately the tea leaves of rumor, to leak an effective leak and to control the interpretation of sly slanders have become business skills as essential as the firm handshake and efficient time management. Take the high road if you wish, but don't be surprised if that unsavory underground traveler, the office gossip broker, gets to the facts before you. When a top officer in a large New York corporation was asked by a reporter to comment on rumors that his job was being shopped around, he snapped, "I don't pay any attention to rumors." Too bad. Three days later he was out, no doubt with a sudden new respect for the ancient sotto voce party line.

According to Graydon Carter, former co-editor of *Spy* magazine, leaks and rumors are "a guerrilla action to counterattack the effects of new and more widespread methods of corporate lying." The upright old notion (always fairly hypocritical) that rumors are categorically worthless has given way to the pragmatic realization that attention had better damn well be paid. Orlin "Chick" Davis, a top headhunter with the executive recruiting firm of Heidrick & Struggles in New York, considers some level of credibility a given. "Anyone hearing a rumor should know that at least a kernel of truth is in there somewhere," he says. But, Davis warns, "the old game of 'whisper-down-the-line' tends to distort a rumor's truth with each retelling. The more convoluted a story gets, the less dependable it is." Davis assured me I could depend on *that*.

Though leaks, rumors, spin control, and plain old idle talk all fall under the heading of gossip, each has a specific coloration and purpose in the workplace. Study them, learn their uses and abuses. They *will* be on the final. Before dissecting gossip's subtle nuances, a brief gloss of the glossary:

• **Leak.** Unofficially official. Can be true or false but is usually meaningful. Contains agenda set by the leaker; frequently destructive. Must be studied carefully by the leakee before being passed along or acted upon. Often sent outside company to reporter for laundering before coming back inside.

• **Rumor.** May be based on a leak or not, but usually based on something. Can in part be judged by its stamina; if still around next week, probably true. If good news, probably false.

• **Spin control.** Essentially, a method of generating half truths to slant extant rumor in favor of spinner (or spinner's superiors). Alters rumor that may already have altered leak. Spun rumors are invariably unreliable, though spinning is a useful ability much in demand by politicians, corporate CEOs, and lawyers of clients under felony indictment. Spinning rumors tend to slow owing to friction exerted by truth and must be respun constantly, leading eventually to erratic behavior (as in George Bush's many variations of the Persian Gulf crisis of 1990–91).

• **Hot tip.** Though always offered as fresh, choice, and instantly useful, temperatures vary widely, usually from absolute zero to tepid. Hot tips are usually signaled by tipper looking left and right, then leaning closer to listener. The phrase "I probably shouldn't be telling you this, but . . ." is another sign. People with little information but deep need to *seem* plugged in tend to be source of (not so) hot tips.

• **Idle talk.** Valueless as information, but one of the few things that make day-to-day corporate life bearable. Idle talkers make ideal lunch companions, as long as they do all the talking. What is said *to* them should be limited to name, rank, and serial number.

Keep in mind that official sources and rumor-mongers are frequently the same people. With straightforward methods such as newsletters, press briefings, and authorized memoranda universally scorned, those who want to get the word out, or create a strategic smoke screen, may leak version Z while in the process of announcing version A. The official story has to be produced—that's an institutional function, after all—but even in corporate PR departments the dissemination of real information often goes underground. (Back when I worked as a junior wordman in a corporate press office, the drill went like this: I cranked out a constant stream of releases and sent them dutifully to every newspaper and magazine on an endless list, while my boss took a chosen few reporters to lunch at 21 and, under the deep cover of vodka martinis, told them the "real" story.)

There are various uses for the well-placed leak—making sure people get bad news while not actually having to give it to them in person, or testing the reaction to a strategy without actually committing yourself to it—but certainly the most curious is what might be called the Deep Throat phenomenon: the nagging itch to tell the truth on the part of someone whose highly paid job is to *hide* the truth.

Ironically, the long-standing corporate "lie-and-let-lie" ethos remains pretty much in place despite a groundswell of change in the willingness of the public to be lied to, and in the acceptance of employees to work for companies guilty of chronic lying (about, for instance, their environmental policies). Even with the *nouvelle noblesse* of the nineties, we're so numb to duplicity as a standard operating procedure that nobody gets riled when official falsehoods are exposed, not even when the time between untruth and consequences is embarrassingly brief. On a given Friday, let's say, the CEO of Lovejoy Small Arms tells a reporter from the *Wall Street Journal* that rumors of impending layoffs are "absolute fabrications." The story runs on Monday (incidentally shoring up Lovejoy's stock), and a little after noon on Tuesday, 2,500 employees of the company get pink slips. Will you see this headline the next day: LOVEJOY DIRECTORS OUST CEO OVER MENDACITY CHARGE? Don't count on it. The directors will approve of their man's approach. In fact, they won't think of what he said as a lie, merely as a tactical evasion, a bit of smoke, some necessary fudging with the meddlesome press. And, amazingly, no one else will be particularly angry, not even those suddenly unemployed. It's the way things are.

Chances are the CEO brought up the layoff rumors in the first place, as a psychological preparation for the firings, knowing his denial would be believed only by those too dumb to be employable anyway.

Occasionally, rumors spring into being through spontaneous generation. The "kernel of truth somewhere in there" that Chick Davis talks about may just be imaginative speculation, not based on leaks but still worth a lot more than Jeane Dixon's stuff. The point is that a rumor doesn't need any foundation at all to become widely believed. Jean-Noel Kapferer, French author of the book *Rumeurs*, contends there's no necessity for some original event to justify a rumor. Like Superman or the cavalry in old westerns, rumors tend to show up when they're needed. Human nature abhors an information vacuum, and fills the gap with hearsay as a hedge against angst. In the late eighties, when the federal government was building its case against the investment firm of Drexel Burnham Lambert, months during which the extent of the case and the planned reaction of the company went undefined, rumors were so rife among Drexel's ten thousand employees that one insider (who spoke to me—you guessed it—on the condition that she not be named) said that anyone could say anything, no matter how implausible, and by the end of the day the rumor was being reported as "absolutely a sure thing." A day or two later, some new rumor would be championed just as credulously. And so it went. As the gossip columnist played by Wallace Shawn in the movie *The Moderns* lamented, "I don't like spreading rumors, but what else can you do with them?"

The ability of rumors to take on a life of their own, and the willingness of almost everyone to listen more closely to leaks than to official news, makes these alternative communiqués powerfully effective as tools of self-promotion and control, or—in a form of sub rosa personnel management—to bring pressure on or raise havoc among those who may be plotting your destruction. Though it might be nice not to need a knowledge of such dubious methods, they are employed daily by others and ought to be understood, if only as a matter of self-defense. To wit, a loose-lips lexicon:

• **The rumor as self-fulfilling prophecy.** Because they are simply more compelling than fact, rumors based on little or nothing can have the effect of actual events. Let's say three executives are equally positioned to succeed to the top spot in a corporation. Somehow, one of the contenders is singled out in a trade publication as "rumored to be the personal choice of the retiring CEO," even though, in fact, the chief has never said anything of the kind. The members of the board of directors read the rumor, or hear of it, and despite denials by the CEO, the rumored favorite magically begins to appear the most logical choice for the job. How did the rumor get into print in the first place? Well, reporters need to sound informed, and if a certain candidate for a job just happens to say something like "I know I'm rumored to be the one, but frankly, I think that's just idle talk," the rest pretty much takes care of itself.

• **The Damocles denial.** Since public pronouncements often mean just the opposite of what is said, the denial of rumors can make bigger waves then the rumors themselves. When former Los Angeles Raiders head coach Mike Shanahan, at the time fairly new in his job, fired his defensive coordinator and another assistant coach, sportswriters speculated that he would fire all of his predecessor's staff (the kind of new-broom sweep that happens in many businesses). Shanahan hadn't done much to quash that prediction, so when he announced that the jobs of the team's other assistants were safe and that "no other moves are foreseen," the effect can only have been to put several of his employees in a state of more or less permanent anxiety. Imagine having your boss pat you on the back tomorrow and say, "Don't worry, kid, whatever you've heard, your job isn't being phased out" when you hadn't heard anything at all. What, *you* worry?

• **The leak as leverage.** Any politician with the necessary instincts for survival knows that going public with private communications, while ethically questionable, can work miracles on a colleague's willingness to get with the program. Lyndon Johnson was a master of calculated indiscretions about who was supposed to be doing what *by next week or else*, and the technique has lost none of its appeal since the days of the late Great Society. When former New York mayor Ed Koch sent a memo to the city schools chancellor (a man whose job many considered impossible) complaining about the decline of grammar in the city's schools, he leaked the note to the *New York Times*, which reported it in detail. The last paragraph of the story pointed out that the chancellor had not yet actually received Hizzoner's testy note. Presumably, of course, the

besieged chancellor had found out about it when he read his newspaper at breakfast that very morning (the yolks curdling on his
eggs), and planned to do something about that damned grammar
thing by afternoon. The same sort of "gotcha!" effect is achieved
when someone at a meeting puts somebody else on the spot by
referring to a certain demanding task outlined in a memo calculated
not to have emerged from the mailroom yet. The ploy is a sure way
to guarantee cooperation, since for reasons of face people rarely
turn down responsibility in public, and will take on the grimmest
assignments with a bravado they soon enough regret.

Learning to read rumors and assess the value of leaks is a semimystical skill, like solving the London *Times* crossword puzzle, but
much more useful around the office. Former *Spy* editor Carter,
whose magazine serves as a lightning rod for every reckless charge
in the Western world, has developed an early-warning system for
bogus bits of intelligence. "Anything that comes in the mail, single-
spaced, crammed with details for several pages, is almost sure to be
no good," he says. Since it is the nature of rumors to be vague, it
follows that when someone tells you a story with all the blanks
filled in, you can reasonably suspect that what you're hearing is
mostly fiction.

Carter is also wary of the high-security, maximum-dramatic-
effect rumor. "Whenever somebody pulls me close and says, 'Listen, don't quote me on this, but . . . ,' I figure I'm in for some bit
of inane gossip." When people have a truly significant rumor to pass
along, they don't have to chew the scenery to make things interesting. "We get about fifty phone-in leaks a week, and maybe one
checks out," Carter says. How do you evaluate such undependable
stuff? A few rules of tongue:

First, consider the source. The higher the better is a good general
measure; inside information from a senior VP is almost always
better—as currency if not fact—than some premonition of Paulie
the security guard. The revelations of assistants are not to be
scorned, however, especially the assistants of men and women with
corner offices and silver coffee services; they have the instincts of
master detectives, and few scruples about prying. And if a company has that newest high-tech blabbermouth, a centralized fax
machine, an impressive lunch is in order for its well-informed
keeper.

Second, consider the beneficiary. Look to the motives if you want to know who leaked what and why, the *New York Times* advises in one of the periodic primers it publishes on the art of interpreting leaks and rumors: "The truth of a leak is usually found not so much in the thing it would destroy, but in the people or ideas it would promote." Of course, in the piranha pond of business competition, the destruction of one party often results in the promotion of another, so in the unhappy event that you find yourself the subject of damaging leaks and rumors, you need only figure out who would rise if you fall to have a pretty good idea where they're coming from.

Third, consider the alternatives. There are various ways to cope with rumors that threaten. Some, alas, are borderline unethical. Like a forest ranger setting backfires, you can instigate counterrumors by using such well-tested methods as leaving unsigned memos in the copy machine, dropping implications into the ears of known security risks, and faking a few loud phone conversations (making sure to leave your office door open). You can also exercise expeditious spin control, reshaping hearsay (that you're in trouble for screwing up the Harris deal, for instance) to reflect well on yourself (the Harris problem arose from philosophical differences between you and the sales manager). No need to tell any lies; just let people supply their own inferences and hope for the best.

Obviously, when you reach a certain level, it helps to have some friends in the press, and there's a press for every trade. Most journalists will still listen to anything as long as you're buying lunch. About the only way *not* to counter a rumor is to deny it, since any denial tends to give the rumor added clout. The more vehement the denial (the more he or she doth protest) the more credible the story becomes. When Arizona senator Dennis DeConcini was accused by a special counsel of helping Charles Keating evade government regulation, he delivered a fierce speech in defense of his rectitude. But as testimony at the hearings of the Senate Ethics Committee wore on, it became clear that DeConcini had been among the most deeply compromised of the so-called Keating Five.

No matter how annoying leaks and rumors may be, there's some comfort in the old saw that the only thing worse than being talked about is not being talked about. A rumor once appeared about me in the *New York Post*, on the deliciously disreputable, gossip-gushing Page Six. The item, based on a mostly false leak, might have jeopardized a negotiation I was in the middle of. All afternoon after the story appeared, I worked my Rolodex to contact just about everyone I knew. Was I desperately trying to quash the rumor to avoid trouble? Well, that's what I told the people I called. But the real truth, I suspect, was that I wanted all my friends to know I'd made it.

17

Marching
Orders

business travel

made bearable, mile

by miserable mile

*T*he Friday flight from New York to San Francisco was crowded, as it usually is, and the nerves of those who had escaped from Manhattan during rush hour were tattered, as they usually are. Under typically dire conditions—the frantic search for luggage space in the overhead glove compartments, the hour delay boarding the plane, the secret fear that this time a wing really was going to fall off over Wichita—the unappealing characteristics of one's fellow humans were grotesquely highlighted. With a minimum of effort, I could find it in my heart to be utterly unforgiving.

A couple of rows ahead of me, a woman dressed in a stern Alcott & Andrews habit was busily stowing her gear, folding her raincoat with obsessive concern, unloading a daunting stack of computer paper and other office paraphernalia, and generally acting as if she were on the corporate jet. Finally in her seat, having filled her tray table with the heavy ordnance of executive action, she threw a hard look at those around her, a look that said, "Yo! I gotta work, so don't try to turn this trip into the goddamn Loveboat."

Inevitably, I suppose, the woman reached into her attaché case and withdrew that Excalibur of overweening ambition, a cellular phone. As she prepared to dial a number, a flight attendant told her that the phone might interfere with the crew's radio frequencies, and couldn't be used. With a scowl, the woman put the phone back and hunched over her calculator. Then, as if just comprehending the full significance of what she'd heard, she shouted down the aisle to the stewardess, "You mean, I can't use it *at all?*" Barred from making calls on her own phone, the woman fidgeted during takeoff, then leapt up as soon as the seat belt sign blinked off, and went to get the in-flight credit card phone, which she used nonstop for the next two thousand miles while consulting yard after yard of spreadsheets. Needless to say, fellow business travelers, this was not a healthy camper. She is one of those relentless workers who carry their grindstones with them, and make the most forbearing row mates wish they were sitting next to a colicky baby. Let her be a lesson to us.

For those who regularly sally forth in quest of profit, business travel can be a hard slog. At its rare best, the working trip can actually be a welcome diversion from the dailiness of the office, but at its familiar worst it is an activity that can wither the souls of decent folk and turn borderline hard cases into absolute lunatics. Done badly, business travel is to traveling what business dinners are to dining: both take something that should be a source of pleasure and turn it into cruel and unusual punishment. But there is no avoiding the fact that most jobs require travel, whether an occasional convention trip or endless treks from one sales call to another. It simply goes with the territory that sooner or later you'll be checking in at the gate for an arduous trip *to* the territories.

At that point, though, you have a choice: you can stoically endure the rigors of a forced march, or follow the Yellow Brick Road and come home with heart, brain, and courage still intact. If you give in to the perfectly reasonable gloom that accompanies planning for a trip, you'll likely have a perfectly gloomy time. But if you take a deep breath and rethink the whole concept, you can make a business trip bearable, and beyond.

There are all sorts of practical ploys to take the sting out of business travel, some of which I'll get to presently. But the first step in eliminating the drear of flying is simply to reduce the amount of work attempted in the span of time allotted. This little revolutionary thought might seem perversely naive—after all, we're not going to Duluth in December for our health, are we?—but it's meant to serve as an antidote for the ambulatory workaholism that has given business travel a bad name. Somehow, whether as a result of jet travel (with its illusion of ease), undue expectations on the part of employers, or the grim climate of aggression in business that is a legacy of the eighties, people have fallen into a Calvinistic habit of measuring the success of a trip by how miserable they are while they're out and how exhausted they feel when they get back.

The insanity of our times (or is it just inanity?) is such that if someone spends two weeks dayhopping across the country, passing those days in windowless conference rooms and the nights in airport hotels, subsisting on in-flight lasagna and reading *USA Today*, then—after the red-eye from LAX to NYC and the shuttle to D.C. ASAP—stumbles into the office hollow-eyed and wasted, everybody will nod approvingly and say, "Way to go!" Thus are bred a caste of road warriors, male and female, who see business travel as combat, and not only expect little more than blood, sweat, and tears, but revel in their own ability to function under hellish conditions. The rewards may be a reputation for Odyssean pluck and, ironically, a bigger territory to cover, but the costs are high. Sooner or later, depending on stamina (or sheer tolerance for pain) such relentless road work can reach a point of diminishing returns, after which the toll taken by travel will nullify whatever benefit the trip may bring. Unfair as it may seem, whatever success you've had in the outback, if you're bumping into the furniture when you return, some mean-minded martinet will decide you really can't cut it. (Odysseus managed to dispatch a gang of competitors when he got back from *his* extended working trip, but don't count on the same luck unless Athena is backing you.)

So what can you do about it? Quit the field, give up the commissions (or the glory), admit that your legs are going, plead to come in from the cold, and settle for the rooted life of a desk jockey? Admit it, that doesn't sound so bad. But let's just say it's not an option (which it probably isn't), that your legs are solid oak, or that forsaking commissions might mean saying sayonara to the Z car or the beach house (or your dreams of same). How can you civilize the business trip so that it doesn't turn you into a pod person by the time it's over?

First, think of it as getting away from it all with a few strings attached. Think of it as *travel*. (You remember, the thing you were going to do before you got caught up in a career?) Even if your destination is a city you've been to twenty times, don't give in to the hotel potato temptation, spending your nights slumped over a meager desk with *Lethal Weapon 7* on Spectravision and a room service club sandwich at your elbow. How would you feel about yourself if you did that on your first night of a vacation in, say, Paris? Okay, so this is no vacation. And one gets few business trips to Paris, but oh, so many to Spokane, Minneapolis, Detroit, and Albany. Yet all is not lost. These are legitimate geographic places, not purgatories (necessarily).

In Spokane, for instance, I once saw a man with waders on over his business suit catch a trout on a fly from the river that runs through the middle of town. In snowbound but scrubbed Minneapolis you'll find two of the greatest art museums in America. Detroit has memorable Deco buildings and Pistons or Tigers home games. And Albany, though aswarm with state legislators and infamous for restaurants that cater to them, is only a trot away from Saratoga's splendid racetrack and lots of picture postcard towns. The point is, few places on your itinerary will have nothing to recommend them (including Oakland, California, despite Gertrude Stein's stinging zinger that there's no *there* there), as long as you commit yourself to the pleasures of travel along with the pressures of work.

If, along with all the other preparations for a trip, you study up on the local color and culture of your destinations, vow not to stay at an airport hotel, and make sure to seek out the best places to eat, track down the jazz joints, and, yes, even make pilgrimages to area landmarks, a trip can't be a total drag. You'd do all this if you were going to Athens, Greece, so why not in Athens, Georgia? A management consultant I know based in New York claims to take in all the things on the road—concerts, plays, sporting events, museums—that he never seems able to find the time (or money) for when he's at home. Another friend, a sales rep in the Midwest who spends a lot of time in small cities where culture is sparse, has become a connoisseur of monuments. She says she has yet to find a city that doesn't have at least one Union or Confederate stalwart astride his bronze steed in verdigris grandeur. She makes Polaroids of these finds and brings them home like prize baseball cards. While this may not seem excitement at fever pitch, the search for commemorative statuary has given my friend a reason to get out and explore towns she might have ignored in favor of watching "Jeopardy" in her hotel room ("I'll take Civil War generals for three hundred, Alex").

But however much you may do to make being there pleasurable, getting there is still likely to be no fun at all if you don't make things better for yourself. Raising the level of creature comfort on any trip is a matter of attending to details, like so much else in life, and comfort is the key to taking the high road in business travel. The first step is to take your travel agent to lunch. The person who is just a voice on the other end of your telephone (or your secretary's phone) can do a lot for you, which is surely worth springing for a steak au poivre and listening to a litany of his or her recent freebies. If you can establish the simple fact that you want certain things—a special meal, complimentary passes to airline clubs, seats with extra legroom—other minor miracles may begin to take place. A good travel agent can provide a postgraduate course in how to get the most out of an airline, an airport, a rental car agency, or for that matter a travel agent.

As far as comfort aloft is concerned, there are just two words you have to remember: first class. Unfortunately, that's a perk most companies are stingy with, or one of the first things to go when the arctic winds of austerity sweep over a once generous management. (Early in 1990, Apple Computers downgraded its executives to coach class—a.k.a. steerage—in a move that many took to mean the company's greatest days were over.) But never mind the parsimony of the bean counters; first-class upgrades can be a bit of private business between you and a consenting airline. If you are a member of the frequent flier plans on the lines you normally take (and why wouldn't you be?), a small extra charge will move you up to the wide seats, complimentary champagne, and smug superiority in the plush end of the plane. You'll have to pick up the tab for the upgrade, but the added pleasure pays off in extra energy (and an effectively gratified ego—"I travel first class therefore I am") by flight's end.

Airlines generally offer upgrades only to passengers who have paid full coach fare, but tickets for business flights are usually unrestricted to allow for schedule flexibility, and are thus the most expensive for a given class. The problem with upgrades is that first-class seats are popular with frequent fliers, so the sooner you make the call the better. Sometimes you can upgrade when you make your reservation, which is the best way to ensure your rightful place in the scheme of things. Even if first class is full, I offer one last, desperate ploy. Check in for the flight in your best Italian suit and Armani shades (or Norma Kamali wrap) and say to the person at the counter, "Your PR department suggested that I ask for a first class upgrade." There may be an opening, and you may just get a VIP boost over some shabbily dressed millionaire.

The countless free miles that business flights earn often take care of vacation trips, a significant blessing that can be worth meditating upon when you're due at an important morning meeting in snowbound Chicago but are eating watery scrambled eggs at the St. Louis airport instead. But those miles can add some fun to working trips, too. A management consultant who spends too much time trying to patch up sinking ventures lightens his mood by renting Thunderbirds when he's staying a few days in another town, and paying the difference with accumulated mileage. For other tactics of the good life on the road, I asked a television personality I know who travels constantly to studios all over the country and needs to arrive with his good humor and telegenic smile intact. What follows are his suggestions:

• Join the airport clubs of every airline you use. Not only do these places offer a comfortable haven to wait for a plane, sipping free coffee and sometimes free drinks, but the staff will check you in and handle reservation problems. If, for instance, a flight is canceled, rather than having to line up with all the other displaced souls, you can retreat to the Admirals Club or the Crown Room or whatever and have your plans revised while you phone ahead. The hub system used by major air carriers has created a nightmarish network of stopovers and plane changes, with increased chances of delays in purgatories like O'Hare or the Dallas airport, so it pays to have a second home wherever you find yourself stuck with a two-hour layover.

• Subscribe to the *Official Airline Guides*. These monthly schedule books cost about $65 a year and contain up-to-date flight information for every airline in the states. My TV pal carries the current issue with him at all times, so that if he's on a plane that's caught in a holding pattern and knows he won't make a connection, he can consult the schedules and use the in-flight phone to make a new plan. He also subscribes to Compuserve, a computer data base that lets him check to make sure his travel agent has given him the best connections rather than the first ones to come up on the screen. (And *you* thought TV personalities got rich with dumb luck.)

• Ask airlines or your travel agent for seating charts of their aircraft. If you don't manage to upgrade, at least you can give yourself the benefit of extra legroom, or make sure you're on the side of the plane with two seats in a row instead of four (as is often the setup in DC-10s, for instance). Even in the fraternal *égalité* of first class, some seats are more *égal* than others.

• When you read the departures list on the airline terminal TV monitors, check to see what plane is arriving at the same gate. If your flight is scheduled out of gate 72 at 5:00 and the flight into gate 72 is half an hour late, relax, go to the club, listen for a delay or gate-change announcement, and let everybody else get the bad news after they've sprinted a quarter mile with luggage.

• And this last, which I serve up with an FDA warning that it might be an entirely specious health claim: my friend says that an oral surgeon sitting next to him (in first class, of course—your dental dollars at work) warned that the overhead air vent should be turned off, or directed away from your face, since germs and viruses circulating through the ventilation system can easily be absorbed through the eyes. (Many of the newer planes don't have movable vents, so the best you can do is ask the flight attendant for lots of orange juice.)

For all business travelers, the most important tip of all is philosophical, not practical: use the time between cities, and between working sessions, as R and R, not extra hours for the grind. Rather than desperately trying to get ahead by turning an airplane seat into a minioffice with a full supply of office angst, take advantage of the rare chance to be out of touch. Read a book, watch the movie, look at the clouds go by as you did when you were ten. You could even talk to the person next to you and learn a lot about what your fellow roadies are up to. (I once got a short course in the joys and frustrations of engineering that was fascinating and extraordinarily useful, and I'm living in anticipation of the flight when I sit next to an IRS auditor.) Though it's true that the relative quiet of an airplane trip provides a tempting interlude for uninterrupted work, if you do feel the irresistible urge to keep at it, at least use the time to think (you remember thinking, surely); leave the spreadsheets and calculator in the overhead compartment, take out a pencil and a yellow legal pad, and try to come up with a new idea. Given the surreal wonder of whooshing along at thirty thousand feet sipping a scotch and eating peanuts while absorbing an extra helping of cosmic rays, who knows what incandescent thoughts might occur to you?

18

Tantrum Art: An Appreciation

sudden outbursts of

temper can work

wonders, if your

form is flawless

*T*he final stage in growing up may be the moment when we stop blaming our parents for just about everything. I fully intend to reach that mature plateau, possibly today, but not before I blame Mom and Dad just one more time.

The particular culpability on my mind concerns a key bit of mis- or disinformation passed on to me at the age of—I'm guessing here—two years and some months, and reinforced from that point on until it stuck. I don't remember the exact words, of course, though I think it's likely my mother must have spoken them. I remember the message clearly, however, so well that I'm still crippled by it. "Tantrums," my mother would have said to a little boy rapidly turning blue, "are very, very bad."

Okay, let's be fair; anyone who has ever seen a two-year-old throw a tantrum will be inclined to acquit my folks on the grounds of self-defense. Having a sparrow-hawk missile loose in the living room isn't an experience anybody wants to undergo twice. Only a parent with a masochist's tolerance for pain or mush for a spinal column will tolerate a kid in a state of sky-high dudgeon. But however understandable their admonition may have been, its blanket indictment of the tantrum was simplistic; while solving a problem for them, it created one for me.

That problem—to use a modern metaphor—is unilateral disarmament. For the sake of my parents' sanity, I was directed to abandon development and testing of a potent weapon that eventually might have become a big stick in a fiercely competitive adult world where personal ambition is often met by resistance verging on hostility. Thus, I entered that world lacking a vital skill that others—those, perhaps, whose parents were less determined than mine, or simply hard of hearing—are able to use with stunning success. Once I began to understand the stormy realpolitik of the workplace, I found myself playing catch-up with my personal arsenal—without any real hope of reaching parity with those who, unhindered by a tantrum ban, had never disarmed.

Rather than quashing my bravura displays of temper without qualification, what my parents should have told me was this: "Tantrums are not going to get you anywhere around *this* house," thus allowing the possibility that elsewhere they might work just fine. Because, according to my observations, they do. I once saw a famous writer throw herself to the floor of an equally famous editor's office, kicking her legs and screaming about cuts made in a cover story. Almost instantly, the cuts were restored. I was appalled, and hugely impressed.

The Harvard Business School offers no course in the Executive Tantrum. I know; I checked. Nor does Stanford. Some other venerable business institution (or war college) may have evolved that far, but I doubt it. Various management courses touch on the subject of anger, but usually with the idea of controlling it, diverting it, "managing" it. They echo the parental approach, as if getting mad and showing it is still very, very bad.

Yet the scorned and neglected tantrum, that sudden, stunning, radiant display of rage, is a management tool that can be faster and more effective than the most bristling memo, and infinitely more energy-efficient than the most elegantly choreographed act of icy disdain. As every two-year-old instinctively knows (before he gets talked out of it), the tantrum gets results—instantly—and then proceeds to reverberate in the minds of the beholders like residual radiation from the Big Bang. Thrown at the right time, in the right place, and in just the right way, the tantrum has more sheer staying power than almost any other management (or antimanagement) ploy.

Because most of us were well brought up (we know who we are), we're not proud of tantrums even if we *can* bring ourselves to throw them. And because we repress our desire to spray emotional shrapnel all over the place, we tend not to understand the true nature of the tantrum, its subtle variations, and the range of methodology of its use. At the office, the difference between a tantrum and protracted anger is one of economy, of how much must be invested to get a desired result. A simmering feud may go on for days, months, even years, devouring more and more time and energy as it builds toward an inevitable climax. The business press never lacks for stories of high-level cold wars that distract corporate management from doing their jobs, with eventual disastrous results.

In the book *Indecent Exposure*, an account of the decline of Columbia Pictures following the David Begelman check-forging scandal, author David McClintick describes Alan Hirschfield and Herbert Allen, two former friends who together had revitalized a fading company but whose gradually widening rift all but dismantled what they had accomplished. Allen, who appeared unable to lose his temper openly, managed to oust CEO Hirschfield after a long period of ill will. Yet the protracted drain on the attention of the board and top executives in a highly hands-on business seems in retrospect pointless and enervating. A well-thrown tantrum gives far more bang for the buck, and can be over so quickly that the thrower (let's just say it's you) won't be diverted for more than a few minutes from the real business at hand.

In fact, the tantrum is so effective that it need not even be specifically directed at anyone to be extraordinarily useful. I recall, only too vividly, witnessing what might be called a psychological-warfare demonstration some years ago, put on by a boss who was about the size of an undernourished jockey but could, by pumping ire, expand to terrifying dimensions. I was on the phone in an adjacent office when I became aware of loud thumps on the wall next to me. Peering into my boss's office, I saw the High Personage, pink of dress and mauve of face, methodically picking up everything on her desk and throwing it full force across the office. The din was tremendous—major concussions in the relentless rhythm of an artillery barrage (military metaphors are unavoidable, I'm afraid)—and everyone rushed to see what was going on.

Gathering at the door (no one was *about* to go in), we watched this ferocious venting of wrath and glanced nervously at one another. It turned out later that the focus of the boss's anger was a malfunctioning dictation machine that had failed to record a long evening's worth of correspondence, but the fact that the victim wasn't human offered little comfort. In everyone's mind, I'm sure, was the same fainthearted hope: Please, please, don't ever let me make her that mad.

What a wonderful accomplishment! Without going to war, without the risk of incurring hard feelings in a face-off with any of the sometimes truculent members of her staff, our top gun was displaying a terrifying capacity to crush those who might displease her. No one who witnessed that outburst would ever afterward be inclined to go one-on-one with the boss if there was any way—including abject groveling—to avoid it.

Of course, the tantrum in question was absolutely genuine—anything ersatz simply wouldn't have had the same unnerving effect. A fake tantrum has the same telltale lack of conviction as a B-movie kiss or the expressions of delight in television coffee commercials, and as soon as people sense there's no real danger the tantrum thrower loses face and power. But more on the rights and wrongs of tantrum art in a bit.

Management by tantrum is a time-honored technique (or time-dishonored, but effective nonetheless). Despots have long been good at it, in large part because a livid despot is a dangerous despot. The later Caesars were given to cranky outbursts that sent underlings off to fall on their swords, Vlad the Impaler could be awfully cross at times, and Hitler frequently reduced iron-willed Junker generals to cringing lackeys with his monumental mad scenes. It may seem odd that dictators need tantrums, since they wield absolute power anyway. But merely being, say, the Sun King may not be enough to make everyone get with the program, so the heat and light of an occasional nova is just the thing to get absolute followers following absolutely.

It's actually when a leader, or a manager, doesn't have the power of life and death that the tantrum makes the most sense. (Shouting "Off with his head" when you actually *can* have someone's head cut off is pretty boorish, in fact.) I suppose the business tantrum is a throwback to more perilous times, when thwarting bosses was frequently fatal, a dramatic reminder that even in a free country, within the constrained boundaries of civilized corporations, there still lurks the danger of demons unleashed. Though the danger is symbolic (you *can* be fired, but only in some segments of the Brooklyn importing business are you going to be dragged outside and shot), sometimes tantrums in the most civilized surroundings can get physical. Who could be more unthreatening than the saintly wimps in publishing? Yet the editor of a famous Aquarian Age magazine is rumored to have punched a photographer when he flew into a rage during a dispute about a picture. Even in Japan, land of ultimate self-control, tantrums can burn through the frustratingly polite layers of group thought. The late Soichiro Honda, shogun of Honda Motors, was called "Mr. Thunder" by his employees because of his incendiary displays. Once, according to newspaper accounts, he hit a worker with a wrench. "In a way, it showed our closeness," he told an American reporter in an admirable use of inscrutable newspeak.

Whether the folks at that particular assembly plant felt any closer to the boss after having seen him lash out is open to question. But be assured, none of them wanted to get him that angry again anytime soon. One of the beauties of the tantrum as a working tool (as opposed, say, to the wrench) is that the better it's wielded, the less often it's needed. Which brings us to certain fundamental points that ought to be understood by anyone who would like to add the tantrum to his management skills.

First, it's important to establish what a tantrum is, and what it isn't. By dictionary definition, a tantrum is "a fit of bad temper." The term "fit" is the operative one here. Sudden. Irrational. Scary. The tantrum is not clenched teeth, a steely-eyed stare, dark mutterings, or the silent treatment. When Achilles retired to his tent and wouldn't come out to fight because he didn't like the way he and his friends were being treated, he wasn't having a tantrum, he was pouting—undistinguished behavior, then and now. When he dragged Hector's body around the battlefield behind his chariot, he was having a tantrum, perhaps at a mere mortal's presumption in challenging him—not a nice way to act, maybe, but it had a way of focusing the attention of those looking on from the walls of Troy. Hence, a working tantrum must be immediate and definitive; anger incarnate, Vishnu the employer.

Second, tantrums are best when they're spontaneous; unless you're a trained actor, rehearsing ahead of time for a supposedly ad lib outburst tends to undercut the fierce beauty of the instant ignition, rapid expansion, and powerful concussion that mark the true tantrum and allow it to flatten egos for miles around. Just as in lovemaking, too much technique can have a decidedly cooling effect on the sensational generation of heat. Standing in front of a mirror and developing a repertoire of baleful expressions (mostly borrowed from old Kurosawa movies) can lead to that hardest of tasks, chewing the rug and thinking at the same time.

However, preparation is not always a bad thing. For those of us whose ability to (as the therapists cutely put it) "express our anger" was stunted by our parents, it's not easy to get into the tantrum mode, and does require practice. To avoid any permanent damage during workouts, it's best to choose simulated targets. But not just any target of opportunity. Friends, lovers, traffic cops, federal investigators, and oral surgeons, for instance, are not good choices. Balky machinery is okay. Dogs are fair game, though it may cost you a small fortune in Milk Bones to make up for a few minutes of unjustified verbal abuse. Telephone operators are terrific for dry runs, especially the ones who, when you dial information, tell you there's no listing for the White House, or worse, the International House of Pancakes. But by far the best simulations are directed at oneself, since even for the tantrum-impaired a certain level of fury over little personal stupidities—cutting one's face (or leg) while shaving with a blade you knew had been in one scrape too many, bashing a thumb while hanging a picture in a dimly lit room, locking the ignition key inside the car—comes quite naturally. Take advantage of these asinine moments; stomp, apply fist to forehead, call yourself awful names, and don't hold back. (Later, you can buy yourself a martini, the Milk Bone of adult humans.) After a while, these incidents will chip away at the parental shibboleth that a stiff upper lip is essential to the anatomy of good little boys and girls. Before long, you'll be ready to take your beefed-up tantrum capabilities out of rehearsals and into the office.

At this point, however, control is everything. The tantrum, as I've amply pointed out, is a weapon, and with its use come responsibilities. The sheer drama of its effect, the pleasures inherent in its power, can lead to tantrum abuse and a distinct loss of utility (not to mention personal decency). All who have earned their black belt in this particular martial art must constantly brush up on the code of Bushido, especially that aspect emphasizing the discipline of restraining deadly skills.

The effectiveness of tantrums in working situations resides in surprise, suspense, and the knowledge of others that crossing you might be very unwise. So anyone who throws tantrums regularly risks diluting the dramatic impact of unpredictability and becoming a mere spectacle, no more threatening than ritual Fourth of July fireworks. Tantrums work when they erupt through the veneer of civility that governs, more or less, the ruthlessness of competition, whether intra- or interorganizational. A flash of unalloyed anger on the part of someone known for equanimity and good humor can be a brilliant coup de théâtre, like the horrible creature that bursts out of John Hurt's chest in *Alien*, whereas a regular Friday afternoon tirade ends up as a running joke.

Another reason control matters so much is the simple fact that tantrums feel so good, especially to those who have long considered public anger taboo. The quantum leap from lashing out at a deserving offender to playing host at a public flogging can take place suddenly, leaving metaphoric blood on the Levelors and making you seem like a heartless bully rather than a good man pushed too far (see Chapter 23). A well-turned tantrum should mean never having to say you're sorry, since no one, including its object, should have any reason to feel an injustice was done. Ideally, in fact, the response to a tantrum on everyone's part ought to be, "Thanks, I needed that."

For those still negotiating the tricky lower rungs of the career ladder, it's important to know that the tantrum *can* be used against those in higher positions, but only if infinitely great care is taken. Timing is everything, or almost everything, and discretion is the rest. It's a disastrous idea, for instance, to fire off a tantrum at your boss after a week or two on the job. He or she has no particular investment in you at that point, and might feel well advised to get rid of you without delay. Nor is it smart to pop off at a superior in public; loss of face is much less acceptable to most bosses than the loss of an employee, however valuable. Against a superior, the purpose of a tantrum is to establish the fact that you can be unpleasant to deal with when you feel badly treated for too long a time. Most bosses know when they're taking advantage of a good employee, but they may play dumb for as long as they can get away with it. Brought up short by a timely detonation, they'll probably deal with you more carefully, and take advantage of someone with a longer-suffering disposition. Almost no one ever gets promoted for taking everything the boss can dish out. (Please do not come gunning for me if this advice doesn't work out.)

When blowing up at a superior, certain things must not be said. Things like "Why, I could do your job twice as well as you any day." Or "If Mr. Dewlip knew how you treated your subordinates, you'd be in big trouble." And especially "If you don't think I'm the person for this job, you'd better tell me right now." If you're throwing a tantrum upward, be sure its message is that you're not there to be whimsically pushed around, never that you're ready for a showdown—unless things have come to the point where you're also ready to lose the job, and don't give a damn anymore. If you're not prepared for out-and-out brinkmanship, your show of temper should bring an end to endless accommodation, not to a working relationship.

Like intercontinental ballistic missiles, the tantrum is at its best when it never has to be thrown, but simply maintains a high level of respect by its ready availability. A veteran correspondent for the *New York Times* once told me that the long and often splendid career of Abe Rosenthal, who retired as executive editor of the paper in 1988, could be viewed as one extended incipient tantrum. And yet by most accounts Rosenthal rarely flew off the handle. "Abe's real gift," said my informant, "was his ability to convey the feeling that if he ever *did* throw a tantrum, it would permanently blind whoever saw it."

If, like the redoubtable Rosenthal, you can get the results of a tantrum, and derive the pleasure of a tantrum, without ever actually engaging in one, you'll have reached the rarest Zen-masterly level of the art, the tantrum of no tantrum, and should be well on your way to legendary status.

19

Good-bye, Miss Phipps

tips on the complicated

care and feeding of

the late-twentieth-century

secretary

*W*hatever happened to Miss Phipps? She was the prim but (one suspected) secretly passionate woman who sat just outside a big corner office, wearing a tweed skirt and a white silk blouse with a cameo brooch at the collar, her shining hair pulled back into a tight bun, typing at virtuoso speed on an IBM Selectric. She answered the phone on the first ring with the voice of a diction coach: "Good afternoon, Mr. Madigan's office." And then, with the skill of a veteran diplomat, managed simultaneously to establish the lines of power and deftly dissemble: "Oh yes, Mr. Ryan, let me just see if he's in." (Ryan knew, of course, that *she* knew whether Madigan was in or not, but her response politely reminded him that her boss reserved the right *not* to be there.) Miss Phipps did everything well—protected the lucky Madigan like a she-wolf, inspired awe among the ranks of hungry young Turks, considered the order "Take a letter" an honorable call to arms, and seemed to have no ambition beyond seeing her boss become emperor.

The Miss Phippses of the business world are, if not extinct, certainly on the endangered list, right out there on the brink with the California condor and the snail darter. There are no doubt readers of this book who have never even seen an example of this splendid and once plentiful breed. When I happened to encounter a formidable Phipps type recently, a woman of middle years with no less confidence than the brash billionaire she worked for, someone frequently referred to in print as "an informed insider" by reporters adroitly thwarted while trying to get to the boss, I realized how much things have changed since the time, not all that long ago, when having a dedicated, selfless, fiercely efficient secretary was every junior executive's birthright. In those days, a young hopeful could screw up ten different ways and be saved by an assistant who was smarter, probably as well educated, far wiser in the ways of the corporate world, and willing to do the grunt work for as long as it took her boss to improve significantly enough to become a credit to them both.

The setup was ironic and lopsided, like the relationship of a veteran sergeant and a lieutenant fresh out of OCS; the pro had to say "Good morning, sir" to the rookie and correct his mistakes while appearing to defer to his putative superiority. But despite this traditional form's presumptive inequality, one thing was sure: daily working life was simpler when secretaries pretended to be impressed by the men they worked for and those men, undeserving though they might be, got to appear brilliantly well organized and never had to make the coffee. This system should be neither mourned nor missed, but it did supply the workplace with a certain simple, solid bedrock. These days, figuring out the tricky etiquette of working with secretaries is tough, now that Miss Phipps has become Ms. Phipps-Carlson, or Jennifer, or for that matter Josh; when movies like *Nine to Five* and *Working Girl* preach a gospel of take-no-crap selfhood; when a young woman is as likely to be an executive as an executive assistant; when changing a coffee filter is considered capitulation; when even the Cosmo Girl, that none-too-bright star in man's firmament, talks like this in a newspaper ad:

> I really like money. But don't get me wrong, I mean my own money . . . the salary I earn . . . My favorite magazine says work hard, aim high, and go for the gold . . .

Secretaries of the Miss Phipps era didn't go for the gold, they worked miracles for small change and a nun's austere satisfactions. Or they were spiritual temps, doing a little time in the workplace without having to care about pay or promotions, while waiting to get married, or pregnant. In my first executive-level position, my secretary was an elegant creature with the high sheen provided by expensive finishing schools. She was married to the heir to a major cosmetics fortune. The irony of having as a virtual slave a young woman who luxuriated in a Park Avenue apartment when I was just scraping by in a Greenwich Village studio was pleasurable in a perverse way, and any uneasiness caused by Christy's two fur coats was compensated for by the cachet of having the secretarial equivalent of an Alfa-Romeo while my friends were making do with Volkswagens.

But modern times are murky for the desk set. Knowing how to get the best out of a secretary, executive assistant, girl friday, or simply—in the decidedly retro nomenclature of a California venture capitalist group—"the ladies" without being seen as a boor (or a boar) is a major challenge. It is a challenge that can't (or shouldn't) be dodged, though, however much some good old boys may sometimes yearn for the unenlightened simplicity of the bad old days.

Given how much things have changed, it's surprising but undeniable that there are still men around (and more than a few women) who scoff at the new era and blithely treat their secretaries like walking, talking household appliances. Thus, it follows that there are certain women (and some men, no doubt) who still take pleasure in being the ultraefficient executor of their boss's every wish and demand. And, since certain men (and some women) have no problem presuming they rate slavish behavior, there still exist symbiotic relationships in which both boss and secretary are addicted to using and being used. One of the classic comical figures in the workplace is the executive who can close megabuck deals with ease but can hardly tie his shoelace without his secretary.

The bonds of dependency are so complex and so taken for granted that both parties to the relationship can behave in ways that verge on the surreal. I once overheard the long-time secretary of a Time Inc. executive (in the heady pre-Warner, pre–debt load days) on the phone with her boss, receiving instructions to make dinner reservations for him that evening at a certain restaurant. Nothing would have been at all unusual about this, except that the secretary was in the company's New York headquarters while the executive *and* the restaurant were in Honolulu. Despite the incongruity of making several phone calls across thousands of miles and five time zones, this executive—someone considered very capable in the communications business—had spent so many years having every little detail attended to for him that he'd simply lost the capacity to grapple with a dinner reservation, or even to trust a hotel concierge with such a straightforward task.

After a while, the all-knowing, all-enabling major-domos who are the Miss Phippses of the business world become fused with their bosses and wield considerable proxy power. As a result, they are often treated with the same deference as the men and women they work for; make the mistake of getting uppity with one of these guardians of order and you'll be lucky to see another office picnic. Some of my most frightening moments years ago at CBS came on the few occasions when I had to encounter the fearsome secretaries of Frank Stanton and William Paley. Having tea with the Furies would have been less daunting than approaching these two formidable sentries at the temple gates. How did one proceed? Arrive with flowers? Lavish the impressive but unimpressible pair with candy and compliments? Or just toss in a few pounds of raw meat before entering the antechamber? Neither I nor any of my colleagues ever figured it out, and simply tried to avoid contact with either of the two women. I suspect that they weren't as terrifying as we boy wonders let ourselves believe, but if they ever smiled we were never allowed to see it, and somehow they managed to give off a whiff of brimstone (or was that cordite?) that kept annoying underlings like me cowering at a safe distance.

But the old fashioned joined-at-the-brain relationships and tacit power-sharing arrangements are dwindling. Smart young women want power of their own, not the proxy variety, and few women are looking for ways to kill time until the right man comes along. The secretary/boss thing has variations that never occurred before, so when the time comes to hire a new secretary, whether your first or your fifth, it pays to think about exactly what you need, and then figure out whether you're in touch with reality. To help out, I offer a mixed bag of suggestions.

• **Two's Company.** Sometimes you can find a spit-and-polish secretary who is also great to have around, but don't count on it. The characteristics that make a Phipps so phippsean—grim efficiency, for instance—are not the characteristics that make someone a lot of fun. If what you want is a pal, and you hire someone on the basis of chummy chemistry, accept the likelihood that precision will not be your assistant's priority. When I once suggested to a successful consultant that she ought to have a more businesslike secretary (the aspiring writer she employed took forever to get mundane but vital chores done) she replied, "I'd rather have somebody who's good to talk to." Her witty, chatty helper has gone on to a big-money career as a sitcom writer, which shows what a hopeless mess he made of his secretarial career. The point is, opt for friendship if that's what you need, but don't expect the trains to run on time.

• **Just Visiting.** Some businesses, such as publishing, are tutorial by nature, and entry-level positions are a convenient way of bringing new people into the company and shamelessly exploiting them at the same time. In these collegial hells, the word "secretary" is replaced by the more prestigious (and less well-paid) "assistant." Thus, editors don't have secretaries, happy to be doing what they do well—they have editorial assistants, muddling through at jobs for which master's degrees in English lit are little use while they wait for someone, perhaps you, to get fired. Be nice to these over-qualified, underskilled assistants; they can't type and they won't make the coffee, but you could be working for one of them by next year.

• **Secs and Violins.** This advice will seem anachronistic, but still applies in enough situations to be worth mentioning. It has to do with a form of bonding, if not quite bondage. Decent men want to make life decent for their secretaries, and all they ask in return is that their secretaries love them unreservedly. It seems only fair, they figure. So, soon after a new secretary starts (assuming here she's a woman and the boss is a man), an after-work drink and maybe dinner takes place, maybe at a restaurant with a wandering gypsy duet. The goal is not seduction, exactly, at least not of the actual moist and clutching sort. The point for the man is to make a spiritual conquest, so that his secretary's endless trips to the photocopier and the alchemical chore of converting stacks of smudged receipts into crisply believable expense accounts will seem like a higher calling. Yet endlessly unrequited love (assuming it remains unrequited) is a kind of cheap trick, one that belongs to an earlier epoch when secretaries might as well have been buried with their bosses like the retainers of pharaohs. The price for loyalty bought with candlelight and cabernet, if you're considering such a purchase, is either the burden of responsibility for a secretary's emotions, or the unpleasant knowledge that you're a rat. Not many women go for the "I'm a great guy, and I love you in a very pure way, so how about working until you drop" scam these days anyway, so forget the dinner and just try to get her a good dental plan.

Of course, a decent man probably will feel genuine affection for a hard-working secretary, and ought to be as loyal to her as he wants her to be to him. As in any working relationship, reciprocity is all. You might still be able to locate a vestigial masochist who longs to be mistreated and will respond with devotion, but would you really want somebody like that? (If your answer is a mumbled yes, it's time for some soul-searching.)

• **Optional, at Extra Cost.** At a certain point on the way up the corporate rock face, usually around the time when the numinous letters VP are affixed to one's name, certain men and women succumb to the temptation to find an executive assistant who functions as a recognizable accessory of success, like a Porsche Design attaché case or a rosewood desk with no drawers. Certain traits identify secretaries who have been hired for status: good looks, usually along classic Grace Kelly lines; a wardrobe as carefully chosen and impeccably designed as the Barcelona chairs in the new office that came with the promotion; a degree in something refined and unbusinessy like art history, or Byzantinology, preferably from a good Eastern school; the ability to make witty conversation on a wide spectrum of esoteric subjects (better for her to have read *The Confessions of Zeno* than "Troubleshooting Your Xerox Machine"); and, if at all possible, an English accent. (Well-bred speech patterns are very important; a friend of mine who works at a Wall Street investment banking firm that handles billion-dollar buyouts once complained bitterly that because the financial district is so convenient to Brooklyn all the secretaries sound like they're married to the mob.) Such humans-as-symbols materialism raises some perplexing ethical questions, especially if looks, wardrobe, and accent are the major considerations in a hire. But the impression a secretary makes on others *is* a factor that can't be ignored, so if a slovenly gum-cracker loses out to someone sleek and chic, the hirer may be forgiven what may seem cosmetic standards. The trouble is, in secretaries as in cars, extras come with a price. A good-looking woman in an Armani ensemble with a BBC accent and a working knowledge of Tang Dynasty politics isn't likely to be much good at such menial tasks as typing and humility. If a conspicuously classy adjunct to your splendid career is what you're looking for, prepare to live with typos, irregular hours, arrogance, mood swings, and the constant, nagging awareness that she knows she's better than you and she knows you know it too. Otherwise, go for the hard worker even if she does pop her Bubblicious and whine sibilantly into the phone, "So I says to this guy, I says . . ."

• **Café Olé!** If what really matters most to you is service with just a hint of that old-time servility, consider hiring a man. Not that men are by nature any happier with drudgery, but having usually done less of it they are not as likely to feel threatened. Reverse equality has brought men into the secretarial market, and they've arrived without ideological baggage, so that making the coffee (and other such politically loaded chores) is just a boring job, not a violation of civil rights. For a while, at least. If you don't push your luck.

• **The Big Easy.** One of the worst mistakes you can make in your daily life with an assistant is to be a bad cop one day and a cop-out the next. On "L.A. Law," the relationship between divorce attorney Arnold Becker and his faithful secretary, Roxanne, presents the classic beastie boy / best friend ambiguity, with Roxanne in a funk or a frenzy as a result. Of course, it's possible to be both friendly and demanding, but not easy. If working for you is hell, so be it; you ought to do all you can to mitigate the daily distress, but try not to sow confusion with sporadic, brief efforts to make life seem beautiful. This is not to discourage flowers on occasion, or praise whenever it's due, just the inconsistent behavior that puts someone perpetually between a rock and an all-heart place.

Ideally, the exec/sec gavotte ought to offer rewards for both parties, and at its best should be a professional collaboration between two people equally good at what they do. That it hardly ever works out this way doesn't mean it never can. You may not end up with a true Phipps, living only to carry out your every command, but if you're ready to show some respect, you can still come fairly (the operative word is fairly) close. And don't worry about who makes the coffee—you've probably been drinking too much anyway.

20

Hello, Boy Friday

a primer for women

who manage men,

and the men who

call them "boss"

*M*en have always worked for women, so let's disabuse ourselves of the idea that every time a woman calls out, "Oh James, could you come into my office, please? And bring your steno pad," the earth moves for either of them. But despite historical precedents for the dominant female, things have changed drastically in the last decade or so, with a rapidity that has left human biology gasping in an attempt to catch up. Where men once did the bidding of Queen Elizabeth I, or rallied to the command of Jeanne d'Arc, they work now for just plain Liz and Joan, who may have gone to Princeton or West Point and joined Cap & Gown or the airborne. And though in the best of all possible business worlds, no adjustments would have to be made and transitions would demand nothing more than substituting "Ms." for "Mr.," such is rarely the case. Despite certain optimistic predictions of a workplace free of the old preconceptions about which gender makes the big decisions and which takes the letters (and makes the coffee), for a woman to be the boss of men is a fundamentally different circumstance than being bossed *by* them, or even working with men as colleagues and equals. The complications can be maddening, for both the women and men involved, and they affect people at every level. James the assistant may be a woman's fondest dream of an enlightened man, refreshingly free of hang-ups about who calls the shots, not threatened by the fact that she can afford Armani suits and he can't, unburdened by complexes about a domineering mother—in short, an ever cheerful, never resentful worker—but he isn't Alice, and the differences can make a working relationship tricky for those pioneering on the frontier of the She Generation.

Most of the complications of the "Me Tarzana, You James" setup can be traced to two causes: biology and conditioning. Assuming the man who works for a woman is interested in women (by no means a sure thing, of course, but a distinct possibility), and the woman for whom he works is interested in men, one of the most perplexing elements in their daily collaboration will be none other than that infamous confuser of simple situations, desire. If the effects of this irrepressible force for mischief were written into a movie script, the result would probably be called *When Harry Worked for Sally*. Just as some men can't believe that there can be friendship between a man and a woman without sex somehow sneaking its lambada beat into what otherwise might be a prim minuet, I'm inclined to suspect that a man can't simply work for a woman without the same thing happening.

The desire in question isn't necessarily the basic stuff that makes otherwise rational people throw caution to the wind (and their clothing to the floor), but the ambient chemistry that drifts around like so much pollen. It triggers a wide variety of stresses, regardless of logic, corporate culture, or survival instincts—regardless even of natural attraction. Whether the problem is desire or the lack of desire, or the desperate desire not to give in to desire or reveal no desire at all, something hovers in the air when James walks in with his steno pad poised, or with his flow charts at full flood, and it just won't go away. Though I've had women tell me—as Sally told Harry—that they have no trouble spending time with men at work without the slightest urge to mix business with pleasure, and I don't doubt that's true, the problem won't go away that easily. When a man works for a woman, however determined he may be to keep

things simple, and however scrupulous *she* may be in trying to establish a straight employer-employee relationship, there is no way to erase the fact that the two are chromosomal opposites that nature fully intended not to remain aloof.

Is it invariably this way? Well, probably not. Some staunch souls manage to put their libidos on hold so effectively that they are as neutered as if they'd had surgery. But few are so inclined. Most men, whatever they may say about being above erotic thoughts between the hours of, say, nine and six, cannot coolly divide their days into a working segment and a wanting segment. They have spent their lives at various levels of lust for women (usually ranging from fairly high to way over the top) and this habit wouldn't be easy to break even if men zealously wanted to—which of course they zealously don't. The state of mind that makes Harry think about getting Sally into bed is about as automatic as being red-headed or having musical talent, and even when rigorously suppressed (does your office have a cold shower?) it's buzzing away in there somewhere.

Usually, the effects of this incessant hum are subtle. A man who works for a woman isn't likely to walk into her office wearing his tightest jeans and torn T-shirt, throw himself across the spreadsheets, and moan, "Take me, Ms. Foster . . . but be gentle." But primordial urges will out, in behavior ranging from puppy-dog stares to constant preening. The annoyance working women rightly feel at being seen as sex objects does not show up among men. A young man who worked for a woman executive at a cosmetics company complained to me that he was treated so unexceptionally by his boss and his all-female colleagues that he began to feel like furniture. "If anything, they were too accepting of my presence," he said. "They talked about their boyfriends and husbands as if I were one of them. After a while, all I wanted was to be treated like an adorable bimbo."

As I've mentioned earlier in the book, flirtation is as native to the workplace as complaining. I'd be the last to call for its eradication; first of all, it couldn't be done, and second, the workday is quite drab enough without any further loss of small pleasures. But when a man can't lighten up when he's around the woman he's supposed to be working for, he can make himself *and* his boss miserable. Firing someone like this can be worse than a messy divorce.

But much as a woman might want to avoid such a situation—

innocent as she may be of flirting to make things more amusing just for the sheer instinctual hell of it—conditioning will conspire against her. After all, being attractive is second nature for a woman. She'll wear clothes and makeup that make her more appealing, not to be provocative, of course (heaven forbid!), but because it feels great to look terrific. The trouble is, a man, even if he knows it's absolutely inappropriate to look at his boss with anything but cool professionalism, will go quietly crazy when she walks in looking like a million. And if her natural inclination to be attractive doesn't dazzle the poor guy, her abilities probably will. Despite much theorizing about men being threatened by capable women, the truth is that some men—the best of the breed, at least—are excited by a woman who can play serious tennis, drive a car with cool precision, choreograph a winning sales presentation, or conceive a brilliant ad campaign.

The better a woman is at what she does, the more likely a man working for her will start casting longing glances when all she wants him to do is run off ten copies of her meeting agenda. There's really not much men and women can do about the attraction and admiration factors, unless they're willing to make themselves as plain as possible and try hard not to excel. But when hiring a man, a woman could do worse than look for someone she feels absolutely no interest in, with the hope that if she's not tempted she'll send out no unconscious signals that prompt unconscionable responses. It's not a very exciting idea, but then that's the whole point.

Some years ago, a man I know was hired by a top woman executive to be her second-in-command. Since his competitors for the job were all better qualified, he suspected that she found him attractive and thought it might be amusing to have him around. His boss was a woman habitually coquettish with men (though happily married and apparently faithful to her husband), and she had a way of always being slightly seductive. My friend, busily making himself appealing, never really managed to understand that despite the traditional male/female interplay this was his boss. Needless to say, the job didn't work out, since she interpreted his attitude as a form of patronizing, which, of course, it was.

But even if no overtones of allure creep into the working relationship of a woman employer with the man or men who work for her, the situation isn't greatly simplified. Men are liable to worry excessively when attraction *isn't* part of the mix. James may be a dead ringer for Woody Allen, and his boss may not be the kind of woman he'd ever approach at a party, but he'll wonder *why* there's nothing going on, then become very boring trying to work up a little chemistry just for the sake of form. A certain strain can arise simply because there's not even a slight edge of sexual tension between a boss and the man with whom she spends most of her days.

As for the conditioning, despite considerable change, the same old problems persist. Some men—and some women, too—still feel, if only subconsciously, that the natural order of things places men in the position to wield ultimate executive power in business. Since more and more women are rising through the managerial ranks, it might seem that such retrograde thinking is on the decline. Yet for all the women at the middle level, the top echelons of Fortune 500 corporations remain mostly male. When a woman is running a company, more often than not it's a company she started. What this reveals, I suspect, is the inclinations (and disinclinations) of corporate boards, also predominantly male. A college administrator on the West Coast who serves on the boards of three corporations generally considered enlightened told me that women are rarely suggested when the boards are considering very high-level appointments. "It's not like we're a bunch of old boys sitting around complaining about uppity feminists," he says. "Most of our wives have careers of their own, after all. But somehow, when we're looking for a new CEO or top financial officer, no woman's name is ever brought up. I think maybe everybody privately figures it will just complicate everything." Curiously, he points out that two of the three boards he is on have women members who seem willing to go along with the practice of tacit exclusion.

Though I don't want to indulge too lavishly in mom-and-pop psychology, a certain automatic deference can be found even in women who daily give orders to men. The western regional sales manager for a Silicon Valley computer company told me, with an ironic smile, that she never takes the wheel when she and her husband are driving anywhere together. Though she denies showing similar deference to the men who work for her, it seems at least possible that her style might be less assertive than the kind of forcefulness men define as "clarity."

Even after the dramatic changes of the seventies and eighties, men and women tend to expect a certain traditional decorum from one another, a decorum that lets boys be boys and requires girls to be sugar and spice and everything nice. Whether it's biology or conditioning or both, lots of men have grown up playing with GI Joe "action figures" and lots of women have grown up with Barbie and My Little Pony. To hope for a fundamental change anytime soon is probably to suffer ongoing disappointment, or a continuation of the unhappy phenomenon of women behaving like men in order to succeed. Rather, declaring *Vive la différence*—and living by that wise acceptance—may be the best solution to reaching a new working relationship between men and women. A publisher in his early thirties admits that it's taken a certain amount of time and training to develop an ability to work well with women. "I've spent most of my career working for women," he says, "as have many men in publishing, since women have achieved an importance in this business unequaled in any other profession. It was an adjustment for me, but it was liberating as well, because for better or worse I don't feel as competitive with women as I do with men."

A woman might be forgiven for deciding that much trouble could be avoided if she just didn't hire men, or found a way to sidestep jobs that require giving them orders. A man would *not* be forgiven for thinking that she might be right. Men still have a lot to learn about working for women, just as many women still have to find a way to get comfortable with the role of top dog (with its unfair risk of being labeled a bitch). But neither sex can learn the new workplace choreography (that minuet with a faint echo of the lambada) if they don't ever get a chance to practice. A reasonable woman with more pride of professionalism than hunger for power may not feel much like adding to her burdens the role of pioneer boss lady. And an evolved man may still be reluctant about taking the time and trouble to decipher the new signals and sensibilities working for a woman requires. But somebody has to do it.

21

The Big Knife

the bloody, boring,

ubiquitous business of

in-house infighting

*I*f what follows has never happened to you, count yourself among the blessed. If it has, I apologize in advance for recalling a moment of pure dread.

You're in a bar. Not a polite place filled with happily chattering young professionals, but slightly tougher turf, somewhere you haven't been before. You go to make a phone call, and when you come back your stool has been taken by a man who has pushed your unfinished drink aside. You size up the situation: the interloper is on the small side, you've been working out regularly, and anyway, who the hell does this guy think he is?

A few uncordial words are exchanged, a civil settlement is obviously out of the question, and you anticipate the ritual step-by-step escalation of hostilities you've been accustomed to since your first schoolyard confrontation. "Oh yeah?" "Yeah!" "Oh yeah? Whaddya gonna doaboudit?" And so on, until everybody's anger winds down, or a few face-saving shoves are exchanged and the bartender buys you both a drink. But when the other guy comes off the barstool, you look into his eyes and realize, with a sinking feeling, that he's not at all reluctant to get into it with you—in fact, he can't wait. His expression tells you two things you'd just as soon not know: that he couldn't care less if he gets hurt, and that putting his fists into the pleasingly formed features of decent, in-the-right citizens like you is his idea of a great time. There are various ways to end this scene (though a negotiated resolution, alas, is not among them), but let's leave before it gets ugly. (If the preceding is too macho to apply to you, there are feminine versions, less incipiently violent, perhaps, but no less unpleasant.)

The point is simply this: some people relish a good fight, and like a bad one even better. They are not always sitting on your barstool—maybe you only go to places as cozy as Cheers—but are just as likely to be in the next office, or across the table in the conference room. And while you—a high-minded team player, let's assume—plan ways to beat the competition on the level playing fields of free enterprise, these office infighters are plotting a hundred crooked ways to do you in. Such bastard colleagues may be even worse than bastard bosses, because they're more likely to masquerade as friends and compatriots.

Aggression is in the air; it was to the eighties what love was to the sixties, and though the nineties have made tough-guy chic seem out of fashion, the ethos of kill-or-be-killed has no more vanished from the office than it has from the NFL. The In-Yo'-Face generation that grew up in the Reagan years, bent on destruction whenever anybody got in the way, is still very much with us (or, in most cases, against us). Witness an advertisement for tennis shoes that ran in men's magazines sometime in 1990, shoes designed for "players who would rather dish it out than be on the receiving end." The copy went on to caution that the wearer of these mean sneaks will have to be patient, while his opponent "checks his gut."

Gosh, what ever happened to such courtly court chat as "Nice shot, Ted! The drinks are on me"? But perhaps if aggression could be limited to good old American unsportsmanlike conduct—the hockey-style fouls routinely committed on NBA basketball players shooting lay-ups, for instance—we could leave meanness and mayhem to the pros and go about our business at work without constantly having to look over our shoulders. But don't get your hopes up.

The fight-or-flight anxiety brought on by our suspicion that certain co-workers would gladly see us facedown in the gutter was illustrated with grim accuracy in a recent series of AT&T television ads in which some poor soul's failure to buy the right telephone system has the office sharks circling, waiting for the inevitable bloody end. What's so remarkable about the ads is the implication that the hapless comrade, having made himself vulnerable by making a mistake, pretty much deserves to be set upon by his colleagues and done in. Of course, the aim of the ads is to instill fear of what might happen if you fail to use AT&T, and the target audience is made up of anxious decision makers, not office assassins. But the message can only be effective if we feel real fear that someone close to us is just waiting for one miscue to make his or her move.

Despite the hopeful impression that the nineties are sure to bring about some sort of bucolic interlude after the past decade's one-for-one-and-all-for-me ferocity, increased global competition in many businesses and tough economic realities in general seem unlikely to make hostility history any time soon.

Like the wording and mood of the AT&T ads and similar Madison Avenue fearmongering, the language of work today is indicative of how business is done. Where once sports terms were the standard clichés—hitting the long ball, going one-on-one, all the right moves, drop back and punt, and so on—now the terminology of warfare dominates: in the trenches, take no prisoners, search and destroy, and other pleasantries of the battlefield. It's no longer enough for a company to outmaneuver a rival, they have to "blow them out of the water," or "waste the bastards." And if skirmishes between rival advertising agencies or computer manufacturers aren't exactly Desert Storm, still there's a lot of bloodlust out there.

You got a problem with that, pal? After all, as a certain hard core of our colleagues sees it, there's a lot of competition, just so much time to make it big, and a finite number of dollars to go around. If the price of getting more than your fair share is behaving like Attila the Hun, they figure, so be it; business has always been a dog-eat-dogfight, anyway, and sometimes the veneer of euphemism wears thin and the clash of combat is heard. The problem is, the actions that follow warlike words tend to be indiscriminate, and that rabid cur clamped onto your ankle (and gnawing its way north) may not be an outside competitor, but someone you thought was on your side. Forget working together against the common enemy—ferocity begins at home. To dedicated infighters, everyone is an enemy.

There are all sorts of reasons for this, most of them well known and chronic: territoriality, ambition, insecurity, revenge, or just plain killer instinct. Rationalization is easy: "Hey, if I hadn't put the idiot out of his misery, somebody else would have." And retribution is rare. But just because evolution often grants survival to the meanest, and treachery isn't invariably a fast track to poverty, the act of going for a compatriot's throat is not okay. Infighting is bad business, and bad *for* business. It diverts energy from the good fight of competition, erodes morale, wastes time, gets good people fired while elevating those with a natural inclination to hit low, and exacerbates the Peter Principle by putting street fighters in jobs where the requisite skill is managing, not mangling.

But deploring infighting will never make it go away, any more than high-minded condemnation of warfare has brought about world peace. Perhaps through a flaw in human design, what Arthur Koestler called "the ghost in the machine," whenever three or more are gathered together in the name of profit, at least one will be plotting to destroy at least one of the others. Try to think, just for a minute, of any working situation you've ever experienced that wasn't complicated by internecine conflict, where someone wasn't trying to pump you for inside information, enlist you in a plot against someone else, or put *you* on ice. If you're in such an uncombative job now, have it bronzed, because chances are you'll never see its like again.

As with all other forms of strife, infighting rises and falls in intensity without ever actually going away. Usually, it's at its worst during economic hard times, when people may be quick to defend their piece of diminishing turf by launching preemptive attacks on co-workers. But good times are not necessarily safe. Though the eighties would seem to have been bullish enough to bring about a general truce, a new factor heated up interoffice conflict: mergers. The fact that the word resembles "murders" is only coincidental, but it provides a handy mnemonic device should you be working for a company that is bought by another and you're curious about what the future holds. When two companies are joined, the standard corporate thinking is simple: If revenue is expanded automatically by virtue of the pairing and overhead is cut, profit increases without any effort to expand market share. It's magic! All management has to do is fire lots of people and get the rest to do more work. Below decks there's carnage, because infighters understand instantly that if they are to keep their jobs, others must go.

The nineties have been tougher sledding than the eighties so far, and will probably stay tough even with economic recovery. Even though the funding for takeovers has dwindled with the collapse of the junk bond market (Michael Milken's mystical Monopoly money), thus easing off the infighting caused by the game of corporate musical chairs, shakeouts in many industries and recession in others have continued to bring out the blades in many formerly congenial environments.

Conventional wisdom holds that when a goal becomes important enough, infighting is put aside and everybody pulls together for the greater good. Certainly that would make sense. But you have to look very hard to find real examples of such noble behavior. The Greeks squabbled for years while supposedly united against the Trojans and thousands of years later fought each other bitterly while resisting the Nazi occupation. The Normans sacked friendly, co-religionist Constantinople on their way to battle the enemies of Christendom. And Patton and Montgomery battled each other with as much determination as they displayed against the Third Reich.

Struggles on a larger front, even for great, historical purposes, mysteriously fail to satisfy a born infighter's limitless appetite for personal confrontation. In the Ridley Scott film *The Duelists*, Harvey Keitel portrayed just such a fracas freak, an officer in Napoleon's army who challenges a fellow officer to a duel for some perceived affront and, in the respites between famous battles, keeps trying to kill him. Keitel's brilliantly malevolent characterization evokes the illogical, implacable fury of the bad guy on the barstool, someone you wish you'd never gotten started with and who won't take "uncle" for an answer.

Let me emphasize that I'm not talking about somebody who likes to get into a little sporting face-off once in a while, then backs off with a laugh when things start to get serious. A classic infighter simply doesn't know when to stop, and will stop at nothing as long as there's a target of opportunity left standing. The Marquis of

Queensbury is not on his Rolodex, just the Marquis de Sade, so the concept of foul play or fair becomes irrelevant, putting at a considerable disadvantage those with ethics and a capacity to be ashamed of dirty tricks. In John DeLorean's autobiography, the former Detroit whiz kid describes a tactic repeatedly used by some of his colleagues at Ford. The ploy involved digging up some obscure piece of information about the operation of another man's department and then finding a way to bring the subject up during an administrative meeting. If the man wasn't instantly familiar with the details (which he probably wouldn't be) the trickster helpfully supplied them, thus implying that he knew more about his victim's job than the department head himself. As DeLorean points out, a cheap trick. But the ability to be a party to such lowjinks and still sleep solidly each night is what marks the naturally gifted infighter.

If "gifted" seems too lofty a word, consider the talents an infighter must display in addition to innate ruthlessness and bloodlust. He or she needs: absolute dedication, since bringing down hard-working, blameless colleagues often demands sustained focus; an actor's ability to project sincerity when seeking the confidence of a victim; great discretion, since infighters never fully reveal their plots even to those they involve in them (thus holding on to deniability even after they have won); a chessplayer's ability to look several moves ahead and anticipate defenses and counterplots; and a perverse purity of spirit strong enough to remain free of doubts and self-recrimination while making bad things happen to good (but unwary) people. Altogether, a rare and formidable arsenal.

Is there anything more annoying than loathing someone and being forced to admire them at the same time? When I see some office shark devour a poor fish (or even a fellow predator) after a meticulously planned and executed maneuver, I'm reluctantly filled with awe for a talent beyond my comprehension. For me, it's like watching someone do a front flip on a high wire or juggle five teacups—not only can't I imagine how such a thing is done, I can't begin to envision the path that led someone to the point of being able to do it. The energy needed to think about all elements in a fight, whether you're winning or losing, is something that few people are willing to expend (which is one of the things that gives infighters an advantage over those who can't be bothered to give their all to ignoble causes).

For instance, when a magazine editor I know, a canny and relentless infighter, lost her job in a much publicized struggle with her publisher, media watchers reported that their long-running squabble had been about professional ethics, namely whether the editor or the publisher would make final editorial decisions. Though I was surprised to see this veteran plotter finally take a fall, it seemed she'd won the moral victory. Though her years of competitive ferocity had left her with few friends, overnight she gained a shining reputation as a stand-up woman ready to sacrifice herself for what she believed in. Only later, after she had landed a far better job (said reputation being a salable commodity) did I discover that the struggle hadn't been about principles at all, but that the editor—characteristically—had been trying to undercut the publisher's position with top management simply to increase her own power. Outgunned for once, she still managed to orchestrate the situation through rumors and press leaks ("I really don't have any statement to make, but . . .") to put the best possible coloration on her comeuppance.

Such Clausewitzian ingenuity is simply more demanding than most working stiffs can find the time and energy for. Or, for that matter, the creativity. But an infighter has to give generously of all three. Nothing can be neglected; sweating the details is a given when you're living by the sword—or at least the dagger—and don't want to die by it.

Those who bemoan infighting's pointless diversion of everyone else's energy may figure that management—given a chance—will step in to make peace. Sometimes this will happen, either because top executives are enlightened and realize the company stands to suffer (don't hold your breath), or because they worry that the likely winner may come after them next. But often, those safely above the fray may actually encourage death struggles among the lower orders. In management courses, where euphemism is a fine art, this is called "creative tension." The stated goal is to heighten intramural competition and thus sharpen company performance, but the real purpose is to keep lean and hungry types so busy with peer bashing that the sanctity of the executive suite isn't threatened.

When top executives begin warring among themselves, the effect on companies can be disastrous. Like onlookers at the Battle of Gettysburg, employees gather to witness the spectacle and profit-

able activity grinds to a halt. Often much of the pleasure in ob-
serving high-level shootouts is the reminder that the same
desperate, black hat tactics apply no matter how far up the ladder
one has scrambled. When the publisher of the *Chicago Sun-Times*
lost a power struggle to his chief financial officer a while back, one
of the directors of the paper's parent company smiled innocently
and called the departure a "friendly parting." But as the story of the
infighting emerged, friendliness didn't seem to fit anywhere into
the picture. The two combatants had apparently been keeping logs
of one another's activities, and the CFO had managed to convince
the company's chairman to oust two of the publisher's allies, no
doubt indicating to the publisher that the handwriting on the wall
was in blood . . . *his* blood. Newspaper employees learned of the
loser's departure from a press release, though dispatches from the
front had preoccupied everyone for months. The public usually
gets the story when the loser writes a book, which, these days, the
loser always does.

And so it goes, with freshly honed blades glinting in every
shadow between the coffee machine and oblivion. If you want to
work without the petty annoyances and major anxieties induced by
infighting, may I suggest a career in lighthouse keeping (though
surely somebody in the maritime section of the Interior Department would probably be out to get you). Otherwise, you have to
learn to live with the daily threat of some in-house duelist making
you his target of opportunity and school yourself on how to live
through it.

There are ways. Not many, and none that are guaranteed; just a
few simple methods for assessing situations, evading those that
offer a high risk of disaster, and holding your own in the fights you
can't duck.

• Listen for the rumor of war. Personally, I have always sub-
scribed to the theory that halcyon times in the workplace tend to be
temporary; if everybody's smiling, just wait, the worst is yet to
come. When the scuttlebutt hints of merger, cutbacks, "downsiz-
ing," a big account or two lost, a shiny new "management team,"
even a steady drop in stock, keep your eyes open (especially the
eyes in the back of your head).

• Identify potential killers. This can be tricky, since serious
infighters don't wear T-shirts that read, "So many throats, so little

time." It's a good idea to start the ID scan as soon as you take a new job, or whenever someone new arrives on the scene. Certain signs are tipoffs. Likely suspects tend to be as interested in other people's work as in their own, and may be noticeably skilled in such intelligence-gathering techniques as upside-down reading (just watch those eyes when they're standing across your desk) and the getting-to-know-you-to-get-enough-rope-to-hang-you drink (a.k.a. the three-martini lynch). A co-worker's tendency to be very friendly in private but cool when others are around, especially the boss, may be a form of social awkwardness or mild schizophrenia, but it's safer to take it as a sign of possible danger.

• Estimate enemy strength. Though there's no precise measure for the malevolence of infighters—at least not before the battle is joined—their abilities in a fight are often in inverse proportion to their abilities on the job. If someone seems to have risen high on limited talent but isn't related to the boss, it's safe to assume the ascendancy is due either to dumb luck, great charm, or evil deeds. Never dismiss a potential threat just because he or she seems too insignificant to be ferocious; keep in mind that pound for pound the weasel, not the tiger, is the fiercest animal on earth.

• Look for high ground in neutral territory. Switzerland, a mountainous land that counts its bullion while other nations count their bullets, has done quite well for itself staying out of fights, and ought to be a model for us all. Work hard, take care of business, and try to get things to go your way without confrontations (even if Chapter 18 has made you think an occasional confrontation might be a nice change of pace). Above all, avoid any expression or appearance of vulnerability; infighters instinctively attack the slow and the weak. Do not, for instance, confide in anyone but a blood relation that you just screwed up royally, that you sometimes get the feeling that the old man doesn't like you, or that you'd probably be better off without this stinking job.

• Calculate the odds. When you've had it up to here with that aggressive little creep Brackish, think hard about what you have going for you in a pitched battle. Has he been spoiling for a fight? If so, watch out; seasoned infighters rarely go into action unless they've got at least a 99 percent chance of winning. Should an infighter outrank you, you'll need serious ordnance to stand any chance—maybe hard evidence of embezzlement or videotape of a cross-dressing party—and recent history indicates neither of those may be damning enough. Management tends to side with the person who's the most expensive to fire (or contributes in profits more than he steals . . . remember David Begelman?).

• Be prepared to do your personal worst. If, no matter how you try to avoid it, the office thug decides it's time to step outside, forget anything you ever learned in Cub Scouts about fighting fair. When the action starts, good infighters are bad, bad people, and if you're not ready to hit low, lie, spread rumors, leak damning information to the business pages, ruin reputations, go public with the smallest enemy infraction, and be so mean your mother would disown you . . . well, you'd better go quietly. Subscribe to the credo "Better dead than ill bred" and you're a definite goner. Getting the best of an infighter may not be a job that brings out the best in you, but keep telling yourself that you're doing it for a better tomorrow. And don't be embarrassed to ask for help from somebody ready to do what needs to be done. If it makes you feel any better, just remember that in *High Noon*, Gary Cooper won the big showdown only because Grace Kelly shot somebody in the back.

22

The Toady Ascendant

beware of those

sucking their way up

the ladder of success

*B*ehold the toady: ubiquitous, sly, infinitely sensitive to the slightest atmospheric shifts, able to change colors with a speed that would make a chameleon blush, as malleable as Silly Putty (and just as useless), universally loathed yet capable of thriving under conditions that destroy more admirable souls. Study the toady well; he or she is a genius in matters of survival and will do anything—and do in anyone, including you—in pursuit of the ancient art of upward servility.

By any other name—suck-up, yes-man, running dog, ass-kisser—the toady is a creature of eminently bad odor with a lugubrious history stretching as far back as the most rudimentary power structures. Can there be any doubt that every Stone Age tribe had at least one self-aggrandizer who grunted and leapt in admiration every time the chief broke wind? The term "toady" itself dates to the Middle Ages, when it was used to describe charlatans' flunkies

193

who, in order to prove the curative powers of their bosses, would pretend to eat toads believed to be poisonous, then make miraculous recoveries.

Clearly, popping a toad into one's mouth, or even pretending to, was not a job for anyone with a normal ration of self-respect. Thus, the very first practitioners established the Toady Code: There is nothing, no matter how unappetizing or demeaning, a toady won't do to make the boss happy. That tenet remains as solid now as it was on the day some medieval groveler smacked his lips and declared, "Zounds, oh great and magnificent wizard, thou hast the tastiest toads in the land!"

Toadies have proved more durable than the magicians who first gave them work, and they've never gone out of fashion as objects of scorn, especially in literature. The cast of characters is long and richly undistinguished, ranging from Lucifer (who was, after all, God's right-hand apple-polisher until he became too ambitious), to the despicable Grima Wormtongue in J.R.R. Tolkien's *The Lord of the Rings*. Perhaps no character symbolizes toadyism better than Shakespeare's Polonius, energetically accommodating Hamlet while at the same time currying favor with the king by hatching plots against the morose prince. The play's quintessential toady moment is worth quoting, since it sums up a classic yes-man's shameless agility:

> HAMLET: *Do you see yonder cloud that's almost in shape of a camel?*
> POLONIUS: *By the mass, and 'tis like a camel, indeed.*
> HAMLET: *Methinks it is like a weasel.*
> POLONIUS: *It is backed like a weasel.*
> HAMLET: *Or like a whale?*
> POLONIUS: *Very like a whale.*

The old smoothie comes to a bad end, of course, as did Lucifer, Wormtongue, and most of the famous toadies of literature. If only it were so. One of the reasons we often prefer books to real life is that things work out better on paper. In actuality, toadies rarely get their comeuppances, for reasons that I will labor to explain shortly.

Into every business life some toadies must come. Typically, they appear quite early in one's career and continue showing up in some form or another (both public and private) until the very end. The first evidence of their presence may be a sibling's whining threat, "You better not or I'll tell Mommy." Later, toadyism appears in the person of a grade-school classmate whose hand is always flailing the air as you struggle to think of an answer to the teacher's damnable question. An unforgettable, unforgivable voice accompanies the hand: "Please, Mrs. Cohen, I know the answer!" Then, all of a sudden, it's twenty years later, and though the words change, the sweaty self-aggrandizement stays the same. "Well, gee, Bob, I think what J.B. is saying—correct me if I'm wrong here, boss—is just that *some* of us don't seem to be doing all we can to land the Framster account."

If you work in an office, no matter how small, the odds are that a toady is at work there, too. It's the Law of Toady Inevitability. The presence of a power hierarchy of any kind spawns the pests through a kind of spontaneous generation. It's as if there's a toady slot in every organization, and somebody has to fill it. Of course, some people take on the job with a notable gusto that marks them as True Toadies, a club about as desirable as a leper colony but never short of volunteers.

Toadies vary in size, gender, plumage, and methodology, but they all behave in certain characteristic ways that make them recognizable. Invariably, their actions are guided by a rapt concentration on the men or women who hold power. Just as a sailor sharpens his senses to understand and anticipate the wind, a toady will strive to attune himself utterly to the mood and the desires of the boss. The toady's determination to become one with Number One is the closest thing to pure Zen in modern American office life. An example of this phenomenon is the Toady Transformation, an instant change that takes place whenever power enters a room. Almost magically, the toady will manage to distance himself from his colleagues, however chummy he was just seconds before, and will somehow give the impression that he'd only been talking with these people at all to keep them from degenerating into the rebellious slackers they naturally are.

The transformation takes place no matter what the toady is saying or doing at any given moment. I remember my wonderment at a Time Inc. meeting some years ago when a fairly infamous corporate toady who had been complaining bitterly about the hopelessness of our fearless leader leapt to his feet when the boss entered the room, broke into a smile that was, frankly, terrible to behold, and exclaimed, "Hey, boss, *great suit!*"

An unmistakable mark of the toady is a complete lack of embarrassment about doing this sort of thing. Embarrassment is a function of ego, and ego (as opposed to overriding ambition) is a luxury the toady cannot afford. The transformation is so complete that a toady literally loses any self to be embarrassed for and without a hint of discomfort will do and say things that cause those around him to wince and shudder. No compliment for or about the boss is too florid, no hype too overblown. When a young upward striver at the Housing and Urban Development Department in Washington, the blond, formidably obsequious Deborah Gore Dean, sent a memo to a colleague describing the notably inept (and possibly felonious) housing secretary Samuel R. Pierce, she wrote of his having the "dedication, insight, relevance, intelligence, charm, strength, sophistication and fortitude of a great leader." Besides a reputation for dispensing lavish patronage, Ms. Dean left behind a paper trail of thank-you notes to lobbyists and administration insiders that give a whole new high-fat meaning to the term "bread and butter letter."

Another way lackeys give themselves away is through their use of toadyspeak. Without a flicker of irony, a toady will refer to the Big Guy, el Jefe, the Man, Top Gun, even (I've heard this, I swear) the Brigadier. As a self-appointed sidekick (with or without portfolio) of the Man (even if the Man is a woman), a toady will devote much of his conversation with others to bossly concerns. "I really don't think the Big Guy's gonna go for that kind of sarcasm in a sales presentation." Or "I'd be careful with those long lunches, pal; the Chief really frowns on that kind of thing." And so forth.

When a toady offers friendship, it is almost always based on the implication that closeness to him is the same as closeness to the boss, and his idea of a favor usually has to do with imparting some secret to help you glean some small part of the favor he already enjoys. A woman on the rise at a major Manhattan investment bank, on receiving a summons to an audience with the top man the next day, was visited by the office toady, who leaned close, looked left and then right, then said, "Make sure to wear a dress. Mr. D likes women in frilly stuff. But for God's sake don't wear yellow. He really hates yellow." In a calculated display of antitoady behavior (a reaction not untypical for decent people) she appeared the next day in her best canary-colored silk suit and now—ostensibly for other reasons—fights the good fight at another company. (The lesson here is clear: Toadies work hard at their studies and are rarely wrong about the foibles of the rich and powerful.)

An important subsection to the Law of Toady Inevitability is the Rule of Toady Distribution. Since toadies are attracted to power—can only be toadies when there's someone worthy of their groveling—it follows that the greater the number of managers, the greater the number of toadies. For this reason, most major corporations are veritable fawning halls, while smaller organizations may scrape by on only one or two bona fide bootlickers. But whatever the numbers, toady distribution remains steady at a maximum density of one per power center. Toadies do not gather in prides (or should that be "shames"?) since they're highly territorial, fiercely protective of their hard-won subservience, and tend not to like one another (though sometimes when a toady becomes important enough, he'll have his own toady). This mutual antipathy has nothing to do with the kind of sensible distaste the rest of us feel for them, but simply the fact that the only natural enemy of a toady is another toady who might get even closer to the honcho. The good news is that once you have identified the toady in your immediate area, you've probably found the only one around. The bad news is that there are usually toadies-in-waiting, so even if the presiding ass-kisser comes to grief (a rare and wonderful event), the spot won't go unfilled for long. Sometimes the new toady turns out to be a person who loudly deplored the vile habits of his predecessor, proving that the urge to curry favor dwells deep in even the most seemingly blameless souls.

Alas, the Law of Toady Distribution is not immutable, and in certain cases it is modified by the fact that toadies love a vacuum, and fill it in whatever numbers are required. When, for instance, a high-level job is held by someone so dictatorial and jealous of his or her power that all subordinates with real ability, individuality, and any hint of ambition are routinely purged (management in the Saddam Hussein style), a circle of sycophants almost invariably forms around the Great One, squabbling among themselves for the kowtowing rights. Companies (and countries) run this way don't often survive for very long, so if you find yourself ousted for a toady along with the best and brightest of your colleagues, take the severance and run. (Gatherings of toadies can occur in less elevated circumstances, as in the entourages of lightweight movie stars or heavyweight champions—but one will inevitably end up as top crawler.)

A note here on a couple of other specimens who may exhibit toadylike characteristics but are not actually toadies. The first is the Complete Loyalist. Once known as the company man, the Loyalist believes unswervingly in the organization and never questions anything it does or anybody who wields its authority (see Chapter 25). Sometimes Loyalists appear ready to do anything to please or protect the boss, but this is just because the boss represents the company. Dan Quayle is a Complete Loyalist, and—in convincing mimicry of toady behavior—protective of his boss and himself in almost equal measure. When confronted by Ted Koppel on "Nightline" with a poll indicating that a high percentage of Americans would feel uncomfortable with him as president, Quayle quite smoothly said that he was sure any American would express discomfort at the suggestion that anything might happen to as great a president as George Bush, but that should such an unthinkable thing take place he was sure people would feel good about him. (In fairness, the vice presidency has become an office for loyalists-cum-lackeys—witness Hubert Humphrey espousing Lyndon Johnson's Vietnam policy despite his own misgivings, Gerald Ford pardoning his former boss, Richard Nixon, and George Bush saluting Reagan policies he'd called "voodoo economics" before he became America's foremost second banana.)

Closer in spirit to the toady, but still not the real thing, is the hero-worshiper, a cryptocultist who elevates someone—and it might just as well be the boss, after all—in answer to some sort of religious impulse. That the hero who is worshiped may not be worthy is beside the point: the act of veneration and the resulting simplicity it gives to life are what matters—the world divides up neatly into what's good for the boss and what isn't. When one of Oliver North's tireless helpers ended his appearance before the Iran-Contra hearings by reciting a poem he'd written to North (in heroic couplets, if I recall correctly), we might have assumed we were seeing a blatant toady show. Yet it was clear by this peculiar act of public veneration that the man was absolutely sincere, and sincerity is one thing a toady is never guilty of.

The true toady feels no loyalty to person or company; his sole concern is looking out for Number Two. If the boss gets canned or the company goes down, the toady wastes no time shedding tears, just tries to land on his feet in a place with some useful big shots and a good bonus package. In fact, because of their highly developed sense of self-preservation, toadies can be useful as early warnings of trouble, like the canaries that miners used to carry with them into coal shafts. In a time of corporate streamlining and an unsettled economy, with resulting management shake-ups, if you happen to notice the office toady Xeroxing his or her résumé, it may be time to bring yours up to date.

Why are toadies allowed to flourish? How can someone whose major contribution to the cause is "Hey, boss, great suit!" move in and move up? It's an obvious question, though you won't like the answer. Toadies thrive because people in power like to have them around. Historians are fond of noting that the Romans pressed slaves into service to whisper into the ears of the Caesars that they, too, were mortal—an excellent practice, though not always very effective. But history does not note an instance when one of those bad-news bearers ended up with a cushy job in the government. What boss really wants to be told he's no different from everybody else, that he puts on his Guccis one at a time like the rest of us, that he's even capable of being wrong? With the beginning of each new administration in Washington, well-meaning presidents invariably bring in someone whose purpose, they announce, is to level with them, to tell them when they're getting puffed up or losing sight of their high purpose. Just as invariably, the designated wet blanket ends up farther and farther down the hall from the Oval Office, until he's forgotten altogether and quietly slouches off to a tenured professorship somewhere far outside the Beltway.

Perhaps only a saint or a masochist (is there a difference?) could feel much affection for someone who comes into the office every day and says, "Chief, you blew it again." Constant negativity is a drag, let's face it. So although anybody with any sense of reality is going to be suspicious of the character who minces in with a daily serving of "Sir, once again I marvel at the elegance of your thinking," it's hard not to be warmed by such sentiments even when uttered by someone who would lick the lint off your blazer if you gave the word. From earliest childhood, we are conditioned to like hearing nice things said about ourselves, and toadies simply supply what most of us go on demanding no matter how tough-minded and realistic we may think we are.

The eighties proved to be a boom time for toadies. When ambition is unskeptically honored and money is the highest priority, people are less apt to condemn any tactic employed for getting ahead. Toadying may even take on a certain legitimacy, as in "Hey, did you hear Snidely telling the boss what a great photographer he is? Smart guy." Such ingratiating achievers as Barbara Walters (who, in a 1990 interview with the American-born queen of Jordan, must have lovingly used the term "Your Majesty" a world-record number of times), Robin Leach, and Ed McMahon have added a show biz gloss to the form's always questionable status. (The holy icon of show biz toadyism is the infamous photograph of Sammy Davis, Jr., hugging an astonished Richard Nixon.) A sure sign of the continued vigor of High Toadyism into the nineties is the success of Arsenio Hall, whose gush sessions with celebrity guests on his late-night talk show might have made Polonius squirm. (Poor Polonius. If only he'd been doing his self-serving nefarious work in our time, he'd have ended up with a corner office and seven figures instead of a rapier through the gullet.)

Assuming a toady is leaving a trail of slime through your office as you read this, what can you do about it? Sadly, not much, short of taking out a contract with someone who looks like three Danny DeVitos. Toadies are tough and tenacious, and they are usually actively engaged in making someone important very happy. Trying to bring one down, though a righteous endeavor, is often more dangerous than the pleasure of success may be worth. Beware of going one-on-one with a groveler in top form. Even if you win (by no means a likely result), the fearless leader is going to bear a grudge about losing a flatterer—unless you step into the role, of course, which you surely wouldn't do. Would you?

At one time or another, most of us are confronted by a Toady Moment of Untruth. The boss calls you into his office, shows you a second-rate design (or whatever) that you happen to know he really likes, and asks your opinion. At this significant juncture, you can (1) tell the truth, (2) feign a severe leg cramp, (3) say what he wants to hear. If you do either of the first two, you may be putting yourself in jeopardy or just putting off an inevitable decision, but you are not toadying. Even if you choose the third you may still be able to evade the moral sinkhole. Let's face it, playing death-before-dishonor if a situation isn't that important may be the principled thing to do, but may not make a lot of sense. So if you answer, "Well, Mr. Perkins, it's probably not the best thing we've done, but I think your opinion is the one that matters here," you can tell yourself that you're really only respectfully acknowledging the boss's greater experience while evading his ire.

But know that you've reached the outer boundary of self-respect. And if you should happen to take a deep breath and say, "Mr. Perkins, this kind of design is the reason certain people in this business think of you as a living legend," then you've swallowed your first toad. It leaves a terrible aftertaste, I suspect, but beware, it's a diet some people actually come to crave.

23

The Fine Art of Kicking Ass

making people do their

jobs—or else!—is

sometimes the toughest

job of all

*A*t the height of the high-rolling days of the Trump Organization, I spent an afternoon with Blanche Sprague, one of the company's top executives at the time, in an effort to find out what made the place tick so profitably. As we were leaving her office in one of the buildings managed by her division, a young man wearing the dark livery of the residential staff approached and handed her an envelope, saying, in a cheerful tone, "This just came for you, Blanche." Without reaching for the piece of paper he held out, she stared hard at him for a few seconds. Then, very quietly—I wasn't meant to overhear—she said, "Do you always call people by their first names?" The young man visibly straightened. "I'm sorry, Mrs. Sprague." She then took the envelope, thanked him, and we went on.

Not a very dramatic confrontation—not a confrontation at all, really. But a significant moment, nevertheless. Because what I was seeing was that ever rarer phenomenon, the meaningful reprimand. In a small but unmistakable way, an executive was practicing the honorable craft of kicking ass. Yeah, sure, you may be saying to yourself. And maybe she was indulging in a little Hapless-Minion Abuse, too. (Don't deny it, the thought crossed your mind.) Leaving aside, for now, the complications that gender still injects into matters of hierarchy (see Chapter 20), the encounter ought to be seen as management at its straightforward best. Of course, to be set straight, even in a relatively mild way, couldn't have been pleasant for the young man—but imagine an alternative scenario: the boss doesn't say anything, just goes on letting the kid use her first name. The new employee notices a certain amount of tension, but figures he couldn't possibly be the reason. After all, she never complains about his work. Then when his review comes up, the peeved boss tells the personnel manager, "Charles doesn't really seem to fit in here," and suggests that he be let go. Out on the street, the kid can't figure out what went wrong. Is that better than a quick, briefly painful boot to the butt? I don't think so.

Yet it happens all the time. In modern life, the art of fan dancing is in better shape than the ability to demand accountability. Hardly anyone tells anyone else to shape the hell up, then takes the trouble to make sure they do. When the customer wants satisfaction, nobody's home. "Give me your supervisor," you growl at some bumbler at the other end of one of those where-am-I 800 numbers, and she sneers back, "I *am* the supervisor." If you think the vaunted "service economy" is going to make life better for us all, just wait until you need to work out a damage claim with UPS or, God forbid, the post office; after four or five fruitless phone calls, you'll be convinced that no one is in charge, when the fact is the people in charge simply don't know what being in charge means. As the confederacy of dunces grows and grows, the hopeless screwups of yesterday are the helpless managers of today.

But there I go, foaming at the mouth. Before I vanish beneath a sea of righteous froth, let me define just what I mean by kicking ass. Or at least what I don't mean. For instance, I don't mean the sort of public humiliation routinely practiced by tyrants who find grim satisfaction in making victims dance by shooting psychological bullets at their feet. (Such bastard bosses are dealt with—harshly enough, I hope—in Chapter 11.) Nor do I mean the by-the-book nitpicking of the office sergeant major, whose rigid insistence on often pointless details is the most dispiriting sort of management (and usually substitutes for useful work). And I don't mean the ritualistic demand for revisions indulged in by people who rule by formula and judge the quality of work by the amount of drudgery it represents.

What I do mean by kicking ass is neither unjust nor personal nor psychologically violent; it is simply the act of insisting that someone take responsibility for doing what they're supposed to do, letting it be known that if they don't there will be repercussions, and then having the guts to follow through. In a sense, it is an act of true managerial decency, a tutorial aimed at helping someone improve in the long run rather than just getting the employee, the manager, and the company through the day with a minimum of fuss. Since kicking ass isn't something that a good person ought to enjoy (well, maybe just a little), and doing it takes precious energy, the chore can only be seen as a form of noblesse oblige.

But these days, it seems, when someone needs calling to account they rarely hear about it. Perhaps, in our frantically litigious age, people are wary of arousing the ire of those whose work is unsatisfactory, and figure that it's better to let sleeping employees lie (or lying employees sleep). Perhaps the relentlessly simulated "niceness" of our advertising messages has sapped people's ability to get tough without getting furious. No doubt there are a thousand good excuses, but what we end up with is a working culture where the only people who ever seem to get mad are the customers. Once, in a San Francisco restaurant, I called the waitress over to ask why an order was taking so long. She sighed and said she really didn't know, as if she and I were in the same boat. I asked her to find out, but when she emerged from the kitchen she didn't return to my table. When I finally complained that waiting on me meant more than just taking an order and bringing the food, she exclaimed, "I don't *need* this!" and strode off.

The food finally did arrive, served by the restaurant manager, who, I speculated, must have sympathized with the waitress for having to deal with such a difficult patron. I told her, ever so civilly, that her waitress had a lot to learn about the standard rigors of the trade, and that legitimate complaints were a long way from abuse. Yes, yes, you're so right, she said, or well-minced words to that effect, as if *she* and I were in the same boat, too. But why did I think she wasn't ever going to say anything to her employee harsher than "Don't worry, dear, he was probably just having a bad day"? Maybe this management-as-therapy approach can be blamed on the touchy-feely folkways of northern California, where— sometimes, at least—employers seem to think they have to be un- swervingly nice to keep thin-skinned workers from wandering off to more supportive surroundings in which they feel good about themselves. (San Francisco, after all, is home to an organization that busies itself helping army recruits get out of their enlistments if they don't like basic training. Somehow, one suspects that likable basic training might not produce the kind of army you'd trust in some unpleasant situation like combat. "Hey, Captain, I don't *need* this!")

But the malaise is nationwide, and extends from the bottom to the top in managerial culture. What is simply annoying (if symp- tomatic) in a restaurant is pernicious and ultimately damaging in business both public and private. Feeble responses are the disorder of the day. When police in another West Coast city had reason to believe several murder victims were buried in the yard of a rooming house, they let the landlady—the main suspect—walk away un- tailed even after they had unearthed the first of several bodies. After she had disappeared, the chief of police couldn't bear to blame any of his Keystone Kops, putting together instead a semi- coherent excuse for everyone's lame performance: "There was not the weight of probable cause to make the arrest. With a crystal ball or Monday morning quarterback, the probable cause could have been stretched and the arrest made." Could you run that by us again, Chief?

In corporate and government bureaucracies, the lines of author- ity are often so blurred that bucks get passed from artful dodger to shameless evader until they just vanish. If you've missed the terror and tedium of trying to track down an expensive error in the dim catacombs of the IRS, you haven't lived . . . or rather, died yet. You're passed from hand to unhelpful hand, starting at zero each time, while the penalties steadily build. And believe me, that an- guish is just a microcosmic speck of the big federal funk. When the brand-new $23 million U.S. Embassy in Moscow turned out to be so riddled with KGB electronic bugs (way back during the cold war, remember?) that it had to be junked before anyone moved in, the chain of responsibility—starting at the top with secretaries of state William P. Rogers and Henry Kissinger—was so unclear, with different government offices pursuing different agendas, that voices of concern about the security problems of Russian construction went unheard. By the time the damage was irretrievably done and the fiasco discovered, the asses deserving to be kicked had been deftly covered, even if anyone had been inclined to do the kicking. Messrs. Rogers and Kissinger did a Gaston and Alphonse routine, declining politely to see the mess as any of their business (Rogers offering the time-honored dodge that he "was carrying out the orders of the White House"). On down the line much shucking and jiving managed to dissipate the wrath that ought to have singed at least a few careers.

A similar managerial disaster scuttled the savings and loan industry, only this time the cost is $150 billion and counting, yet even with a legion of bumblers and villains scrambling for the hills, far too few heads have rolled.

In business, it's almost impossible to find anyone who'll ever admit to being part of the problem, whatever the problem may be, and just as hard to find somebody to do what it takes to be part of the solution. Go as far up the power ladder as you want, but you'll still have a difficult time locating any power. A dependable informant once told me the story about the CEO of a major manufacturing company who made a personal call on the chairman of General Motors and happened to mention the difficulty he was having getting his Cadillac properly serviced. In the movie version, of course, where life can be beautiful and justice swift, the GM honcho picks up the phone and says a few choice words to someone well below him on the food chain and the problem gets solved pronto. But that was then. Now, the GM chief sympathized with his fellow CEO, then gave him an 800 number to find the nearest place to take his troublesome car.

This is hearsay, I'll admit, but it sounds believable, and it isn't reassuring. Men and women who once ran their companies personally are now so busy fending off hostile takeovers and conjuring quarterly earnings increases there's not much time left for checking on whether people are doing their jobs. The effect on the quality of American products and the productivity of American companies is well known. From a management standpoint the results are nothing short of disastrous, with the unsettling outcome that when asses do get kicked, it's not always our fellow Americans who do the kicking.

How is it that something as basic as holding people responsible for their work has atrophied so drastically? There are many reasons. For one thing, the idea simply went out of fashion. I'm reluctant to blame yet another societal ill on the legacy of the sixties, but a central credo of that tumultuous time was "Do your own thing," and somewhere along the way it became uncool to be on somebody's case or in their face. In the new utopia, lots of us decided, people would do their best work without being hounded by fascist pig overlords. And if our best wasn't so hot, well, wow, like what do you want?

The climate grew especially ambiguous during the Reagan years (I'm not reluctant to blame old Ron for everything). Though the president could play the tough guy at an ideological distance, firing air traffic controllers by the hundreds or backing a mercenary force in Nicaragua, up close he couldn't bring himself to say an unkind word to the worst miscreants. Maybe it was the effect of a career filled with cream-puff, nice-guy roles, maybe—like a lot of us—he just wanted to be loved. But with such an avuncular presence as national figurehead (and management exemplar), the fundamental concept of raising hell when people dope off declined dramatically.

The list of woeful examples is long. When a shipmate of Captain Hazelwood, Exxon's allegedly dipso factotum in charge of the ill-fated oil tanker *Valdez*, repeatedly warned the company about his boss's heavy drinking as far back as 1982, nothing ever came of it. When a doctor in a small Wyoming town was sent to prison for raping scores of women and girls who were his patients, his accusers were ostracized by townspeople who just wouldn't have such things said about lovable old Doc.

Sometimes it seems we've lost the capacity to make harsh judgments (except during campaign years), even to point the finger at someone and say simply that what they've done is wrong. Upon the arrest of John List, accused and later convicted of killing his mother, wife, and three children eighteen years before in Westfield, New Jersey, one of his current acquaintances said, "This is not a man with a history of murder, but a man with a couple of murders in his history." (This acquaintance might consider a career in corporate public relations.) When a bystander videotaped the prolonged beating of a man stopped for speeding by Los Angeles police officers, Chief Daryl Gates seemed to treat what he called "an aberration" as a glitch in the smooth operation of his departmental machinery—saying at one point that he hoped the incident would help the victim (a parolee) find a more productive life.

With the loss of clarity about wrongdoing has come a loss of will to exact retribution that sometimes becomes almost comical. Not long after Corporal Clayton Lonetree, a marine embassy guard in Moscow later convicted of giving vital information to Soviet intelligence, was found asleep on duty one night, he was promoted to sergeant. (Though this wasn't a case of cause and effect, it was a perfect example of ineptitude being ignored in the evaluation process.)

The ethical cloudiness of our times isn't solely to blame. A disdain for what one advertising campaign calls "sweating the details" has grown in business as in politics, a sense that real men don't pick nits and women don't do windows. Even if somebody urgently needs straightening out, the folks in charge will let him go on bumbling until he's vulture bait rather than risk being accused of micromanagement. And as belt-tightening has thinned the ranks of middle management, the number of people able to keep track of small, unglamorous, crucial matters has dropped, and isn't likely to rise again. Currently popular managerial wisdom dictates picking good people and leaving them alone to do their jobs. This sounds enlightened, and when it works it is. But as an invariable principle it can backfire. Sometimes the people we pick don't turn out to be as good as they could be, and the result of benign neglect is an inability to make improvements in an organization without draconian measures.

On a more immediate, push-comes-to-shove level, tough leadership has lost momentum in the workplace because it takes energy and guts. In our have-a-nice-day-or-die ethos, it's easier and far more pleasant to get quietly mad and later get even than to look right at someone and tell him or her to shape up. Kicking ass means, at least in the short run, not worrying at all whether someone likes you. For most of us, playing the heavy is hard work, with delayed gratification at best. We prefer affection to respect. Sure, we can all remind ourselves that the only high school teachers we remember are the ones who demanded the most of us and aroused a certain amount of dread, but saying "Someday you'll thank me for this" just doesn't fill our need to be adored.

Today, fewer and fewer executives arrive at positions of power and responsibility via that classic leadership prep school, military service. The result is that a generation or two of young managers have the mistaken idea that coming down hard on people who badly need—and in fact deserve—correcting will wreck morale. They worry that those chastised will sulk, others will sympathize, and everything will slide downhill from there. But just the opposite is often true; the best approach to building morale is to demand that people do their best, and not let up until they do. Esprit de corps is built by effort and excellence and killed by easy living, not the other way around. Some people know that secret, whether they've ever seen the business end of a drill sergeant or not. Millard Drexler, CEO of the Gap, the billion-dollar chain of clothing stores based in San Francisco, is a genial man inclined to wear jeans to work and not at all put off when his employees call him by his nickname, "Mickey." But he feels no hesitation when it comes to jumping all over high-level executives when he isn't happy with their work. Once, after a meeting at which Drexler had been particularly pointed in expressing his displeasure, his personnel director complained privately to him that his verbal floggings were sure to have a disastrous effect on the company's upbeat mood. Drexler told her that he knew precisely how hard he was pushing, and just as precisely the effect his words were intended to have. Neither a bully nor a bastard, Drexler is just a CEO with a clear sense of what he's about, and the willingness to enforce his standards no matter what it takes. Significantly, the company has grown and prospered since the early eighties, when Drexler arrived and proceeded to shake up management with both pep talks and purges. No less notable, the atmosphere at Gap headquarters (where the cafeteria produces made-to-order individual pizzas) is about as tense as that at a surf beach on Maui. If Drexler is doing any damage with his insistent demands for championship performance, it's hard to see what it could be.

Despite all the factors that militate against kicking ass, an appropriate use of the educational toe is good business. For those ready to participate in a much needed revival, a few helpful hints:

• If it feels good, don't do it. The purpose of kicking ass is not to satisfy momentary anger (though anger at careless or lazy work may motivate you) but to make someone else better at what they do. If, in the course of a stern dressing-down, you find yourself warming to the task, it's time to cool off.

• Make sure it matters. Since kicking ass really is an effort, and essentially a favor to the kickee, don't squander your psychic resources on somebody not worth improving, or whose resentment will make you wish you hadn't bothered.

• Make the kick count. A boot in the tail is a lesson, so be sure you know what you intend to teach, then don't back down just because you feel like a bad guy. Kids have been ruined because their parents give them three to get something done, and then end up counting, "One, two, two and a half, two and three quarters . . ." A half-hearted reprimand, filled with doubt and guilt, invariably confuses whatever the issue may be, and causes more harm than reform. If in the process of telling someone to pull themselves together you go to pieces, how effective can the message be? Tough it out; remember, very few people are in their jobs because they were drafted, so don't imagine that it's somehow immoral and cruel to lean on them.

• Ten rights don't make a wrong all right. No matter how splendid someone's track record, a major blunder is still a major blunder. In fact, the better somebody is, the more worthwhile it is to keep him or her in top form. When a player gets too big to be coached, it may be time for a trade.

• Go private with your reproofs. Meetings are many and unavoidable, so it's not always possible to close the door and reprimand someone without any witnesses. Sometimes, too, a public chastisement serves as a message to all. But generally, specific problems should be pointed out privately to the underachiever, since embarrassment can create long-term resentment. Showing off while kicking ass is distinctly third-rate behavior.

• Don't worry, be snappish. Certain people may be infamously thin-skinned about being criticized. In an age rife with employee lawsuits for sexism, racism, ageism, and a daunting bouquet of other isms, it's not unnatural to consider ignoring unsatisfactory performance in order to avoid trouble. But if somebody wants to make trouble, they'll find a way, and in a damned-if-you-do-damned-if-you-don't world you might as well get in your licks. In a 1991 ruling in a U.S. district court in California, a woman won a discrimination suit against her employer because her supervisor—knowing her reputation for litigiousness—had avoided confrontations over her inadequate work. When she was eventually fired, she successfully charged that she hadn't been given an opportunity to improve her performance.

Now that the kid glove-ins of the Reagan years are past, there's a chance that demanding the best work from people may no longer be politically incorrect or socially uncool. George Bush is hardly the tough manager he would like us to believe—despite his Desert Storm camouflage, the president lets Sununu deal with no-nos—but he's made the goal of "kicking a little ass" something of a personal rallying cry. With the HUD scandal and the savings and loan disaster taking money out of our pockets more or less till the end of time, with malingerers being turned up at (if not always out of) the Pentagon, and with U.S. business being scolded for sloth by the punctilious Japanese, kicking ass may well be the miracle discovery of the decade. Watch for it at an MBA program near you.

24

Eat, Drink, and Be Wary

surviving the office

Christmas party

with (moderately)

good cheer

*C*harles Dickens can rarely be accused of not going far enough. His splendidly sappy endings make the finales of Italian opera seem almost antiseptic by comparison. But at least once, at the end of *A Christmas Carol*, Dickens lowered the curtain an hour or two before the story's real dramatic denouement. In order to preserve a necessarily happy finish, the author gave Tiny Tim his immortal tag line—"God bless us, every one!" for any grouch who doesn't remember—then faded to black while the scene was all tinkling glasses and twinkling smiles.

Any veteran of gatherings at which employers mix with their employees can easily imagine how things would have progressed had Dickens let us linger a bit later into the evening. Scrooge, filled with uncharacteristic good spirit and more than a little ale, would give a series of embarrassing little speeches about how much each of those present had meant to the company's success during the

213

previous year, and how it was the little people who'd helped lift him onto the pantheon of the Forbes A list. Bob Cratchit, several wassails to the wind, would sling an uninvited arm intimately around the boss's shoulders and confide in him that, hey, he wasn't such an old son of a bitch after all. Mrs. Cratchit, tears in her eyes and ale on her breath, would tell the CEO that her husband deserved a hell of a lot more than he'd been getting all these years, and ought to have any raise made retroactive to compensate for all the grief she'd had to take when bitter Bob came home from the office every night. As the spiral of the evening's frolic wound ever downward, someone would sooner or later ask Tiny Tim to dance.

So it goes with the annual ordeal by alcohol, hypocrisy, and pratfallen camaraderie known as the office Christmas party, that fraught festivity given for those whom the gods would punish. As if the corporate wars were not perilous enough, the Christmas party finishes the year with a long walk across a minefield—a chardonnay in one hand, a sprig of broccoli and dip in the other, and a ghastly smile on one's face. (All company outings, from softball galas to farewell fetes, are harrowing experiences to some extent, but given the stress of the season, the Christmas party is by far the most concentrated and formidable. Anyway, even companies that never have social gatherings at other times of the year succumb to Yule fever.) The best you can hope for with most of these agons is simply to get through them, perks intact and not remembered by anyone who matters as "that loudmouth idiot from sales." Like a major battle, the Christmas party is something many otherwise sensible people actually look forward to, then—if they survive—spend all their energy plotting how to get out of next time.

What humbug, you say? An office Christmas party, you protest, is just a well-deserved letting off of steam, a lighthearted frolic that gives the seven dwarfs from accounting a chance to rub whatevers with the Snow Whites of personnel. Well, maybe things *were* once that innocent. But it's the nature of most cultures to go from simple fun to hellish rites in disturbingly short order. Gather a few nice folks together at the solstice for a little therapeutic bonding and before you know it they'll be deep into sacrificial altars and obsidian knives and complaints of how hard it is to find a virgin anymore. Though corporate culture shies away from such obvious ritual carnage, the urge to slather ever darker shades of meaning onto lighthearted celebrations is no less powerful now than what the Druids must have felt. What once might have been no more than the happy clink of sherry glasses around some grandee's desk and a plate of Triscuits with Cheez Whiz has grown inexorably to become one of the truest tests of executive mettle.

The sheer size of Christmas parties has become a trial for corporate endurance as well. Like fireworks displays and movie special effects, company holiday gatherings have a way of creating greater and greater expectations, so that each one has to outdo the one that came before. And, of course, must resoundingly surpass the parties of rival companies. The price tag for these hoedowns can make grown treasurers cry, and yet once the escalation begins, no one seems to know how to wind it down. Just as companies feel compelled to declare profit and growth at the end of each relentless quarter, so do they seem compelled to throw the holiday party to end all holiday parties, year after year. Where will it all end? Sometimes, as we see every day, in bankruptcy court, an infamous squelcher of Yuletide spirit. And sometimes in a sobering memo from some corner-office Scrooge announcing that "due to projected end-of-year deficits, it is suggested that in place of the company Christmas party, individual sections hold their own celebrations on premises, with the expenses shared equally among employees." So much for that second lump of coal, Cratchit!

But such things are more exceptions than a visible trend, even in what are proving to be the high-fiber, low-fat nineties. It seems that no matter how dire a company's stock picture, or how much euphemism is needed to prop up the annual report, parties just go on growing bigger and more arduous for all involved, as if corporations suspect that every second person at the hors d'oeuvre table is a reporter for the *Wall Street Journal*, there just to make sure the setting is still as dramatic as the year before and the Moët & Chandon hasn't been replaced by Asti Spumante. Often, nothing is quite so stimulating to the management's party-as-big-as-the-Ritz mentality than tremors of discontent on the Big Board. Eat, drink, and so forth, or tomorrow our stock dies!

Christmas parties tend to grow despite frequently intense animosity toward them on the part of the people who pay for them. Like Christmas itself, which long ago went madly out of control, these affairs have lives of their own and are harder to kill than the

Terminator. I was once given the job of planning the holiday fes-
tivities at a corporate division I'd recently joined. Veterans at the
place told me that the party had grown bigger each year, so naturally I threw myself into making my mark with the biggest and best
yet. What no one told me (the nest had more than its share of
vipers) was that the boss considered all company parties a plague,
a pointless way of wasting money and taking the time of a staff that
ought to be hard at work late into Christmas eve. Thus, the more
successful the party, the more dismal the party planner's fate.

Though the division was tremendously profitable, the annual
party, to which important clients and the media were invited, was
still held in the utilitarian office space where we all labored un-
glamorously day after day. Since the overhead fluorescent lighting
was all wrong for atmosphere, I arranged to have Chinese lanterns
with low-wattage bulbs hung in rows along the ceiling, and hired a
pricy caterer to provide dim sum to go along with the effect. I went
over budget, but the added expenditures seemed well worth making in the cause of the company's image. If everyone went home
humming "Some Enchanted Evening," what could it hurt?

When I announced my plans to the boss (with more than a trace
of clearly justifiable pride), she narrowed her eyes ominously. Sens-
ing that all was not well, I quickly added, "I really think this is a
way to make sure everybody has a good time."

"The point, my dear," she said with a sneer, "is not to make sure
everybody has a good time, but to make sure everybody goes the
hell home as soon as possible."

Thus the Chinese lanterns were consigned to that small dustbin
of history reserved for things that never got a chance to happen, and
the caterer was asked to swap the dim sum for bacon-wrapped
chicken livers. In the face of this kind of high-level resistance, one
might assume that particular division's Christmas party had a dubious future. Yet the next year, with another just-arrived fall guy
in charge—someone obviously less easily discouraged than I—the
fete was held in a recently vacated midtown Manhattan auto sales-
room, complete with gilded columns and, yes, romantic lighting.
Attendees in the past few years tell me that the party has continued
to grow, despite the continued disapproval of the person signing the
checks.

Not everyone hates the company party, of course. But then not
everyone has to. Generally, the less a person has to lose, or at least

the less strategically he or she has to maneuver through the obstacle course of office politics, the more fun that person can have. Just look around at the next Christmas party or Fourth of July cruise you're dragooned into attending. The receptionists and mailroom troops are happily wolfing down the shrimp and dancing their little Reeboks off. They've anxiously awaited this affair and view it as a major perk, something like a stock option but a whole lot more fun. Without the energy they bring to the company party—and voyeuristic possibilities—the institution would surely have vanished long ago. Inevitably though, as people have grown more cautious about how they behave in the workplace and the traditional frivolity of the get-together has stiffened, the mixing of the managers and the managed that sometimes actually did engender a we're-all-in-this-together spirit has become guarded and artificial.

Take, for instance, that great source of company loyalty and employee morale, lust. Not the major trouble-making sort discussed in Chapter 10, but the evanescent, party-long variety that used to lend a certain illicit excitement to annual sock hops. Back in the days when most companies were male chauvinistic châteaus and boys just wanted to have fun, the Yuletide encounter was nothing more—or less—than a singles bar with tinsel. What were known back then as junior executives went to ogle the "gals" of the typing pool and, with the help of the free bar, to say a few things that had been squirming restlessly in their libidos all year. The frank hope of each enterprising gray flannel buck was to ambush some beauty under the mistletoe and give himself something to come to work for until life got back to normal in the joyless funk of February. Nowadays the gorgeous creature making a man's reserve melt (helped along by reserve malt) is as likely as not to be above him in the hierarchy, and putting the moves on her may be a fatal career move.

Not that I would wish us back in those dark ages of office dalliance—haven't I already warned against that sort of thing?—when all was vanity, nothing was fair, and secretaries were fair game. But it's only human to feel a bit of nostalgia for the Christmas parties of auld lang syne, with their all-rules-waived frenzy of carnival in Rio or revelries on the eve of war. I go on accepting my share of Christmas party invitations, I'll admit, but what once was adamantly an interlude of *not* working has taken on the unmistakably drab aura of networking, further dividing those who may not be able to afford a BMW but can afford to get down and boogie from those who can't waste a minute in their pursuit of power, gain, and glory. At a party given at a hip dance club by a top New York PR agency a Christmas or two ago, the small dance floor was surrounded by vice presidents, account executives, copywriters, and other wearers of the white collar. They chatted earnestly with one another, and with the select outsiders there, about how tough the image-burnishing biz is these days, making plans and talking deals just as they did every day at work, all the while casting envious sidelong glances at some of the splendid, heedless young underlings on the dance floor who were—no question about it— actually having a great time.

Whether or not the Grinches of ambition, politicking, and corporate tension have stolen Christmas fun forever, when the season rolls around you inevitably find yourself at one or more obligatory company functions, so a brief survival guide for the Christmas party of the nineties may be in order. What follows are thirteen basic rules of conduct. If you end up hating yourself in the morning, don't say you weren't warned.

• If you're invited, go. Trying to avoid the pitfalls of a Christmas party by feigning illness, or claiming to be too busy, is the coward's way out. No-shows are liable to be considered disloyal or, worse, unwilling to suffer along with their colleagues. Then again, if you can manage to be out of town on business, or persuade a favorite uncle to grow gravely ill . . .

• Wear more or less what you would wear for any office occasion. Don't use the party as an excuse for a personality transformation; being the person you've always wanted to be for a couple of hours on the twenty-third of December tends to complicate life for the person you actually are. If a man whose normal style is conservative shows up as if prepared to ride to the hounds, he'll only cause confusion (if not an outbreak of ridicule). And if a woman known for quietly elegant good taste wriggles into a spandex minidress just because this is a once-a-year chance to create a sensation, the memory of that sensation is likely to hover in the air like a Tina Turner video when the same woman, back in character in oh-so-sober January, gets up to present the new pension plan. So that duck decoy corduroy vest or the Victoria's Secret fishnet stockings you got last year for Christmas and wouldn't be caught dead in any other time should go to the thrift shop *now*, before it's too late. The ghosts of Christmas parties past will *always* come back to haunt you.

• Try to arrive about half an hour late, so you don't seem desperate to be there (and to imply that breaking away from work is tough for someone so key to the well-being of the company as you). But don't be an hour late, since certain people (who *will* be watching) think of office parties as a form of business meeting, with the same rigorous obligations.

• Leave just before people start saying things they'll regret. There's no known scientific survey of just when that witching hour is, but in my experience it's about 143 minutes into the bubbly. Hearing a true confession from a subordinate may be embarrassing. Hearing one from a drunken executive vice president can be deadly if, on Monday, he remembers what he said and to whom. Someone else's loose lips can definitely sink your ship.

• Dance a bit, so as not to seem stiff, but not so much (or with such abandon) that you seem to be having a far better time than anyone else except the office temp in the black tights and the fuchsia mohawk.

• Drink very little. Very, very little. And never anything from Russia, Scotland, or Tennessee.

• Try to appear to be drinking as much as the CEO, which will be very little anyway because those *Journal* spies will be watching, and because he's picking up the tab.

• Do not, under any circumstances, even if the walls of workaday propriety seem to have come tumbling down, let your libido be your guide. Remember, whoever you are flirting with has been on someone else's mind for the past year, and that someone may be in a position to make you pay for even the most innocent pleasures. Be strong!

• Do not make a toast unless absolutely required to do so. Hardly anyone does this well, and you are almost bound to say too much or to hurt someone's feelings by omitting him or her. And if you do succeed, you'll be pressed into duty as the company toastmaster, giving you many more chances to screw up.

• Ditto with jokes. The dangers of humor have been dealt with at unfunny length in Chapter 5. Read it again. Nothing is more perilous than an offensive punchline among those who have previously done their best to respect you. Better to tinker with a live grenade.

• Should someone start to sing carols, do not attempt harmony. Stay close to dead center on the melody, and sing ever so softly.

• Do not call the boss by his or her initials, unless you always have, and not even then. Christmas may be a season of good cheer, but don't be misled into thinking that goodwill toward men invariably applies to you.

• Look as if you're having a good time, even if you aren't, which will probably be the case if you're abiding by all these rules. When you begin to wonder why you came in the first place, remind yourself that it happens only once a year, and smile. It's almost over.

In the slightly sodden, somewhat rueful aftermath of the holiday season, as the new year stretches endlessly ahead, bear in mind that however daunting and tedious those parties have been, they have one truly worthwhile use. Within ten months or so the impending annual rite will give you a chance to say once again, "I'll be sure to get the Smedlap marketing plan done. Right after the Christmas party."

In the meantime, God help us, every one.

25

Staying Power: The New Loyalty

signing on for the long

haul may be smart,

or honorable, or (who

knows?) even both

*S*omething funny is happening on the way to the millennium: loyalty, a quality as warm and fuzzy as a fifties sitcom—and, you might think, just about as relevant to the lean-and-mean, globally competitive nineties—seems to be making a comeback. Job hopping, once the restless dance of the hippest self-agrandizers, is becoming decidedly unfashionable; even Me-generation masters of the strategic bugout are weighing the benefits of trading the glitter of perpetual novelty for the steadier returns of staying the course. There may even be reasons to believe that companies, as well as employees, are getting that old family feeling again. To wit, an updated look at the loyalty logbook:

• Los Angeles Laker megaguard Magic Johnson offered to defer a few hundred thousand dollars of his 1991 salary so that his team could attract other key players without going beyond the league's salary cap. Similarly, NFL All-Star safety Ronnie Lott announced his willingness to take a significant pay cut in order to finish his career with the San Francisco '49ers.

• Michael Korda, editor-in-chief of Simon & Schuster and the author of tooth-and-claw texts on power-playing, celebrated thirty years at the same company, an astonishing feat in what has traditionally been a highly migratory business.

• Honda Motors announced a 1991 production cutback at one of its main U.S. plants, but said that no workers would be laid off as a result—the assembly line would simply be slowed down.

• In what may be the most inexplicable act of loyalty in recent political history, George Bush made sure to include Dan Quayle in the big photo opportunities during the Gulf war, thus implying that the vice president was part of the decision-making apparatus despite polls universally indicating America's vast discomfort with the idea of Dan as the Man.

• Though not necessarily a scientific indicator of anything at all, recent polls have shown a diminishing number of married couples who consider divorce an acceptable option when things get rocky, and actual divorces are down about 10 percent since the breakup high in 1979. Whatever it means, the young and the restless are obviously longing for stability.

Everywhere, people seem to be looking at their jobs—jobs they might have viewed as mere stepping-stones in the fast-paced eighties—with a new sense of involvement and permanence. As the wind blows cold, it would stand to reason we'd look for the warmth of familiarity of an established working relationship. But before you rush out into the lobby and kiss the company logo, or send the chairman of the board a Father's Day card, or tack up that needlepoint sampler JOB SWEET JOB, a reality check may be in order. However much we may desire to bring order out of the chaos that has followed the end of the gilded, guilty decade just past, skepticism is still useful. For every example of the new loyalty paradigm, one can easily come up with a bit of antimatter from the old paradigm.

Loyalty in sports? The once sweet rituals of baseball spring training have become a dissonant chorus of whining, with disloyalty on the part of players and teams making the sports pages read like the grimmer columns of the business section. Bobby Bonds, in a huff about his $2.3 million salary, sulks at practice and shouts at his manager. Rickey Henderson sits out most of the 1991 exhibition season because a four-year, $12 million no-trade contract just doesn't sit right with him anymore. And lest we think such churlishness is strictly a player attitude, the Kansas City Royals drop Bo Jackson like a worn out cross-training shoe when a football injury sidelines him for the '91 season. And the '49ers ignore the loyal Lott's offer and send him packing to the L.A. Raiders.

Loyalty in politics? Ambassador to Iraq April Glaspie is expected to show her loyalty to the State Department by uncomplainingly taking the blame for her boss James Baker's failure to comprehend Saddam Hussein's wicked ways—while State unfaithfully lets her twist slowly in the wind during the entire Gulf crisis.

Loyalty in high places? One of Queen Elizabeth's beloved Welsh corgis, in a regicidal snit, bites the royal hand that feeds him. (We are *not* amused.) The Soviet foreign minister publicly resigns, abandoning his old friend Mikhail Gorbachev in the midst of a growing crisis. And enterprising provocateurs on the Democratic National Committee desperately try to convince General Norman Schwarzkopf to run for president against his commander in chief.

Loyalty in business? The unions and management at the *New York Daily News* go at each other with a vehemence unmellowed by any sense of mutual obligation. Even big insurance companies, traditionally the most paternalistic of employers (lifelong security in exchange for a gray life in the actuarial flatlands), have begun laying off thousands of workers and casting unnerving looks at thousands more.

But despite all this, there is *something* going on. "There's no question that from a recruiter's perspective the glamour is fading from high mobility," says Chick Davis of Heidrick & Struggles. Yet even a soupçon of cynicism should warn that lack of movement is not the same as willing allegiance. Isn't it possible that this born-again fidelity is just a response to unsettled economic times and the corporate streamlining that has become as trendy as the Ultra Slim Fast diet? When people jumped from job to job, moving laterally upward and making changes whenever the in-box simply got too full, it was because there was always someplace to go. If the last decade was a time of golden parachutes for some, it was also a time of golden drop zones for just about everybody. But as the Spartan cast of the nineties reveals itself, the prospect for happy landings is dwindling.

"These days, most companies are clearing out from the bottom up," says Davis, "and good candidates for management positions are very risk aversive." Taking into account that four million white-collar jobs have simply ceased to exist in the last couple of years, it's not hard to see why the grass has begun to seem badly parched on the other side of the fence (if there *is* any grass, or even another side of the fence). When corporations were as fat and jolly as the un-fallen Falstaff, an MBA or law degree was the ticket to a limitless shopping spree in the job market, and having a situation go sour was no big deal. Ambitious young tricksters zipped through com-panies like neutrinos, barely leaving an impression on their ergo-nomic desk chairs before moving on and collecting better money with each ricochet. Now, if that six-figure gamble doesn't work out, the next stop may be driving a diaper service truck.

As a result, the unpredictable aspects of a new job—assimilating oneself into a new (and possibly resistant) culture, proving to com-petitive colleagues that you're as good as you've claimed to be, and facing up to the danger that you'll be rejected like a transplanted heart by a body impolitic—now loom as major gambles instead of mere rolls of the dice. Boredom or nagging discontent, strong mo-tivations for a change of scene not all that long ago, have become facts of life people are learning to live with. "This may be a dead-end job," former quick-change artists may now be saying, "but at least it's *my* dead-end job."

Let's hope there's more to staying put, in most cases, than fear of the unknown. As the economy has cooled from the high-profit, bull-riding heat of recent times—with economists predicting that such heedless good times aren't likely to be seen again in this cen-tury, if ever—it's beginning to seem apparent that the wages of constant movement were higher wages and not much else. With the game of executive musical chairs coming to an end, people who have dazzled employer after employer with their footwork ("He must be good, look at all the places he's worked") may discover that they're more skilled at working out career moves than at working in their professions. "People who moved too much," says the person-nel director of a major West Coast manufacturing company, "were never in one place long enough to really prove anything. Their real talent was getting hired." The quick-cut rock video version of work-ing life didn't demand the kind of stolid effort that staying the course requires, and the new trend to stability is going to force some of the free-climbing stars of the eighties to concentrate for a longer span than many ever have before. Hammer in those pitons and watch out for bodies plummeting from above.

When the pace of corporate arrivals and departures was so hectic that house organs began to read like train schedules, the sheer busyness of all the motion created the illusion of business. But just as all the leveraged buyouts of the eighties were a distraction from the real work of making better products or improving service, the constant shifting of people from one place to another tended to blur company identity and sow confusion, with staffs put on hold while new managers acclimated themselves (or simply updated their résumés). Firings were rife and often gratuitous as newcomers brought in their own staffs (then moved on and left them to the undependable kindness of strangers). So much change for the sake of change often had dire side effects. When someone who had been running a technology corporation one week was deciding how to program a television season the next, quality usually ended up as what the military likes to call "collateral damage." In other words, it was dead. Anyone who tried to get anything real accomplished during those fidgety days can remember the frustration of waiting for a decision from someone who had just taken over and was probably thinking about taking off. Antsy executives and wandering bands of leverage samurai had a grim effect on American business—even when anything *did* get done, it was often wrong, sometimes calamitously so, and great companies were broken up or just plain broken with sad regularity. But not until the chastening effects of a recession slowed down the collective heavy breathing could the extent of the damage be assessed.

Two years into the nineties, the sins of instability are raising eyebrows and ire for the first time in a generation or so. In the spring of 1991, when Martin S. Davis, the chairman of Paramount Communications, named producer Stanley Jaffe as CEO of the company, precipitating the departure of thirty-year loyalist Frank Mancuso, virtually every report on the appointment attributed Paramount's growing problems to the high turnover of executives (including current Disney president Michael Eisner and Barry Diller of Fox Television) that has characterized Davis's management. In the eighties, turnover like that was so commonplace it would hardly have been noticed.

But however deleterious the quick change era was and however salutary the effects of a more settled time may prove to be, the question remains as to whether the nineties will be characterized by true loyalty, or just various loyalty-like substances. Understandably, one may wonder why such a fine distinction matters. If life improves, quality rises, and you can count on steady employment and learn to live with a résumé that doesn't look like a Byzantine mosaic, who cares what the motivations are? Not everyone, perhaps, but you should, because it's okay to have other reasons, more strategic reasons for sitting tight than loyalty, but not okay to kid yourself. There's no way to know for sure whether, in a stressful climate, a given corporation will get the message that stability works for everybody, or will just obsess about the bottom line and let the pink slips fall where they may. If you delude yourself that your allegiance is of the purest kind, with nothing but noble motives, and you discover that your employer ultimately couldn't care less about you, the feeling that you've been a chump will be crushing. If you've really been loyal, at least you can walk away with your self-esteem intact (and, one hopes, a good settlement based on President Reagan's favorite Russian slogan, "Trust, but verify"). If your loyalty is just for appearance's sake, with other factors really at work, you'll be a better person (sorry, but after all these pages, I have to make a blatant pitch for virtue) if you acknowledge the fundamental difference.

So the time has come to take an unsentimental look at what being loyal is all about. Real loyalty, of course, is as virtuous and unimpeachable as any other part of the Boy Scout oath. But like patriotism, it can serve as the refuge of scoundrels, as camouflage for baser motivations, or as a justification for actions that, while not exactly culpable, are something less than honorable. It's important to keep in mind that artificial loyalty is used more-or-less equally by employees and employers, so even if you're not faking it, the company might be. Curiously, even large and mercilessly pragmatic institutions can become self-deluded by their own proclamations of loyalty.

Perhaps the best way to understand what loyalty is is to know what loyalty is not.

• **Loyalty is not fealty.** Being loyal to a company, or an individual, is not the same as playing vassal to a feudal lord. The divine

right of kings is passé (despite how deeply the idea pleased kings and comforted courtiers), and so is the concept of "My company, right or wrong." You may have signed a contract, but you didn't sign away your rights. Or did you?

• **Loyalty is not naivety.** The kind of robotic behavior that gave loyalty a bad name in the fifties—womb-to-tomb, gray flannel, time-clock obedience in return for a gold watch and a monthly pension check—could make a comeback if people allow themselves to believe again in the employer as a benign and all-powerful presence, a piece of the rock immune to changes of fortune or philosophy. Remember, nothing is forever, and it never was. Pension plans go bust, blue-chip companies go bye-bye, enlightened leaders retire, so fidelity must still be guided by the rule of "Let the hired beware."

• **Loyalty is not charity.** Some people are loyal because it makes them feel good, like going to church or watching MacNeil/Lehrer. Giving their all to their employers, not worrying overmuch about whether this loyalty is returned to them, these folks are the monks and nuns of the workplace. Everybody knows at least one secular saint who delights in being called a "company man" (never mind the gender, they're long past that) and can't imagine life beyond the corporate walls. There's no point pitying people like this; they're happy enough, for all the wrong reasons. What's important is to make sure you never give in to the temptation to become one.

• **Loyalty is not slavery.** Certain companies, often those that are family owned (or at least closely held), value loyalty above all other employee attributes. By throwing a couple of parties a year and jury-rigging some child care facilities, they figure they can produce an aura of Norman Rockwell coziness without too much cost. After all, a true-blue employee wouldn't be so unfriendly as to demand a raise, or want a share of the profits—what kind of loyalty would that be?

• **Loyalty is not knavery.** Utterly trusting, all-giving company people may start out simply cheating themselves, but their true belief in the worthiness of the organization (it *has* to be deserving of their sacrifices, after all) can lead to Goldwaterish thinking: Moderation in the defense of the corporation is no virtue, and all that. Out of this can come toadyism, complicity in the exploitation of others, and a willingness to do the company dirty work. Though to some, loyalty means never being able to say no to anything the employer does or requires, playing the henchman role perverts the concept in ways both silly and chilling.

• **Loyalty is not cupidity.** All right, it's true . . . money *can* buy loyalty, of a sort. There are people—quite a few people, in fact—who will offer their fidelity unstintingly just as long as the pay is sufficient. Thus, the essential dynamic of the boxer's entourage, the mobster's henchmen, and the campaigner's political consultants: Sign my check, rent my soul. But leased loyalty is spurious stuff and debases the currency drastically. The depressing teamlessness that besets professional sports these days is symptomatic of loyalty for hire, as well as the obsession of the sports press with contracts rather than athletic performance. Money is a perfectly legitimate reason to do many things, but not to put your hand over your heart and pledge allegiance to something you otherwise wouldn't care much about. Like love, loyalty should be above commerce; if money is all there is to hold you, then hard work is all you ought to owe in return.

• **Loyalty is not frailty.** The worst possible motivation for loyalty is fear. If you find yourself lustily harmonizing the company song or favoring a tie with the corporate trademark just because times are tough and somehow it seems that sufficiently public zeal will provide protection, back off. Though this may explain why George Bush is so loyal to Dan Quayle (his unimpeachable impeachment protection), it ought to be the last reason for anyone else to keep the faith. Obviously, intense competition for survival, a harsh hallmark of the times, is a respectable reason to avoid public displays of disdain for everything that Buzzington Power Tools International (or whatever) holds dear. But timidity makes for mediocre, uncritical thinking and predictable decisions, so loyalty born of anxiety is as likely to bring you down as it is to keep you safe.

If staying in one place and patiently proving yourself fit to move up is unglamorous compared to the pyrotechnics of job-jumping that characterized meteoric rises in the eighties, get ready for a severe glamour famine in the coming years. No doubt there will always be high-level office temps who manage to keep moving too fast to be found out. But they will be exceptions. Sticking around will be the rule (albeit a voluntary rule). And loyalty may well turn out to be a reward far more satisfying than a career distinguished mostly by its abundance of teary, beery good-bye lunches. What matters most, for the rest of this decade, is to make sure that hanging in there isn't a cosmetically upgraded form of just hanging around.

Index

Madden, John, 121
Mancuso, Frank, 225
Mao Tse-tung, Madame, 136
Marcos, Imelda, 136
Marine Corps, 1, 9–10, 55–56, 97–98, 120
Marshall, George, 48
Martin, Steve, 38
Marx, Groucho, 32, 124
Mason, James, 138
McCarthy, Joe, 28
McClintick, David, 161
McEnroe, John, 78
McFarlane, Robert, 28
McKay, Jim, 129
McMahon, Ed, 200
Meese, Edwin, 58
meetings
  adaptability to, 51
  criticism, responding to, 45–46
  dislike of, 44
  focus in, 51–52
  military metaphors applied to, 48–49, 50
  passion and risk in, 52–53
  performance in, 44–45
  preparation for, 47
  women's effect on, 49–51
Melnick, Dan, 98
memos
  angry memos, 59
  as CYA devices, 60
  effectiveness in, 55–56
  guidelines for, 61–62
  memophobes, two types of, 60–61
  reasons for, 57–58, 59, 60

as substitutes for action, 58–59
mentoring
  dangers of, 25–26
  guidelines in, 31–33
  motivations in, 26–30
  serial protégé phenomenon, 27–28
  traditions of, 30–31
Metropolitan Opera, 104
Michael, George, 89
Milken, Michael, 187
Moderns, The (film), 145
Montana, Joe, 131
Montgomery, Field Marshal, 187
Moynihan, Patrick, 40
Murphy, Eddie, 118

NBC, 30
Neuharth, Al, 97, 99
Newsweek, 96
Newton, Wayne, 126
New York City Transit Authority, 77
New York Daily News, 223
New York Post, 120, 148–49
New York Times, 97, 146, 148, 166
New York Times Magazine, 75
Nicholson, Jack, 108
"Nightline" (TV show), 198
Nine to Five (film), 170
Nixon, Richard, 68, 117, 198, 200
Nofziger, Lyn, 127
North, Oliver, 11, 28, 57, 198